Love Never Fails

I0038960

A Journey Through Forgiveness, Patience, and Lasting Connection

Published by: Ronald D'Haiti

Year: [2025]

ISBN: [979-8-9933956-1-6]

This book invites readers to embrace love as the greatest force in life. By highlighting its healing, enduring, and transformative power, Love Never Fails encourages readers to create relationships and legacies that stand the test of time.

In contrast to other self-help or relationship manuals, Love Never Fails integrates spiritual profundity with pragmatic applicability. It provides not just motivation but also practical measures, rendering it both introspective and transformative. Every chapter culminates in the fundamental theme: love is everlasting, potent, and deserving of daily commitment.

Dedication

To everyone whose love, support, and life have shaped my heart and inspired every word, I dedicate this book with all of my heart. For everything you are and everything you mean to me

To my beloved wife **Guerda J. D'Haiti**, you have my sincere gratitude. Your unwavering support, kindness, and patience have been the cornerstones of my life. Your kindness, bravery, and effortless expression of love amaze me every day. Without your support and example, I could not have written this book. You exemplify the enduring strength of love, and you are far more than merely my spouse.

To my late mother, **Vilioda D'Haiti**—though you are no longer physically here, your voice, your values, and your life lessons continue to guide me. You taught me what genuine love for people looks like: unconditional, generous, and without boundaries. Your legacy lives on in me, in the way I strive to love others, and in every word of this book.

Thank you to my dear sisters, **Marie Y. Eliacin, Marie Meda D'Haiti, Charlene Gray, Geralda Theodor, Gerda Rosembert, Marie Mirlande, and Marie Nadine Jules-Fils,** for your everlasting love, support, and faith in me despite my failures. Your presence has repeatedly emphasized Love Never Fails and the power of family.

This book is for every reader who encounters it—especially for those who struggle in relationships, family, friendships, or even within themselves. If you've ever wrestled with forgiveness, longed for patience, or searched for a connection that lasts, may these words remind you that love is still the greatest force in life.

Finally, to all the men and women who choose to forgive with their whole hearts, who lay down pride and pick up grace, and who give relationships a second chance for the sake of love—this book is for you. You are the living proof that **"Love Never Fails"**, and your courage to begin again inspires hope for every heart still searching for connection, healing, and lasting love.

Disclaimer

This book, Love Never Fails: A Journey Through Forgiveness, Patience, and Lasting Connection, solely serves as a source of inspiration, education, and information. The author has drawn upon personal insights, life experiences, research, and stories to share lessons and reflections on love, forgiveness, patience, and the power of human connection.

This book is **not a substitute for professional advice** in areas such as counseling, psychology, mental health, legal matters, or medical treatment. Readers are encouraged to seek the guidance of licensed professionals for personal challenges or decisions that require expertise in these fields.

The author and publisher make no guarantees about the completeness, suitability, or applicability of the material provided, despite efforts to ensure accuracy and reliability. Any reliance you place on the content of this book is strictly at your discretion and responsibility.

The stories and examples included may reflect a blend of real experiences, illustrative composites, or fictionalized scenarios designed to convey the broader truths of love and forgiveness. Any resemblance to actual individuals, living or deceased, is purely coincidental unless otherwise noted.

The author and publisher shall not be held liable for any direct or indirect damages, losses, or consequences arising from the use or application of the ideas presented in this book.

By reading *Love Never Fails*, you acknowledge and accept this disclaimer and understand that the purpose of this work is to encourage reflection, growth, and inspiration in your journey toward cultivating lasting love.

Preface

Love Never Fails was not written in a single flash of inspiration but rather after years of introspection, observation, and life events that demonstrated the true power of love. In a world that frequently seems rushed, divided, and unsure, I felt compelled to take a moment to think on the one force that never fades: Love.

I have witnessed both the most beautiful and the most difficult types of love. I've seen patience keep individuals going through protracted periods of hardship, how forgiveness restores relationships that appeared irreparable, and how real connection can inspire hope in even the most hopeless hearts. Families, friendships, communities, and faith are all settings where life's everyday realities impart these lessons, not just theoretical concepts. Time and again, life may be confusing, but love remains an unchanging, straightforward reality that never falters.

I hope that as you read these pages, you will be encouraged to reaffirm your faith in the certainty that love endures, a promise that has sustained countless generations through both happiness and adversity.

With thankfulness and optimism,
Ronald D'Haiti

Introduction

Love it's a word we use so often, yet it's one of the most misunderstood and underestimated forces in our lives. We hear it in songs, see it in movies, and say it in conversations, but when life gets tough—when forgiveness feels impossible, when patience runs thin, when connections are strained—love reveals its truest form. And it is in those moments, not the easy ones, that we discover whether love really has the power to endure.

Love Never Fails: A Journey Through Forgiveness, Patience, and Lasting Connection was written with a simple but powerful truth in mind: love is not just an emotion—it's a choice, a commitment, and a way of living. This book isn't about fairy-tale romances or picture-perfect relationships. It's about real love—the kind that forgives when it's easier to walk away, the kind that waits when impatience screams louder, the kind that chooses connection when life tries to pull us apart. Throughout these pages, you'll be invited to look at love in all its dimensions. Romantic love, yes, but also the love that exists in families, in friendships, in communities, and even the love we learn to give ourselves. Each chapter is built to help you see that love is both the gentlest and the strongest force on earth—it heals wounds, restores trust, and builds bridges across divides we thought could never be crossed.

This book is not here to give you quick fixes or unrealistic promises. Instead, it's an honest conversation about what it really takes to love well: forgiveness that goes deeper than words, patience that stretches farther than we think possible, and connection that weaves our lives together in ways that outlast hardship. It's about discovering that the legacy we leave behind is not measured in what we've achieved or collected, but in how deeply we've loved. So, whether you're holding this book because you're searching for healing, want to strengthen your marriage or relationships, or are simply curious about how love can change the way we live, I want you to know this: you are in the right place. These words were written for you. For the weary heart needing hope. For the one wrestling with forgiveness. For the person who longs to love fully and be loved in return.

Because here's the timeless truth: when everything else fades, love remains. And if you let it, love will change you—forever.

Chapter Outline

Chapter 1: The Meaning of Unconditional Love

Chapter 2: Love in Action

Chapter 3: The Power of Forgiveness in Love

Chapter 4: Love Through Trials and Challenges

Chapter 5: The Sacrifices Love Makes

Chapter 6: The Importance of Trust in Love

Chapter 7: Love and Communication

Chapter 8: Love and Respect

Chapter 9: Love as a Choice, Not Just a Feeling

Chapter 10: Love and Faith

Chapter 11: Love and Vulnerability

Chapter 12: Love Beyond Romantic Relationships

Chapter 13: Love as a Healing Force

Chapter 14: Love and Patience

Chapter 15: Love and Forgiving Yourself

Chapter 16: Love Without Expectations

Chapter 17: Love in Parenthood

Chapter 18: Love in Aging Relationships

Chapter 19: Love and Boundaries

Chapter 20: Love in Times of Loss

Chapter 21: Love and Selflessness

Chapter 22: Love in Service to Others

Chapter 23: The Joy of Loving Fully

Chapter 24: The Legacy of Love

Chapter 25: Love Never Fails

Chapter: 1

The Meaning of Unconditional Love
Defining Love Beyond Emotions

L ove has always been one of the most powerful words we know. People make pledges, pray for it, and write about it in many songs. Even though love is beautiful, people often get it wrong. People often think of love as an emotion that comes and goes, like a wave. Unconditional love, on the other hand, isn't based on how we feel; it's based on something much more substantial. It's a choice, not a response. When we realize that love is more than just feelings, we discover that real love isn't about butterflies or excitement; it's about being loyal. It's about choosing to stay there, even when the emotions have faded or the situation has become more difficult. Emotions pass, but long-lasting love is a choice.

Love is more than just how you feel. Even if you love someone a lot, you could still feel irritated, fatigued, or even distant at times. Love isn't gone; it's simply being tested. To understand love beyond feelings, you need to learn to see it as stable instead of tumultuous. It's the kind of love that stays the same even when moods change. It speeds up and slows down, yet it never stops, just like a pulse. That's how love without conditions looks: solid, vibrant, and faithful. It keeps coming back, no matter what. What matters is endurance, not intensity.

To love beyond feelings is a sign of maturity. It means saying, "I will love you even when I don't want to," or "I will forgive you even when it hurts." It takes a lot of bravery and humility to love that way, which is why it's so unusual. It's easy to follow our feelings because they don't tell us to do anything. You have to be patient, give up things, and be nice to someone you love. It tells us to be kind when we want to pull away and to stay when it would be easier to go away. Love that goes beyond sentiment isn't blind; it sees everything fully, but chooses to be kind rather than judge. That's how unconditional love begins.

Chapter: 1

When we say that love is more than just feelings, we don't mean that emotions aren't important. All we mean is that they ought to be in the proper location. Emotions are like the colors in a painting; they bring love to life and make it genuine. The canvas is a promise; the colors fade without that basis. Deep love lasts because it's not about how easy or good it is. It comes from knowledge. It goes deeper and says, "I'm still here, even when things aren't perfect." This is the kind of love that stays even when you're sick, going through bad times, not getting it, or being quiet. It doesn't need much excitement to keep alive; it finds meaning in the quiet corners of loyalty and compassion.

To comprehend love as more than just a feeling, we need to know that it's not about what we get but what we give. Real love provides without asking anything in return. It's not easy, but it's real. It's the sort of love that listens even when it's exhausted, forgives without keeping score, and believes in others even when they don't do their best. It doesn't wait for love to be flawless; it flourishes in the defects. We start to comprehend what keeps relationships going when we love like that. Love doesn't last because of the huge things or the passionate times; it lasts because of the little things we do every day to be kind, patient, and understanding

God's love is like love that transcends feelings. The kind of love that stays the same no matter what. God loves us no matter what we do wrong or how we feel. His affection stays the same. That's how to demonstrate love without strings attached. We start to love individuals for who they are, rather than what they do, when we follow that example. We begin to view people as they are, not as they should be. We start to see that loving beyond our feelings doesn't make us weaker; it makes us stronger. It makes us smarter, nicer, and better at making friends.

Chapter: 1

Loving beyond feelings means recognizing that love can be both wonderful and unpleasant. Real love will push us to our limits, make us question our pride, and reveal our weaknesses. That's where its power comes from, though. It helps us improve. Love that lasts teaches patience in a culture that emphasizes speed. In a society that prioritizes self-interest, people are encouraged to put others first. It tells us to build things up rather than tear them down, and to take care of things rather than ignore them. To love beyond emotion means to know that relationships aren't supposed to be flawless; they're supposed to change and grow. It takes time to grow, and love without conditions provides it. It states, "I'm not just here for the fun times; I'm here for all of them."

Changing how we think about love also changes what strength implies. The most powerful love isn't the loudest or most passionate. It's the one that forgives quickly, listens quietly, and stays true without getting any accolades. It doesn't mind being nice. Being gentle is one of the finest things about love. People sometimes think that love is weak because it is soft, but anyone who has chosen to love even when it hurts knows that kindness takes more strength than coldness. Staying cool takes more strength than fighting back. And that's what makes unconditional love so strong: it's not a reaction; it's a choice.

The beauty of love that goes beyond feelings is that it affects how we see other people. It lets us love somebody because we care about them, not because we want something from them. Love is patient when things go wrong, forgiving when they hurt, and hopeful when they don't know what to do. It is a form of love that makes both the person who gives and the person who gets it feel good. You stop trying to be perfect and start accepting who you are when you love beyond how you feel. You start to realize that you don't find love; you make it.

Chapter: 1

At its core, unconditional love is something you do every day. We don't just do it once; we learn to live it by making choices every day. Every day, we have new possibilities to demonstrate love that aren't reliant on how we feel, how easy it is, or how much we can get out of it. It's how we listen when someone needs to be heard, how we forgive when it's hard, and how we care even when it's hard. This type of love doesn't need to be noticed; it expresses itself by being steady. When we love beyond feelings, we start to see that the little things, like a kind word, a quiet moment, or a simple act of service, often mean the most.

Defining love in a way that goes beyond feelings also provides you with freedom. We don't have to feel flawless love all the time. It reminds us that love isn't just about being excited all the time; it's also about being there all the time. The best relationships aren't the ones where people are always in love; they're the ones where people trust one another and are kind to each other. Love that goes beyond sentiments lets people make errors. It gives two people spaces to breathe, fail, and grow together. It turns disappointment into discovery and weakness into strength. It's the kind of love that says, "We're not perfect, but we're still good."

When we accept unconditional love, we learn to love the way we were designed to: with purpose, calm, and no fear. Loving beyond feelings is caring even when it's hard, staying when it's easier to leave, and giving when no one is looking. What keeps a relationship going is love that goes beyond feelings. Things change and feelings fade, but genuine love never dies. The kind of love that lasts is the calm, strong kind that is built on commitment rather than feelings. And that's the kind of love that will always be there for you.

Chapter: 1

The Meaning of Unconditional Love
Exploring the essence of love that never fails

L ove that never fails is more than a nice saying; it's a way of life that alters how we see ourselves, other people, and even life itself. This kind of love is constant, steady, and long-lasting, even when everything else seems to be changing. It doesn't matter how you feel, what's going on, or how easy it is. People get through hard times in relationships with the quiet strength they have. This love persists even when everything else fades away, like the thrill of the new, the excitement, and the passion. It doesn't break when you test it; it gets stronger. The heart of love that never fails is that it can forgive, keep going, and keep believing even when it would be easier to give up. It doesn't make a big issue out of it or yell, but it is quite loyal.

To comprehend what this love is really about, we need to first realize that love isn't about being flawless; it's about being with it. Love that never fails doesn't mean it never has issues. It merely implies it won't stop. It's the steady heartbeat that keeps going even when the body is feeble. This kind of love occurs when couples stay together and work through their differences, friends keep supporting each other even when they don't understand each other, or a parent keeps praying for a kid who has drifted away. Love is what makes you think there's still something to hold on to. This love is strong because of the tremendous faith behind it. It's built on hope, not feelings.

The best part about love that never fails is that it doesn't depend on anything. It doesn't say, "I'll love you if you deserve it" or "I'll stay as long as it's easy." It states, "I love you because I want to." That sort of love is like God's, since it offers everything and asks for nothing in return. When we love like that, we start to feel something really rare: peace that doesn't depend on how other people respond. We can stop keeping score when we have love that never fails. It is compassionate, patient, and keeps its word even when things change. Love lasts because it is built on something that will always be true, not just how you feel at the moment.

15

Chapter: 1

The strength of love that never fails is what makes it strong. It bends but doesn't break. It can get harmed, but it won't die. Real love was created in fire, so it's not simple to break. It gets stronger over time. It learns, moves on, and grows. We often think of love as something that makes us feel wonderful, but the truth is that love that never fails is often hard to handle. It tries our patience, makes us proud, and teaches us to give instead of ask for things. It pushes us to get better. It makes us better, kinder, and more caring people, which is what makes it sacred. Love really shows itself when things are bad. This indicates that true love isn't based on how simple things are; it's based on how dedicated we stay when things get hard.

A lot of what people call "love" doesn't last long, and it's plain to see that. It is built on sentiments that come and go, like the waves. But real love, the type that lasts, doesn't change with the weather. When others pull away, it's the steady hand that reaches out. It's the decision to be honest in a world that makes leaving seem like a smart idea. When doubt threatens to tear us apart, that voice answers, "I still believe in us." In a society that prizes getting what you want right now, love that never fails moves at a slower, deeper pace. It doesn't rush; it takes its time. It puts being present ahead of being flawless, faith ahead of feelings, and consistency ahead of ease.

Love that never fails also sees the good in people. It recognizes that everyone has imperfections, but it still loves them. This love doesn't turn a blind eye to reality; it accepts it. It's not blind; it's brave. It looks at the disarray and declares, "I still see beauty." That's how love lasts: by looking at the heart instead of the scars. Love learns to listen before making a decision, to comprehend before acting, and to forgive before getting angry. Love is unbreakable when you forgive. It learns to let go of its pride and replace it with understanding. The secret to love that never fails is that it doesn't try to be right; it tries to be pleasant.

Chapter: 1

To truly grasp never-ending love, we must first understand that it begins within us. You can't contribute if you don't know how to care for yourself. Grace and patience water the love seed that has been placed in the heart. When we accept unconditional love from God or other people, we begin to express it to others. It evolves into a way of life, a set of beliefs and behaviors. Love that never fails does not imply that we will never be wounded; it just implies that hurt will not have the final say. Love gives us the strength to keep going, even when we're tired, since it believes there's still something to try for. It's not about being flawless, but about not giving up.

Humility is an essential component of genuine love. To love genuinely, you must be willing to say sorry, accept your mistakes, and learn from them. Pride destroys what love creates, but humility protects it. Never-failing love seeks peace rather than victory in battle. It does not keep a note of wrongdoing; instead, it forgives and moves forward. It trusts rather than attempting to control things. And, perhaps most crucially, it does not vanish when things change; rather, it evolves alongside them. The calm strength of lifelong love is that it does not shatter under pressure; instead, it bends and changes shape, constantly finding a way to keep giving.

People perceive love in the small things they do every day, rather than in grand gestures. It's in the smile you give when you're tired, the kind word you say when you'd rather not say anything, and the tolerance you have when someone pushes your buttons. These small things are what keep love going. In regular existence, love takes on exceptional qualities. When things go well, it's easy to love; when things are tough, it's more difficult but more significant. That is the kind of love that can transform your life. It is steadfast, loyal, and graceful.

Chapter: 1

Forgiveness is another way to see the timeless core of love. It is necessary for the survival of any connection, friendship, or family link. Forgiveness revitalizes love and sustains relationships. When we forgive, we recognize that the connection is more important than the conflict. That option does not alleviate the agony, but it does initiate the healing process. Love that forgives lasts. It converts betrayal into understanding and disappointment into growth. The more we let go of our anger, the more love can flourish. Love dies without forgiveness, but it grows stronger because of it. That is how love never fails: it learns to get back up again after time.

Love that never fails knows when to let go of things rather than people. It allows others the freedom to be human. It does not anticipate perfection, but rather celebrates progress. It understands that loving someone entails accepting their entire journey, not just the pleasant moments. This love is not domineering; rather, it is soft and patient. It understands that loving sincerely entails offering freedom rather than fear. The longest-lasting relationships allow love to breathe—grow, adapt, and stretch without breaking. Love endures indefinitely because it allows grace in.

In the end, the core of unfailing love is that it resembles God. God's love never ceases, grows tired, or gives up. The same love that instructs us to keep our hearts open, trust in redemption, and find hope where others see only the end. When we live by this love, we become healers in a world that desperately needs it. It is not easy, but it is always worthwhile. Love endures when all else fails—when words fail, promises shatter, and sentiments shift. That is what never-failing love is all about: it endures all and has the capacity to rebuild, restore, and regenerate every heart it touches.

Chapter: 1

The Meaning of Unconditional Love
Biblical and philosophical perspectives on love

L ove has always been one of the most enigmatic aspects of being human. Faith and philosophy have both attempted to explain it, yet words alone will never fully capture its profundity. The Bible describes love as being patient, compassionate, modest, and long-lasting. It is an unchanging force that reveals God's identity. From ancient Greece to the present day, philosophers have seen love as the best thing a person can do, the thing that makes them good, moral, and purposeful. These points of view combine to provide a magnificent picture: love is more than a sensation or a notion; it is a spiritual and moral calling. It is what connects heaven and earth, soul and soul, and man and God. To understand love from both sides, you must recognize that it is a condition of being rather than an experience.

According to the Bible, God is the source of love. According to the Bible, God is love, not just loving. That fact serves as the foundation for everything in God's relationship with humans. His love is not conditional or preference-based; it is complete, unselfish, and redemptive. It is the type of love that provides even when it is not desired, forgives even when it is hurtful, and endures even when it is forgotten. Jesus exemplified this love perfectly, not only through words but also by actions. He demonstrated that true love is costly when He washed His disciples' feet, cured the sick, and died for others. The most effective method to express love is via service. Humility in action. And this is why biblical love is so powerful: it transforms both the giver and the receiver.

From a philosophical standpoint, love has traditionally been considered the best method to demonstrate virtue. Plato described it as a bridge between the human and divine, elevating the soul above its selfish desires and toward the pursuit of truth and beauty. Aristotle regarded love as the purest kind of friendship, based on respect, goodness, and development. Love is not about owning or dominating another person; it is about creating, connecting, and giving without expecting anything in return.

Chapter: 1

When we combine what the Bible says with what philosophy teaches, love becomes more than a sensation; it becomes the foundation of moral and spiritual existence. The Bible says love is the law, and philosophy says love is the goal. They both believe that love makes life worthwhile. Without it, everything else, including power, money, and knowledge, sounds hollow. Love balances justice and mercy, reason and compassion, faith and action. It teaches us to look beyond ourselves and treat others with the same respect and value. When we act out of love, we leave a lasting impression. When we fail to exhibit love, we lose a piece of what makes us human.

Love, according to the Bible, is something that is given rather than earned. It provides the foundation for both grace and forgiveness. God's love for humans is not based on transactions; it transforms them. He loves us not because we deserve it, but because that is His nature. This type of love inspires us to love others the same way. That's why Jesus told us to love our enemies. It isn't natural; it's spiritual. It is simple to love people who love us, but it takes divine strength to love those who hurt us. That's where love becomes sacred. It disrupts the cycle of rage, pride, and vengeance. Words alone cannot do what it does: softening hearts and healing wounds. In a society filled with judgment, love is the only thing that can transform darkness into light.

From a philosophical standpoint, love is also the foundation of morality. It gives life significance and elevates relationships to divine status. Immanuel Kant once stated that you cannot force someone to love you, but you may choose to love them. That choice is what distinguishes love as moral; it demands consideration, responsibility, and dedication. Love that is not thought about might become an obsession, and love that is pondered about can become knowledge. That is why philosophy advises us to love on purpose, not merely because we feel like it, but because we believe it is the right thing to do. When we act out of love, we align with truth, beauty, and purpose—all of which make life worthwhile.

Chapter: 1

In philosophy and religion, love is regarded as a power that transcends time and space. It endures because it stems from something other than feelings. According to the Bible, "love never fails," which suggests that true love cannot be broken; it transforms, forgives, and endures. It is eternal because it emanates from God, who is eternal himself. Philosophers have stated the same principle in several ways: love is eternal because it lives on in the hearts it touches. When we love sincerely, we leave a legacy that lasts longer than ourselves. Kindness, compassion, and sacrifice are all manifestations of love that transcend generations. This is why love is sometimes said to as divine: it lasts eternally, rather than just for a brief period.

One of the most fundamental biblical realities about love is that it cannot be separated from truth. Without love, truth is harsh and frigid; without truth, love is blind. Jesus demonstrated how to find that balance by telling the truth in love. His love mended, healed, and revived everything at once. Biblical love is revolutionary because it does not tolerate wrongdoing and instead seeks redemption rather than vengeance. It views people not just as they are, but also as they could be. Love recognizes the good in others, even when they make mistakes. It sees potential and helps it blossom. That is why love remains the most important commandment: it is both the beginning and end of all wisdom.

Love has a similar philosophical meaning. Philosophers like Søren Kierkegaard believe that love is the defining characteristic of true existence. He believed that in order to truly live, you had to love with a purpose rather than just because you had to. He believed that love was not merely moral, but also spiritual, a vocation that provides meaning to daily existence. Martin Buber and other philosophers taught that love alters our perceptions of others, transforming them from "I-It" (as objects) to "I-Thou" (as sacred). That kind of thinking is consistent with the Bible's teaching that love honors rather than uses. It transforms strangers into friends, rivals into brothers. Caring family. Love is the most excellent form of wisdom because it teaches us how to live for others.

Chapter: 1

When we combine biblical and philosophical views about love, we discover that they all say the same thing: love is what makes life worth living. It gives everything its significance. It is the soul's breath, the reason for every nice act and sacrifice. According to philosophy, it is the best thing you can do, and the Bible agrees. They both agree that love is something you choose to do on purpose and with creativity. It develops, forgives, and endures. The junction of God's grace and human decision produces unfailing love. It brings faith and reason together, as well as spirit and will.

As we reflect on different points of view, we realize that love is more than just a feeling; it is a way of life. The Bible defines love as serving, forgiving, and lifting up. Philosophical love entails seeking virtue, intelligence, and harmony. When we combine those two elements, we obtain a whole love: emotional and rational, passionate and patient, earthy and divine. This love does not perceive life as a race; rather, it sees it as a shared journey in which each act of kindness is a modest reflection of something that will never end. When we love in the same way, we can see why the Bible teaches that love never fails. It is not constrained by time, logic, or circumstances.

In the end, love is the only reality that both religion and reason can accept. It is the foundation of morality, the purpose for being, and the hope that holds the world together. The Bible and philosophy use different language, but they both convey the same thing: love is more than something we give; it is who we are supposed to be. Loving without expecting anything in exchange is the finest calling we can have. In our daily lives, we reveal the divine image in ourselves and the eternal light. The most significant aspect of never-failing love is that it reveals both God's heart and what humans are capable of.

Chapter: 1

Unconditional love is one of life's most misunderstood treasures. It goes far beyond emotions or fleeting feelings—it's a conscious choice to love without limits, conditions, or expiration dates. This chapter explored how love that never fails is rooted not in temporary happiness, but in commitment, grace, and truth. It also reminded us that both Scripture and philosophy agree: real love doesn't demand perfection—it calls us to a higher understanding of compassion and purpose. Take a moment to slow down and reflect on what this kind of love means in your own life.

Reflection Questions

1. How would you define unconditional love in your own words? Has your understanding of love changed after reading this chapter?

2. Think of a time when you loved someone even when it wasn't easy. What motivated you to keep showing love in that situation?

3. The chapter mentioned that love is more than emotion—it's an action, a commitment, and a choice. How do you personally practice that kind of love in your relationships?

4. Do you believe love can truly exist without conditions? Why or why not? Reflect on what makes love "unconditional" rather than temporary or transactional.

5. How do you handle moments when love is tested—when someone disappoints or hurts you? What does "love never fails" look like in those moments?

6. In your opinion, what's the difference between loving someone because of who they are and loving them despite their flaws? Which type of love do you think is more enduring?

Chapter: 1

From biblical to philosophical views, the idea of unconditional love invites us to look deeper than feelings. It's love that seeks truth and justice, love that forgives, and love that remains steady even when emotions shift. This section encourages you to reflect on how divine and human love intersect—and how practicing unconditional love can transform the way you live, give, and relate to others.

Personal Reflection & Application

1. The Bible describes love as patient, kind, and enduring. How does that description inspire you to change the way you treat people in your daily life?

2. Philosophers like Aristotle and Plato spoke of love as the pursuit of goodness and virtue. How do those ideas connect with your personal beliefs about what it means to love well?

3. Who in your life has shown you unconditional love? What did their actions teach you about compassion and commitment?

4. When it comes to self-love, do you find it easy or challenging to offer yourself grace? What would unconditional love toward yourself look like?

5. Think about the phrase "love never fails." What do you think keeps love from failing, even when circumstances or emotions change?

6. How can understanding love from both biblical and philosophical perspectives help you build stronger, healthier relationships—with God, yourself, and others?

7. Write a personal affirmation inspired by this chapter—something you can carry with you daily. For example: "I choose to love beyond emotion, to forgive freely, and to stand firm in love that never fails." Then create your own version that reflects your heart's truth.

Chapter: 2

Love in Action
How love is demonstrated through actions

Love is a nice word, but it is only a sound if nothing is done. What we do, not what we say, is the most effective method to demonstrate love. It's easy to say we care, but genuine love goes beyond words. It is shown in regular actions of generosity, sacrifice, and understanding. Love in action can be seen in the small things that happen every day, such as a warm dinner after a long day, a friend who listens without judgment, or a parent who works quietly to improve their child's life. These may not seem like significant events, but they are examples of love in action—steady, humble, and compassionate. loyal love is quiet; it stays loyal. It's not about showing off; it's about investing money.

Love becomes real when you put it into action. It can be seen in the eyes of someone who decides to let go of anger or to wait rather than becoming angry. You can sense it in a kind remark, a delicate touch, or when someone shows up when you least expect it. True love doesn't need an audience; it manifests itself through quiet persistence. It's the kind of love that cleans up after others without grumbling, prays for someone after they've been injured, and continues to demonstrate grace even when others might abandon them. Love in action is more concerned with objectives than with feelings. It is a drive to do good, even when it is difficult.

According to the Bible, faith without works is dead, and the same is true of love. Lovely words are crucial, but they are even more powerful when accompanied by actions. Love is not about waiting for the appropriate emotion; it is about making the correct choice. It's holding someone's hand when they're terrified, forgiving them when you'd rather argue, and giving them your time when you'd rather relax. You can see love there. It doesn't matter how you feel or what's going on, since it's founded on something more profound: the choice to care no matter what. It is the beating heart that sustains all connections. They have meaning because of the activity of love.

Chapter: 2

Looking closely, we can see that love takes numerous forms. It appears to be both service and sacrifice at times. It is how we treat others when no one is watching and how we deal with adversity. Love involves doing the right thing even when it is simpler not to. It is assisting someone who is unable to help themselves, without asking anything in return, and being kind rather than cruel. Love does not require recognition; it flourishes in quiet areas where kindness is valued more than acclaim. When you express love through your actions, you become part of something holy. You become a beacon of hope for someone who has forgotten what it's like to be cared for.

Love in action is about being present rather than being flawless. Being present wholly and entirely, even when words fail. When you're battling, love may be patience, and when you're feeling down, it can be gentleness. Sometimes it's forgiveness, bestowed repeatedly, not because someone deserves it, but because love gives without expecting anything in return. When times are difficult, we demonstrate our love the most. It's when you choose kindness over revenge, honesty over arrogance, and humility over victory. In those moments, love reveals its genuine power—not as a passing emotion, but as a healing force. That is what makes it so powerful: it affects both the person who receives it and the person who offers it.

Jesus taught us the finest way to love. He was always compassionate when He performed miracles, cured people, and spoke. He didn't just talk about love; he experienced it. He washed His disciples' feet to demonstrate love's service, forgave His adversaries to demonstrate love's redemption, and offered His life to demonstrate love's sacrifice. His actions were more powerful than any sermon. We are required to embody that sort of love: love that moves from comfort to bravery, from words to actions. Loving in that way reveals God's heart.

Chapter: 2

We often believe that love must be grand and dramatic to be meaningful, yet the small things we do daily are what truly matter. These tiny things, holding the door open, smiling, or checking on someone who is quiet, add up to something significant. Love does not necessarily alter the world immediately, but it does change people's hearts one by one. A tiny act of compassion may not seem like much, but it can mean everything to someone who is suffering. When we demonstrate love via our deeds, we sow seeds that develop slowly but deeply. Once planted, compassionate seeds can heal wounds we may never see again.

Consistency is crucial in love. It is not something we do once and then forget about; it must be done daily. We lay the groundwork for love in our lives every time we choose to be patient instead of angry, to understand instead of assuming, or to be kind instead of harsh. It is not a spectacle; it is a discipline. People who love sincerely do not always succeed; instead, they keep trying. Even when things are tough, they keep coming. And that is what love in action is all about: it is not about being flawless, but about never giving up. Love stays, listens, and perseveres through the agony. That's how it stays.

Love in action is what keeps partnerships alive. It is not enough to just declare "I love you." You must demonstrate it in small ways each day. The partner who listens rather than fights, the friend who visits at midnight, the child who forgives a parent, or the stranger who provides assistance. You don't simply talk about genuine love; you embody it. When love transforms into action, it fosters trust, heals, and makes others feel secure. It is a living monument to humanity's capacity for compassion in an often-unsympathetic environment. What makes hope come true is love put into action.

Chapter: 2

Love in action means having the courage to show vulnerability, to take the chance of being rejected, and to care deeply even when it is painful. To love by deed means to let your heart open, even if it is not recognized or understood. True love gives without anticipating anything in return; it doesn't wait for promises. Unrestricted love and selflessness, prioritizing others, require bravery. The question, "What will I receive in return?" is not asked in this kind of love. "How can I make a difference?" is what it asks instead. This kind of love raises people, mends relationships, and promotes peace wherever we go because it is an example of grace.

The true test of love is how it responds when it is most difficult. It's easy to love when things are basic and people are pleasant. But love manifests itself in the tension—in the misunderstandings, disappointments, and unseen sacrifices. When you choose kindness over harshness, when you offer mercy instead of judgment, or when you assist someone who has previously injured you, you are showing compassion. That's when the power of love shines brightest. They remind us that love is not weak, but rather strong. It can address suffering and loss while remaining pleasant.

In the end, love in action is what holds the world together. It converts faith into evidence, words into comfort, and promises into tranquility. Every time you choose to love—by giving, forgiving, serving, or remaining—you make the world a better place. When you love someone, it affects not only your relationship but also your life. It demonstrates that there is still good in the world, that hope exists, and that love never fails when lived day to day. Don't simply state, "I love you." Let your actions communicate the language of love that words can never fully explain.

Chapter: 2

Love in Action
The role of patience, kindness, and selflessness in love

Patience, kindness, and selflessness are the three key components of true love. Without them, love is nothing more than a fleeting emotion that is fragile and easily shattered. Love is made genuine not only by how we feel, but also by how we respond when things do not go our way. Patience enables us to slow down and look at others with understanding rather than wrath. It serves as a reminder that love takes time and that people do not change suddenly. When life looks harsh, kindness softens our words and warms our hearts. Selflessness is a higher form of love, as it entails placing another person's needs ahead of our own. These three characteristics make love not only conceivable but also robust.

One of the most challenging aspects of love is patience. It's easy to love when everything is going well, but true love emerges when we have to wait, endure, and trust. Being patient does not mean doing nothing; it means doing the right thing without haste. It entails being quiet when we want to speak, forgiving when we want to fight, and remaining calm when things become tense. Patience allows for relationship growth. It allows others to make mistakes while also providing them with opportunities to improve. Every long-lasting love tale includes instances when the couple must wait. These were occasions when being impatient could have ruined everything, yet patience saved the day. To love slowly means to love wisely. It demonstrates that you value the relationship more than your own ego.

Kindness, on the other hand, is love's gentle voice. It's not about large things; it's about small gestures that show you care. A pleasant remark can repair the damage caused by rage. When silence hurts, a friendly gaze can help. Kindness is the most authentic kind of love; it feeds the hungry, consoles the lonely, and forgives those who are imperfect. People do it for love, not for attention or appreciation. Kindness is a subtle revolution in a world where pride and aggression are frequently rewarded.

Chapter: 2

The third pillar, selflessness, may be the most difficult to follow. Being unselfish in love does not imply surrendering one's identity; rather, it entails ceasing to consider the cost. It's being willing to help others even when it's difficult for you. It's staying up to listen when you're sleepy, assisting when no one's looking, and forgiving even when no one apologizes. Selflessness converts love from a feeling to an action. It is what keeps love alive when feelings fade. True love does not question, "What's in it for me?" It asks, "How can I help?" That shift, from wanting to give rather than receive, is what makes love eternal.

Patience, kindness, and selflessness are like threads on a single piece of cloth. When one person is missing, the relationship begins to erode. When the storms come, patience keeps love steadfast. When life becomes cold, kindness keeps it warm. And when selfish wants threaten to break it apart, selflessness holds it together. Each characteristic benefits the others. Being patient makes you inherently friendlier. Being compassionate helps you prioritize others. And being unselfish improves your patience. They create a cycle of grace that keeps all healthy relationships running. These virtues do not come naturally; you must strive for them, be humble, and have trust. However, once they take root, they transform love into something unbreakable.

The Bible expresses this nicely in 1 Corinthians 13: "Love is patient, love is kind... It is not self-seeking." Those phrases have endured for hundreds of years because they depict what real love is like. They remind us that love is more than simply a feeling; it is something we can cultivate. Patience makes love last; kindness makes it warm, and selflessness makes it strong. When we follow these guidelines, we begin to demonstrate God's love, which never fails, believes everything, and bears all. It is difficult, but the effort is worthwhile. When these qualities are at its core, love can withstand anything.

Chapter: 2

Patience is frequently tested in situations of misunderstanding. It's that period of silence before you do or say something. When everything inside you wants to burst, love's most powerful act of strength is being quiet. Being patient does not imply pretending you are not hurt; it entails prioritizing tranquility over your first inclination. It allows you to listen and understand rather than make assumptions and blame others. Patience builds trust over time. It demonstrates that love is powerful and can withstand adversity without breaking. And when two individuals learn to be patient with one another, they create a safe love. Mistakes in this love do not imply the end of the relationship; rather, they mark the beginning of progress.

Kindness also has a subtle power. It can tear down the barricades of fury. It transforms anger into dialogue and healing. To truly be kind, you must be humble enough to choose the other person's sorrow over your own. It is the kind of love that gives someone a second opportunity, even if they disappoint you. Kindness is lovely because it expands with each act of generosity. Every pleasant thing you do sends out a ripple that reaches hearts you can't see. Kindness is the language of love in relationships; it demonstrates how much you care more than words could.

Selflessness is what keeps love together when all else fails. It is the most crucial aspect of any relationship since it is about giving rather than receiving. Being unselfish does not imply placing yourself last; rather, it involves prioritizing your own needs while still caring for others. It is the willingness to sacrifice comfort in order to connect with others. When we love without expecting anything in exchange, we begin to demonstrate divine love. This love doesn't mind how many times it's been hurt; it keeps coming back. That is the love that endures, the love that evolves, and the love that never fails.

Chapter: 2

To love maturely implies being patient, kind, and prioritizing others. It is about prioritizing depth over drama, peace over pride, and giving over taking. It entails understanding that love is not about doing everything perfectly; rather, it is about remaining in love even when things go wrong. Not all relationships are based on perpetual excitement. The best ones are based on consistent effort. People who forgive readily, give generously, and remain loyal quietly make them. This type of love is not easy; it requires effort, but it is extremely gratifying. When you love with patience, kindness, and selflessness, you improve your character and your relationship.

These three attributes also demonstrate how to love ourselves in a healthy manner. Patience serves as a reminder that growth requires time. Kindness teaches us to speak to ourselves respectfully rather than criticize ourselves. Selflessness tells us that love is about finding equilibrium. It is not necessary to give everything away; rather, give from a point of totality. When we practice these characteristics, they become second nature. We become gentler, more stable, and more receptive to others. In this sense, love takes action beginning with us. It starts with how we treat our own hearts before sharing them with others.

In the end, being patient, compassionate, and unselfish are not simply characteristics; they are choices. Every day provides an opportunity to practice them in fresh ways, such as waiting without complaining, speaking with kindness, and giving without keeping score. This is how love transforms from words to acts. This is how love strengthens, grows, and heals. Quiet faithfulness, not grandiose demonstrations of love, is what changes the world. So, love patiently, be kind to everyone, and give without expecting anything back. When love is lived this way, it is unstoppable. It endures through everything, hopes through everything, and never fails.

Chapter: 2

Love in Action
Real-life examples of enduring love

L ove isn't always found in grand gestures or in movie love stories. It often manifests in ordinary individuals who choose to care, forgive, and persevere during the most difficult periods of their lives. Real-life experiences of long-term love demonstrate that love is more than a fleeting emotion; it is a daily decision to be faithful, kind, and compassionate, even when it is difficult. One such narrative could be about a couple who have been married for decades and have faced illness, financial difficulties, and the death of a loved one. Their relationship has evolved from a youthful, passionate love to a steadfast companionship. They've discovered that love isn't about being flawless; it's about sticking to it. Every wrinkle on their faces tells a narrative about their challenges and successes together.

Long-lasting love frequently shines brightest when times are tough. Consider a spouse caring for their ailing mate. The days are long and the nights are frightening, yet love continues to flow with every medicine, kind word, and act of service that says, "You're not alone." That kind of love cannot be faked or forced; it is the result of genuine dedication. It is love that has moved beyond "what's easy" to discover "what's right." Enduring love says, "I'll carry you when you can't walk," and it means it. It understands that love is not about what we get from others, but about what we offer, even when no one is looking. It's love with rough hands and worn eyes, but a heart that never gives up. Forgiving someone who has badly injured you is sometimes necessary for long-lasting love. Rather than leaving, some people choose to repair what was broken. It could be a betrayed marriage or a friendship that has been silenced for years. But, through patience and kindness, love was able to repair the cracks.

These stories demonstrate that love is more than just avoiding pain; it is also about overcoming it. Even in the face of failure, true love can envision the future. It believes in redemption even when others only see ruin. It is not silly; it is brave. And this is the kind of love that endures, demonstrating to the world that forgiveness is not a sign of weakness, but of sheer power.

Chapter: 2

Families that remain close during both good and bad times can demonstrate enduring love. Consider the parent who works long hours to provide a brighter future for their children, or the child who grows up and continues to care for their aging parents. These acts of devotion are more than just an obligation; they demonstrate true love in action. A mother's love does not go away when her child leaves, and a father's love does not cease when he makes a mistake. Instead, their love evolves, grows, and lasts. It anticipates revolt, accepts failure, and celebrates reconciliation. This type of love demonstrates that endurance is something we do on purpose and with great attention.

We also see long-lasting love in friendships that withstand time, distance, and change. Friends who have been through a lot together over the years—breakups, new jobs, losses, and wins—understand that love in friendship is being there for each other. It's a sign when someone remains silent or recalls a minor detail that no one else does. Even if you don't entirely understand what they're going through, it's important to be supportive. An enduring friendship is built on a deep bond rather than constant conversation. It doesn't go away when you don't speak; it gets stronger when you trust someone. This kind of love is calm and devoted. It states, "I'm still here, even if we don't talk every day."

Long-lasting love can also be found where people aid others without expecting anything in return. The neighbor who checks on the elderly couple next door, the teacher who stays late to help a struggling student, or the stranger who displays generosity for no reason—all of these people demonstrate the same truth: love transcends relationships. It's the type of love that believes in others. These everyday heroes demonstrate that love is more than an emotion; it is something you do. Its legs represent compassion, while its hands represent empathy. When we choose to be kind, we become part of a larger drama in which love triumphs over apathy.

Chapter: 2

Another great example of long-term love is a couple that has learnt to love each other as they grow and evolve. People, dreams, and seasons all change over the course of their lives. However, long-lasting love evolves without losing its essence. After years of misunderstandings, the pair learns to communicate more effectively. After the kids leave the house, the spouses look for new ways to interact. Enduring love acknowledges that people change, but commitment need not. It welcomes change rather than hating it. It learns to fall in love with the same person over and over again, not because they haven't changed, but because love chooses to view them in a new way.

Long-lasting love can be silent and unseen, such as when a widow speaks fondly of her late husband. Time may have taken her spouse, but the love endures. She demonstrates her love by assisting others, telling stories, and keeping the memory alive. Love that endures does not die; it lives on in the hearts of those who remember. It demonstrates that love is constant; it does not fade; rather, it evolves. It becomes a heritage, a source of faith, and a source of solace. That is the power of lasting love: it transcends time and geography. Even as circumstances change, love remains constant.

Second chances can also indicate long-term love. Some couples ended their relationship but eventually reconciled. It wasn't because life was easy; it was because they recognized that love was worth the effort. These stories remind us that love is about loyalty, not perfection. It entails choosing grace over ego, and connection above comfort. When two individuals resolve to recreate what they have lost, they demonstrate that love can return from the dead. Love lasts because you choose to heal together, not because there is no pain. That is what makes love endure: the willingness to remain and grow no matter how many times it is tried.

Chapter: 2

Faith can also lead to lifelong love. People who continue to love even when life does not make sense, when prayers go unanswered, and hope seems distant—demonstrate a love that transcends emotions. Even when it hurts, love relies on God's goodness and continues to aid others while waiting for its own breakthrough. This type of love stems from your personality rather than your actions. It believes that love is never wasted and that every good deed, no matter how tiny, has a purpose. Love endures, not because everything is flawless, but because it is founded on something eternal.

One reality is true in all cases, whether romantic, familial, friendly, or spiritual: lasting love always accomplishes something. It provides, forgives, makes sacrifices, and remains. It is unconcerned about going through difficult times because it understands that storms do not destroy love; rather, they demonstrate its strength. People who have long-term love do not seek temporary enjoyment; instead, they create something that will stay. They understand that love is about finding meaning in pain rather than avoiding it. Love endures because it is founded on understanding, faith, and hope. It is unaffected by what is going on; it becomes stronger as a result.

The world needs more models of enduring love, love that is consistent, kind, and brave. This type of love inspires individuals to believe again, whether in lasting couples, devoted friends, or simple acts of compassion. It emphasizes that love is more than simply a word; it is a way of life. When love lasts, it leaves a trace on hearts and footprints for generations. It does not dissipate with time; instead, it grows deeper, stronger, and more beautiful. Everlasting love is ageless because it never ends, never gives up, and never fails.

Chapter: 2

Love is more than an emotion; it's a way of life. This chapter explored how love manifests itself in the decisions we make, the patience we demonstrate, the small things we do for others, and our willingness to prioritize others even when it is difficult. As you reflect on what you've read, consider how love manifests itself in your daily life, such as what you say, what you do, and how you treat others.

Reflection Questions

1. What does "love in action" look like to you personally? Think about one specific example where your actions spoke louder than your words.

2. When was the last time you showed love without expecting anything in return? How did it make you feel afterward?

3. The chapter described patience as the "first teacher of love." In your relationships, where do you find patience most challenging—and what might love be trying to teach you in those moments?

4. Reflect on a recent situation that tested your kindness. How did you respond? If you could go back, would you do anything differently?

5. Love often requires us to pause before reacting. Think of a time when holding back, listening, or showing understanding changed the outcome of a situation.

6. The role of selflessness in love can feel hard in a world that often says, "Put yourself first." What does healthy selflessness mean to you? How do you balance caring for others without losing yourself in the process?

7. Describe one small, consistent act of love that you can practice daily. Maybe it's checking in on someone, saying thank you more often, or offering forgiveness faster

Chapter: 2

Patience, kindness, and selflessness are not simply concepts; they are the modest actions we take to keep love alive when feelings wane. Real-life examples of lasting love demonstrate that partnerships last not because they are perfect, but because someone chooses love over and over again.

Personal Application & Growth

1. Think about someone in your life who has shown you patient love. How has their example influenced the way you give love to others?

2. What does kindness look like when life gets busy or stressful? How can you remind yourself to act with compassion even when it's not convenient?

3. In moments of conflict, do you find it easy or difficult to be selfless? What helps you move from frustration to understanding?

4. Reflect on a real-life story—yours or someone else's—that reminds you of enduring love. What lessons can you draw from it about faithfulness, resilience, and grace?

5. If someone observed your daily actions, what would they learn about the way you love? What do you hope they would see?

6. Imagine the kind of love you want to leave behind—a legacy of compassion, patience, and understanding. What steps can you take today to start living that kind of love?

7. Finally, write your own affirmation inspired by this chapter. For example: "My love grows stronger through action." Then craft one that feels personal—something you can carry with you as a reminder that love is most powerful when it's lived, not just felt.

Chapter: 3

The Power of Forgiveness in Love
Forgiveness as a cornerstone of lasting love

Forgiveness is one of the most difficult yet powerful ways to express love. Letting go of suffering and choosing peace over pride requires courage, humility, and faith. Love and forgiveness combine to become something unbreakable. Every long-term relationship, whether it's with a spouse, a friend, or a family member, includes moments of disappointment and hurt. But it is forgiveness that keeps love alive in those moments. Without it, resentment spreads like a weed, choking the roots of connection. Forgiving does not imply acting as if nothing happened; rather, it involves letting go of the bitterness so that love can breathe anew. It reads, "You hurt me, but I won't let that pain control us." You are not weak for making that decision; you are liberated.

Forgiveness is not a single event; rather, it is a journey. It can happen quickly at times, but it usually takes a long period since we have to cope with our emotions. The heart desires justice, but love prefers kindness. When we choose grace, we allow love to heal what anger could never do. Forgiveness does not erase the past; rather, it transforms our perception of it. It rebuilds what was broken, making it stronger. Couples who have been cheated on, families that have been torn apart by misunderstandings, and friends who have grown away due to pride can all find healing when forgiveness is involved. Forgiveness transforms not only the relationship but also the individuals involved.

Forgiveness has the potential to transform sorrow into wisdom. We regain control of our hearts once we forgive. We cease letting grief teach us how to love. Forgiveness is essential for the longevity of love because it preserves its purity. In contrast, failing to forgive someone progressively poisons love. It hardens the heart and converts love into indifference. But forgiveness softens the sharpness. It restores warmth and movement, much as sunlight melts ice. True love understands that there is no future without forgiveness.

Chapter: 3

When you love someone sincerely, you must learn to communicate forgiveness effectively. Everyone makes errors, and every relationship goes through ups and downs. But forgiveness is what makes love last, not fade. It is what transforms adversity into an opportunity. The best love stories are those that have overcome obstacles. When everything else is breaking apart, forgiving is what holds love together. It is the option to declare, "I still believe in us," even when trust has been violated. It's not about getting rid of the hurt; it's about developing trust, brick by brick, with kindness and patience.

Love requires humility. Pride teaches us to hang onto the wrong and make the other person pay for it. But humility makes us aware of our own flaws. No one is flawless, and love grows when we show others the same grace that we wish to receive. That is not to say that allowing individuals to be unpleasant or act in agony is insignificant. It entails being gentle while setting boundaries and preferring peace over punishment. Forgiveness does not imply forgetting; it entails remembering in a fresh way. It is choosing to see the individual not through the prism of their error, but through the possibilities of who they can be. That is when love becomes stronger: when it chooses to see hope instead of grief.

According to the Bible, "Love does not keep track of wrongs." It is simple to read those words, but difficult to live by them. However, they do hold the key to long-term love. When we keep reliving prior hurts, we deplete the delight of the present moment. Forgiveness opens the door for love to begin again. It doesn't mean the past didn't happen; it just means it has no influence over the future. True love does not keep track of wrongs like trophies; rather, it lets them go. Every time we let go of our anger, we come closer to liberation. We break the cycle of wrath and allow compassion to lead the way. That is how love endures through the storms: it does not hold grudges.

Chapter: 3

Forgiveness strengthens the emotional bonds between people. When you forgive, you reveal your deepest love. Instead of building barriers, you open your heart. Being open in this way brings individuals closer together and increases their trust in one another. It reads: "I still choose you, even after what happened." Love becomes real at that point, not because it's flawless, but because it's genuine. Forgiveness does not immediately alleviate suffering, but it initiates the healing process, and improving relationships makes them stronger than before. When two individuals learn to forgive, they provide a safe space for love to grow and evolve without fear of failure.

Being able to forgive requires bravery. It takes fortitude to let go of anger, especially when you believe it is justified. The individual who refuses to seek forgiveness is frequently the most difficult to forgive. However, forgiveness is not necessarily about reconciliation; it can simply be about liberation. Even if the apology never arrives, it is a decision for peace. Forgiveness allows us to move on from our past. We offer love, strength rather than anguish. Forgiveness is so wonderful because it restores balance to our hearts. Because love and hatred cannot coexist, they develop when one is diminished.

Forgiveness towards oneself is also nice. We carry regret from our past mistakes, making many relationships difficult. We keep going back to occasions when we failed, convinced that we do not deserve love. But love, in its purest form, reminds us that grace is available to all people. To really love others, we must first learn to forgive ourselves. Forgiving oneself teaches us kindness and humility. It allows us to love with empathy rather than dread. Accepting that we are not perfect makes us more likely to accept that others are not perfect either. Forgiveness is a gentle strength that restores both relationships and souls.

Chapter: 3

Forgiveness in lasting love is not a one-time event; it is a fundamental part of life. This concept permeates daily life and takes the form of small deeds, such as letting go of anger after a fight, choosing to be kind when words could be hurtful, or showing patience when a partner fumbles. A garden without water is like love without forgiveness; it may be alive for a while, but it will eventually wither. Love is revitalized by forgiveness, which keeps it alive and encourages its growth in the face of hardship. It emphasizes that love is grounded in steadfast trust rather than in vengeance. Every act of forgiveness lays the foundation for future peace. Moreover, forgiving is the most profound expression of love's resilience. More bravery is required to heal than to hold grudges.

The natural reaction to emotional suffering may be to retreat, yet love always invites vulnerability. Rather than being a sign of weakness, forgiveness is a display of courage. Despite hardship, it represents a decision to reaffirm one's belief in love. Every act of forgiveness is an act of narrative alteration, bringing hope in place of bitterness. Love gains new meaning in this process of rewriting. Not perfection is the foundation of enduring love; grace—the ability to make mistakes, get back up, and start over—is what keeps it going. In the end, the secret to the eternal nature of love is forgiving. It is the process that turns grief into healing and pain into meaning. Without forgiveness, love becomes ephemeral, brittle, and conditional.

On the other hand, when forgiveness exists, love has no boundaries. Instead of ignoring the truth, forgiveness redeems it. It turns hurt into understanding and pain into tranquility. This is forgiveness's power: it makes it possible for love to thrive rather than endure. We represent God's nature when we learn to love fully and forgive without conditions. Thus, forgiveness is really love in its purest and most enduring form, not merely an act of love.

Chapter: 3

The Power of Forgiveness in Love
How love leads to reconciliation

One of the best aspects of love is how it draws people back together. It is the time when humility and forgiveness come together, allowing two hearts that were once apart to find peace again. But it does not happen right away. Healing, rather than hating, is a long process that begins with love's silent decision. Love that forgives naturally seeks to make things right rather than retaliate. It recognizes the possibility of peace, even if it hurts. When love is in command, walls dissolve, pride disappears, and understanding takes its place. That is the marvel of reconciliation: it restores something that was before broken, making it stronger, more profound, and more important than before.

Love pulls people back together because it is more concerned with connection than correctness. It states: "Our relationship is more important than my pride." It's difficult to accept that truth, especially when the suffering is severe, but love is intended to heal, not harm. A phone call, a letter, or just expressing "I miss you" can be the initial steps toward reconciliation. It may not solve everything right away, but it does begin the healing process. Real love does not rush things; it understands that reestablishing trust requires time and honesty. It's not about pretending the suffering never occurred; it's about creating a new story in which grace triumphs in the end.

In reconciliation, love becomes an active force. It listens before speaking, attempts to comprehend before requesting to be understood, and provides without asking anything in return. This type of love is uncommon since it necessitates vulnerability. Even when it appears hazardous, it communicates, "I still care." However, being open is where real healing begins. When both hearts choose openness rather than closure, reconciliation is possible. Love does not forget the past; it brings it back. It transforms moments of disagreement into moments of kindness, and forgiveness opens the door for two individuals to reconcile.

Chapter: 3

Reconciliation thrives in an atmosphere of honesty and humility. Love doesn't sweep problems under the rug—it brings them into the light with tenderness and truth. It says, "Let's talk about what hurt us so we can move forward." Without love, conversations about pain become arguments, but with love, they become opportunities for understanding. When we allow love to guide our tone, our words become tools of healing instead of weapons of defense. The goal of reconciliation isn't to win—it's to restore. And that can only happen when both people approach each other with the intention to listen, learn, and grow together.

Sometimes, reconciliation takes time because healing hearts is delicate work. Love must be patient in that process. There will be moments of doubt, fear, and even frustration. But every small act of grace—every apology offered; every effort made—builds a path toward peace. Love that leads to reconciliation doesn't demand perfection; it celebrates progress. It understands that reconciliation isn't about returning to what was before—it's about creating something new. The cracks that once divided become lines of strength when filled with forgiveness. Like gold repairing a broken vessel, love makes the relationship even more beautiful after healing.

The Bible beautifully captures this truth in 2 Corinthians 5:18, reminding us that God "reconciled us to Himself through Christ." That means reconciliation isn't just about human relationships—it's a reflection of divine love. When we reconcile with others, we participate in something sacred. We mirror God's heart. Love becomes the agent of restoration, turning separation into unity, and bitterness into blessing. It's not just about peace between people; it's about peace within ourselves. Because every time we choose reconciliation, we heal a part of our own heart, too.

Chapter: 3

Love brings people back together by allowing us to see beyond our grief. Love alters how we perceive others. We start to view the person who made the error rather than the fault itself. We begin to recall moments when we laughed, assisted each other, and felt close, which defined our connection. Love demonstrates what we should fight for. That does not imply abandoning boundaries or rejecting pain; rather, it means believing that individuals can improve and relationships may be saved. Love adds, "This mistake will not be the end of our story." That's how reconciliation begins: one heart chooses hope over pain.

Taking the lead in reconciliation requires humility. Pride will always strive to keep us angry, keep us safe, and close us off from others. But love talks in a unique manner. It declares, "Pride is worse than peace." It takes a lot of guts to reach out after being hurt, and much more humility to admit we've hurt someone. However, individuals who have gone through reconciliation understand that the end result is worthwhile. Peace's lightness replaces anger's heaviness. Reconciliation improves rather than erases memories. It transforms grief into understanding and provides the connection a new cause to exist.

There are several real-life stories of how love can bring individuals back together. After years of not conversing, parents who are no longer connected to their children reconnect. Couples who used to be strangers are now friendly again. Friends who let anger separate them finally get down and understand why they were so important to each other in the first place. Each story centered on love. It came not from threats or disputes, but from being compassionate, gentle, and prepared to start over. That is what makes love so powerful: it will never give up on things that are worth keeping.

Chapter: 3

Making up is not always simple. Old scars can haunt you. Forgiveness can be more complex than you realize. But love comes back, one small step at a time. It is a subtle choice to remain in the discourse rather than leave. It is the willingness to try, listen, and trust again. Love is not naive; it understands that making things right requires effort. But it also understands that every ounce of effort is worthwhile because love provides tranquility. Reconciliation heals what is broken and brings new life to what seemed lost. It restores not only relationships but also the hearts.

When love inspires us to forgive, it has a knock-on impact. Having peace in one relationship might lead to peace in another. Families get better. Communities improve. People who watch people reconcile believe that love can still work. Reconciliation spreads because it demonstrates something everyone desires: connection. It serves as a reminder that love will always bring us back, no matter how far we have strayed. There is a lot of division in the world, but love has the power to bring people together. That is why reconciliation is so important: it not only mends broken relationships, but it also gives individuals new hope.

Ultimately, reconciliation is the most significant victory of love. It demonstrates that love is more than simply an emotion; it's a decision to forgive rather than be furious. Love enters through the door that forgiveness opens. Love holds the hand of the one who has injured them and says, "Let's start over." That type of love can reunite families, save marriages, and rekindle friendships. It is the kind of love that can transform ashes into beauty. When love is in command, reconciliation is both feasible and powerful. And in that power, we find the most authentic type of love: one that forgives, builds up, and endures forever.

Chapter: 3

The Power of Forgiveness in Love
Stories of forgiveness that sustained relationships

Every long-term relationship has a forgiveness tale. Love is beautiful, but it can also be terrible, perplexing, and disappointing at times. Relationships are strengthened by forgiveness, not the absence of dispute. True love understands that no one is flawless, and that harboring resentment is equivalent to swallowing poison and hoping the other person suffers. Forgiveness is what allows love to flourish. Every story of reconciliation, no matter how common or odd, reminds us that forgiveness is not only a nice thing to do; it is also the first step toward healing. These stories reveal what love looks like when it chooses kindness over judgment.

One of these stories is about a couple that had been married for more than twenty years. They'd been through a lot together, but a spell apart nearly broke them up. People said things that were difficult to forget, and laughter faded into silence for months. However, love remained deep within. Instead of arguing the next night, they sat at the kitchen table and spoke. They expressed their fears, accomplishments, and feelings of regret. Anger transformed into tears, and resentment turned into forgiveness. That one chat, despite its difficulty, altered everything. They discovered that forgiveness did not erase the past; rather, it restored the bridge that pride and time had destroyed. Their love not only survived but thrived as a result of their forgiveness for one another.

A mother and daughter, estranged for years due to stubbornness and misunderstandings, finally reconnect when the daughter has a baby. The mother, who had always harbored love for her daughter, reaches out after realizing the power of forgiveness. Their reunion, marked by emotional acceptance and joy, teaches them that love can flourish when forgiveness is granted, regardless of past grievances.

Chapter: 3

Forgiveness is also effective in friendships. Two buddies who had always been close were at odds due to betrayal. They appeared unable to reconcile due to harsh words and damaged feelings. There was no communication for years. Then one of them had to deal with a significant sickness, which altered everything. Suddenly, another friend texted, "I heard what's going on, and I'm here if you need me." That one gesture broke years of stillness. The sick friend replied, and their bond eventually returned. They laughed and sobbed again, realizing that love, not time, had healed the wound. Forgiveness restored a friendship that both people thought was lost for good. It reminded them that love in friendship isn't about being perfect, but about being nice.

One of the most powerful examples of love and forgiveness is when lovers reconcile after being betrayed. Betrayal causes significant pain and undermines trust. However, some relationships survive because of a unique type of love. There is a story about a husband and wife who are disloyal to one another. It hurt so badly, but they both wanted to start fresh. They communicated openly, prayed, and went to counseling every day. It was painful and time-consuming, but each act of forgiveness made a small difference. Trust was eventually restored, not because the grief subsided, but because forgiveness made way for fresh beginnings. Their love demonstrated that, even when things are damaged, forgiveness can transform shame into strength.

Then there's the story of a brother and sister arguing over their parents' money after they died. For years, money and hatred kept them apart. Neither of them wished to go first. However, one Christmas, the brother declared he couldn't take it anymore. He contacted his sister not to argue, but to say, "I miss you." She cried not because the situation was resolved, but because love had triumphed over pride. They met, hugged, and decided that peace was more essential than possessions. Forgiveness reunited their family and helped them feel like a unit again. A small act of humility can repair what appeared to be irreparably shattered.

Chapter: 3

When life reminds us of our own frailty, we typically find forgiveness. A story is told about a father and son who haven't spoken in almost 10 years. The boy said his father was too strict. They exchanged words, burnt bridges, and parted ways. Then the father became ill, and the son discovered this. The son visited the hospital because he was angry and adored his mother. When his father entered, he remarked, "I'm glad you came," with a weak smile. No need for apologies or explanations—just love. That moment dispelled years of rage. The boy clutched his father's hand, and the quiet was infused with forgiveness that words could never express. When his father died, the son replied, "We didn't have much time, but love was enough."

There's also a story of two best friends who grew up together but lost touch due to a misunderstanding. Years later, one of them experienced the loss of a family member. The other person decided to attend the funeral without hesitation. There was no need for words; simply being there was sufficient. That kind gesture expressed "I'm sorry" louder than any words could. Sometimes love doesn't have to fix everything; it just needs to be present. Forgiveness does the following: it goes where the pain was. Their friendship did not continue where it had left off; instead, it began with a new foundation of humility and understanding. Love once again triumphed over pride.

Forgiveness is what helps couples deal with the ups and downs of life, even when they are married. One elderly couple revealed that the secret to their 50-year marriage was forgiveness, not passion or luck. They had occasionally clashed, disagreed, and even doubted each other. However, every night before going to bed, they promised each other that they would never go to bed angry. The husband laughed and replied, "We've said sorry too many times to count." "But that's why we're still here." Their experience demonstrates that forgiveness is a practice you do daily. Love becomes unbreakable when it chooses to forgive daily. It develops into a love that can endure everything.

Chapter: 3

Forgiveness does not alleviate pain, but it does change it. In every reconciliation story, love is the thread that binds torn hearts. When you may be angry, choosing to forgive is a sacred act. "I value this connection more than my pride" is a statement of affection. That is when the healing process begins. According to one couple, forgiving someone was similar to caring for a garden. Their reply was: "You have to keep pulling out weeds before they take over." That image truly captures the truth: love requires ongoing care, and part of that care includes forgiveness. Bitterness rises in its absence. Beauty blossoms once more.

Some forgiveness stories do not lead to reconciliation, but they do bring peace. A woman forgave her ex-husband not to reconcile, but to let go of years of resentment. "I realized forgiveness wasn't for him—it was for me," she explained. "It set my heart free to love again." Forgiveness provides closure, but reconciliation does not always occur. It enables us to love without feeling furious. It's a gift we give to ourselves and others. Her experience teaches us that love does not always imply staying together; it may also mean wishing the other person well from afar.

At the end, all of these stories agree on one thing: forgiveness, like grace, keeps love alive. It makes broken things beautiful and transforms endings into fresh beginnings. Without forgiveness, love becomes conditional and ineffective. It is the source of eternal love. Forgiveness, no matter how minor, helps to sustain relationships. It brings hope to those who are down and reminds us that no wound is too deep to heal. The most powerful act of love is forgiveness. It is the act that keeps families together, friendships alive, and hearts in tune. And in every story, when forgiveness is granted, love not only survives but grows stronger.

Chapter: 3

Forgiving someone is one of the most difficult but liberating acts of love you can do. It transforms stories of grace and growth into ones of broken relationships. This chapter examined how forgiveness serves as the foundation for long-term love, facilitates reconciliation, and, in real-life examples, may even strengthen the most fragile ties. Stop, breathe, and reflect on what forgiveness has meant in your life and relationships.

Reflection Questions

1. When you think about forgiveness, what's the first feeling that comes to mind: relief, fear, anger, or peace? Why do you think that emotion rises first?

2. Is there someone you've struggled to forgive? What holds you back from releasing that burden? Write honestly about the emotions that surface when you think about this person or situation.

3. In your relationships, do you tend to forgive quickly, or do you hold on to pain until it fades on its own? How has that affected your ability to love freely and fully?

4. What do you think it truly means to "forgive but not forget"? How can you honor your healing without reopening old wounds?

5. The chapter mentioned that forgiveness is strength, not weakness. Reflect on a time you chose to forgive someone. How did it change your relationship, or perhaps, how did it change you?

6. Think about your personal definition of love. After reading this chapter, how would you describe love that forgives?

Chapter: 3

Forgiveness and reconciliation are two aspects of the same principle. One enlarges the heart, while the other restores the bridge. This page encourages reflection on the restorative influence of love and the transformative effect of forgiveness on your own narratives.

Personal Application & Growth

1. Can you recall a time when reconciliation seemed impossible, but love found a way to heal the divide? What did that process teach you about patience and grace?

2. How do you respond when someone asks for your forgiveness but hasn't yet earned your trust? What steps could you take to rebuild a connection without reopening pain?

3. Think of one story of forgiveness from the chapter that moved you most, perhaps a mother's grace, a friend's courage, or a couple's second chance. Why did it resonate with you personally?

4. What lessons about love and forgiveness would you want to pass down to someone younger, a child, a friend, or a future generation?

5. If love could speak directly to your heart right now, what do you think it would say about forgiveness and peace?

6. Write a brief personal affirmation inspired by this chapter. For example: "I choose to forgive not because it's easy, but because peace is worth it." Then create one that feels true to your own story.

7. Finally, reflect on this: What kind of love are you building—one that holds on, or one that lets go? How do you want forgiveness to shape the legacy of your relationships?

Chapter: 4

Love Through Trials and Challenges
Navigating difficult times with love

C elebrating love is effortless when circumstances are favorable and align with one's desires. The true measure of love is revealed during challenging circumstances. Adversity can reveal the authentic and the superficial. During tumultuous times, superficial affection diminishes, yet profound, unconditional love endures. Love does not disregard adversity; rather, it flourishes in its presence. Adversity does not extinguish love; it fortifies it. They instruct us to cultivate patience, enhance compassion, and recall the reasons we chose one another in the first place. When two individuals endure adversity together, they discover that love transcends mere emotion; it is a deliberate decision to remain, assist, and maintain faith even in uncertainty.

Every relationship experiences fluctuations. At times, financial difficulties challenge your patience; at other times, illness tests your fortitude; and occasionally, emotional detachment assesses your heart. During such moments, love must transcend mere words and manifest as action. In times of difficulty, love manifests; in moments of fatigue, it attentively listens; and in states of emptiness, it generously bestows. In uncomplicated circumstances, expressing "I love you" is effortless. When circumstances appear to be disintegrating, existence becomes more challenging. However, that is where the essence of love truly radiates. Love does not await the opportune moment; it manifests as illumination in darkness. Love is the force that unifies when all else disintegrates.

In challenging times, loving someone entails perceiving them as an ally in the issue rather than the issue itself. It signifies maintaining awareness of shared interests, especially within tension. You learn to advocate for one another rather than against one another. This mindset transforms challenges into opportunities for learning and development. Enduring love is characterized by the choice to remain united rather than separated, to seek understanding rather than assign blame, and to embrace faith rather than succumb to fear.

Chapter: 4

Communication is essential at challenging times. Numerous relationships end due to a lack of communication rather than the severity of their issues. Love under adversity entails the ability to communicate when inclined and to heed when desired. It signifies expressing, "I lack omniscience, yet I am present." Exercising patience at moments of anger is the most effective demonstration of love. It is the capacity to pause and contemplate before responding, and to choose empathy rather than wrath. Challenges can either unite individuals or create distance between them. The distinction lies in the expression of affection during those periods. When love endures adversity, it cultivates an unbreakable trust.

It is crucial to recognize that love does not include pretending that all is OK. Love acknowledges suffering but refuses to be defined by it. It permits vulnerability. By acknowledging our worries and vulnerabilities, we create space for love to provide solace. Providing support for someone is among the most affectionate actions one can undertake. While you may not resolve the issue, your presence demonstrates your concern. That solace can hold greater significance than any response. Love need not articulate; it merely must exist. It resides in the silent fortitude of clasped hands amidst tears, in prayer at moments of diminished faith, or in softly imparting hope to a shattered heart.

True love perceives challenges not as dangers, but as opportunities for growth. Each struggle reveals insights about our character and values. Love instructs us on perseverance, especially in challenging circumstances. It demonstrates that genuine intimacy is founded not on convenience, but on dedication. It is the decision to persistently return each day, despite fluctuations in emotions. Such decisions provide the foundation of enduring love over time. Couples, friends, and families who endure adversity together often reflect on and recognize that these challenges were not the end; rather, they marked the beginning of a profound connection.

Chapter: 4

Enduring love requires faith, faith in one another and in a greater purpose beyond oneself. In overwhelming circumstances, love encourages you to perceive beyond the visible. It signifies, "I believe we will overcome this," despite the uncertainty over the method of resolution. Faith prevents love from disintegrating due to fear. It contextualizes sorrow by illustrating that adversity is transient, whereas love endures. When individuals ground their relationships in faith, challenges cease to be catastrophic and instead become opportunities for growth. They define our identity, fortify us, and affirm that love is not a sign of weakness; rather, it is a manifestation of strength.

Forgiveness can often be the most arduous aspect of loving someone throughout difficult times. Stress induces negative behavior, and words uttered in anger can have a lasting impact. However, forgiveness enables love to continue. "I prioritize our relationship over my pride." Forgiveness serves as a restorative remedy during such instances. It alleviates anger and bestows grace in its place. Each "I'm sorry" and "I forgive you" serves as a thread that reunites hearts. Love need not be flawless; it merely requires perseverance. Forgiveness softens relationships when life endeavors to complicate them. It subtly conveys that those errors do not characterize love; rather, it is redemption that does.

Numerous narratives of love that persevered against insurmountable odds exist. Couples who endured adversity and discovered resilience in one another. Parents who remained resilient together following a loss and maintained their faith in the face of despair. Friends who remained steadfast despite betrayal, opting for understanding above judgment. In every narrative, love must endure suffering and emerge more resilient. These individuals discovered that love endures when it possesses a purpose. Conversely, they discovered that adversity may fortify love, compassion, and faith. Love is peculiar as it intensifies in the areas where it has been most rigorously challenged.

Chapter: 4

To navigate difficult times with compassion, it is essential to learn to let go of control. There will be times when having faith—confidence in the process, in each other, and in love being enough—is your only option. Even the strongest hearts are frequently weakened by life, highlighting our interconnectedness. We learn from love to rely on grace instead of perfection. It is not about having all the answers; it is about negotiating the unknown together. Love is beautiful because it only needs dedication to last; it doesn't need clarity. Love is your compass through uncertainty when faced with obstacles.

Gratitude is essential during challenging times. There is perpetually something for which to express gratitude, especially during challenging times. A collective laugh, a serene moment, or a minor act of benevolence can all contribute positively. Gratitude shifts your focus from what you lack to what you possess. It alleviates anxiety and sustains affection. When you cultivate the habit of seeing the positive attributes in one another, the challenges that arise lose their capacity to create division. Gratitude does not alleviate suffering; it merely serves as a reminder that love persists. Merely acknowledging that can suffice to sustain you. Gratitude transforms adversity into learning and suffering into significance.

The profundity of a relationship is determined by the extent to which you support one another throughout challenging times. It is easy to love in favorable circumstances, but it takes bravery to love amid adversity. Enduring love amidst adversity is love that truly embodies grace. It remains, pardons, and relinquishes. It does not evade challenges; it advances towards restoration. When two individuals, or even two souls, choose to endure adversity together, they forge an unbreakable bond. They forged a lasting relationship, not because life was perfect, but because they persevered in their commitment to one another. Enduring difficult periods with love entails prioritizing faith over fear and love over all else.

Chapter: 4

Love Through Trials and Challenges
How love remains steady through hardship

W hen all other aspects of your life are uncertain, love remains a reliable constant. When circumstances are favorable, love appears effortless, but the true measure of love is revealed during challenging times. In the face of storms, genuine love does not flee; it entrenches itself further. It remains composed among change; it adapts, maintains resilience, and preserves its essence. Adversity unveils the true nature of love. If that foundation consists solely of emotions, it will disintegrate. However, if it is founded on trust, faith, and genuine dedication, no adversity can dismantle it. Enduring love adapts without fracturing. It does not disregard the difficulty; rather, it opts to recognize the positive even within adversity.

Love possesses a beauty that endures even in challenging circumstances. It is unobtrusive, consistent, and reliable. Envision a pair seated in a hospital room, one grasping the other's hand in silence, yet conveying profound emotions without words. Such love is beyond verbal expression. It is presence that communicates. The parent who, while working extended hours, nonetheless reads a bedtime tale to their child, even when fatigued. That exemplifies the perseverance of love. Enduring love may lack glamour, yet it possesses strength. In challenging times, this type of love chooses fidelity, and in moments of emotional scarcity, it chooses patience. It serves as a reminder that love is not contingent upon favorable circumstances; rather, it is defined by our willingness to persevere during adversity.

Love endures despite adversity because it is rooted in a sense of purpose rather than the pursuit of perfection. Adversity does not extinguish love; it reveals its profundity. They remove the superficial layer to reveal the underlying reality. Individuals discover latent strength during challenging times when supported by others, such as family. The tears, the stillness, the forgiving, and the daily decisions to remain exemplify that love is not feeble. It may require substantial effort. It is in challenging times that love intensifies, forged through adversity and sustained by grace.

Chapter: 4

Love that stays strong through tough times is patient. It doesn't want you to heal quickly or perfectly. It knows that there are good and bad times in life, some of which are bright and joyous and others of which are dark and dangerous. When things go bad, patient love waits for hearts to mend, hope to return, and trust to be reestablished. It doesn't stop when things take a while. Instead, it says, "I'm here for as long as it takes." That type of love not only makes it through tough times; it gets stronger during them. Love learns to be patient as it waits. It learns to rely on love that lasts rather than on feelings that come and go.

Faith is what keeps love strong when life gets hard. Faith that believes there is a reason for the sorrow. Faith that says, "We'll get through this," even when it appears like we can't. Faith-based love is unbreakable because it is not based on what happens; it is based on hope. You can see it in couples who have lost everything but yet smile because they have each other, or in families that hold hands through loss but refuse to lose their kindness. People who love with faith know that every storm will pass and that even when they lose something, they can learn from it, get closer to someone, or start over.

Another vital technique to keep strong during hard times is to talk to each other. When people don't talk, pain can easily turn into distance. But love that talks, even when it's painful, keeps people close. Mature love includes being honest about your anxieties, talking about the hurt, and choosing to understand rather than blame. It's not about who wins the fights; it's about keeping the link strong. When you say, "I may not agree, but I'm not going," you develop trust. That's what steadfast love looks like: it's not flawless, it's messy and emotional, but it never stops trying. It's a love that says, "We're in this together."

Chapter: 4

Difficult times can help us understand what love is. It's not the good times or the butterflies; it's the strength to cling on when you want to let go. People who love each other know that tough times don't imply they have to give up. Every challenge we confront together is a memory that illustrates how solid our relationship is. When things are tough, love gets stronger. People who go through sorrow, loss, or uncertainty together become stronger. Not because things grew easier, but because they learned how to be there for one another when it was toughest.

Love is quietly heroic when it stays strong during tough times. It's not as flashy as major romantic gestures, but it's considerably more effective. It's the love that comes back every day, even when it doesn't feel like it. The partner who keeps believing, the friend who keeps calling, and the parent who keeps praying. It's the love that lasts even when things get tough. Even if the world doesn't see it, this type of love lasts. It's the kind of love that kids remember, that friends need, and that time can't take away.

Of course, unwavering love doesn't mean disregarding pain or pretending that everything is okay. It's about being truthful with each other. Sometimes, love requires having tough conversations, letting go of things, or facing facts that make you feel bad. But it still doesn't leave the boat. It stays, listens, and learns. A strong love realizes that how you deal with problems is what makes or ruins the relationship. When two people resolve to work through their problems rather than run from them, they build a sturdy foundation that no storm can break. That's when love becomes unbreakable—not because it never had to go through harsh times, but because it did.

Chapter: 4

Love that lasts needs grace. Grace is what keeps love gentle, even when circumstances get hard. It helps people forgive, come back, and see one another with understanding rather than judgment. Grace reminds us that everyone makes errors and that love is about supporting each other, not keeping track of who has done what. Grace cleans the wounds when life becomes dirty, not perfectly, but with love. It turns "I can't believe this happened" into "We can still get through this." Grace is always there in steadfast love because it gives love the power to begin again.

Love stays strong when it chooses to be grateful instead of mad. Even when things are hard, there is always something to be grateful for. It may be the person next to you, the things you learnt, or the strength you got. Being grateful affects the way we think about problems. It doesn't make the pain go away, but it reminds us that love is still there. When couples or families are having a hard time, they practice thankfulness to focus less on what's wrong and more on what's still right. That one simple difference in how you see things keeps hearts connected and hope alive. Thankfulness gives you strength, and strength is what makes love last.

Love stays strong during harsh circumstances because it understands who it is. It doesn't need good days to show how strong it is; it shows how strong it is when things are hard. It is strong, loyal, and forgiving. The best sort of love is one that has been put to the test and made stronger by terrible circumstances. It's the kind of love that says, "I still choose you" after you've been let down, failed, or scared. That love will continue forever. That steadfast, unchanging love will always be there, even when all else slips away. It's a love that not only lasts through tough times but also shines through them.

Chapter: 4

Love Through Trials and Challenges
The role of perseverance in enduring love

Perseverance is the steady beat of love that lasts. It's what keeps love alive when feelings fade, situations change, and life doesn't go as planned. In every meaningful connection, whether it's with a partner, family member, or God, there will be times when it's easier to give up than to keep going. But perseverance says, "I'm not going to leave." It's the option to keep loving, even when it's hard. The wonderful part about perseverance is that it makes love more than just a feeling; it makes it a promise that will last forever. It's love's promise at work. It's not flashy or thrilling; it's steady, faithful, and resolute. That's what makes it so strong. Love is powerful and indestructible because it lasts through hard times.

Perseverance doesn't mean disregarding pain or pretending that everything is alright. It's about going through tough situations and choosing to be strong regardless. Love that lasts doesn't deny reality; it just won't let it win. Life will throw things at you that you don't understand, such as money issues, illness, death, and times when you don't know what to do. But if you keep going, love can persist through the storm. When the wind blows fiercely, the roots of a tree grow deeper. The roots of the tree get stronger as they move deeper. Love is the same way. When things get tough, love makes us more patient, faithful, and kind.

Enduring love recognizes that being persistent doesn't equal being perfect. It doesn't mean never falling; it means always helping each other get back up. Every relationship has weak points at times. There are days when words hurt, hopes don't come true, or dreams seem too far away. But love that lasts doesn't let those instances tell the whole story. It keeps coming back. It continues believing. It is constantly pushing for connection, even when feelings wane or hope seems far away. "I love you" is a promise that lasts forever, not just a word spoken once. It is expressed every day by sacrifice and consistency.

Chapter: 4

When things get tough, it's evident how important it is to persevere with love. Sometimes you'll have to be patient, and sometimes loving someone will feel more like labor than love. But that's where love really starts to bloom. Endurance promotes character, and perseverance teaches how to keep going. Testing love makes it stronger. "It's not always easy, but it was worth it," is something people who have been together for a long period often say. They've learned that being persistent doesn't mean never having problems; it means never giving up on each other because of them. That's what helps others believe in you, mature, and feel more deeply.

Love that lasts knows how to move on. If you don't forgive, being persistent becomes being stubborn. But love can't be stopped when it has both strength and grace. For love to last, it needs forgiveness. It lets go of anger, accepts mistakes, and sees the whole picture. Love that lasts states, "I know you're not perfect, and I'm not either, but I still choose you." That single choice, repeated over and over again, makes love stronger than anything else. Forgiveness clears the heart, making it possible to keep going even when feelings change.

Having faith is a big element of sticking with something. It offers love something to cling to when it doesn't make sense to keep on. You can get through the process if you think that love has a purpose. Faith reminds us that every situation can help us grow rather than make things worse. It informs you that the fight is worth it and that no season lasts forever. Faith-based love lasts because it looks beyond the suffering of the present. It wants things to go better, even if the road ahead looks long. Faith gives you the strength to keep going, making love a journey that lasts a lifetime rather than a short-term bond.

Chapter: 4

Love that lasts isn't only about being together; it's also about growing together. There is a distinction between living and performing well. People stay in relationships out of fear of the unknown or because they're used to them. On the other hand, real perseverance comes from making a purposeful effort. It is a love that adapts to the changing seasons. It learns from the past, changes with the present, and looks forward to the future. It doesn't hold on to the past; it invests in the future. When two people talk about their concerns, they learn more, understand each other better, and become stronger. They know the battle wasn't for nothing; it was where they learned to trust one another more and grow closer.

When things become tough, perseverance teaches you to wait. It serves as a reminder that love does not develop as swiftly as one would like. It can take time to heal, work to understand, and faith to grow. Being patient is important. It's being willing to stay even if you don't know what will happen. And as you wait, love evolves from a feeling to a decision you make every day. When things are fun, it's easy to be dedicated, but love that lasts shows itself when things are boring, uncomfortable, or inconvenient. That's where commitment really shines.

Perseverance can also be for others. It's the capacity to put your partner's needs ahead of your own. Love that lasts says, "I'll choose peace over pride," "I'll choose patience over control," and "I'll choose understanding over anger." This humility is what makes endurance so lovely. It's not about winning; it's about protecting what's important. In any long-lasting relationship, tenacity is the silent hero, the force that keeps hearts united through every season. It doesn't have to be loud or well-known; its strength lies in its steadiness.

Chapter: 4

Perseverance also teaches us that love is a process, not a destination. The journey of love is filled with numerous turns, ups, and downs. But the trip is worth it because you keep going. When we've been through the lows, the highs are more enjoyable. Love gets stronger when it hurts and keeps going. It becomes harder when you share memories, lessons, and wins. You become stronger every time you tackle an issue. Love that lasts doesn't attempt to be perfect; it makes you stronger. It realizes that staying together isn't about never having problems; it's about always being able to come back to each other with grace.

Sometimes being persistent means letting go of fear, pride, or unreasonable expectations, and other times it means holding on. It's knowing when to keep going and when to let things happen. Being persistent doesn't imply fixing what's broken; it means taking care of what's still beneficial. It provides space for healing, growth, and starting over. Love that lasts isn't fixed in stone; it changes, bends, and keeps faith alive. It does not currently seek solutions; it simply refuses to stop believing that love is worth the effort. That kind of thinking will last longer than a few weeks.

In the end, the best thing you can do for love is to keep going. When the world urges you to give up, it's believing in "us." It means being there for someone when things are rough, forgiving them when they don't deserve it, and staying hopeful when things seem bleak. If you keep going, love lasts longer. It turns short-lived feelings into deep loyalty. Love is like a spark that goes out if you don't keep it going. With love, it's like a flame that never goes out. That type of love can transform lives. It is the kind of love that endures steadfastly and affirms, "No matter what occurs, I will not release my hold."

Chapter: 4

There are always challenging periods in love stories. Some are modest, like misunderstandings or stress from everyday life, while others feel like storms that may break everything apart. The most crucial question to ask is, how can we love when things are hard? Think about the issues you've had with your partner, friend, or family member. Did love help you get through the tough times, or did it show you where you needed to improve? Trials can teach us how powerful love really is. What do you think kept love alive when you reflect on your life? Was it talking, waiting, having faith, or simply being there? What did those times teach you about yourself and the people you care about?

Reflection Questions:

1. When life becomes difficult, how do you personally respond in your relationships—do you shut down, withdraw, or reach out for understanding?

2. Think of a time when love helped you navigate a personal challenge. What did that experience teach you about strength and vulnerability?

3. How can you remind yourself to respond with patience and compassion the next time love is tested by adversity?

4. What practical ways can you show love even when you're emotionally drained or uncertain about the future?

5. In your opinion, what does "steady love" look like in real life?

6. How can you practice emotional steadiness when your relationship is under stress?

7. What role does forgiveness play in maintaining stability during hard times?

8. Think of one area where your love could become steadier. What small change could you make this week to strengthen it?

Chapter: 4

Perseverance is the unseen weapon of love. It's what keeps partnerships going despite suffering, time, and doubt. It doesn't always feel like being brave; sometimes it looks like small acts of loyalty, like listening when it's easier to dispute or remaining when it's easier to leave. Persevering love doesn't imply disregarding issues; it means believing that affection is worth fighting for. Consider how your connections have evolved as a result of your persistence. Did you ever want to quit, but persevere? What gave you the strength to keep going? Sometimes love instructs us to stay still while we recover or to keep going even when we don't know what to do next. What does perseverance mean to you? How does it affect the decisions you make, the words you say, or how patient you are?

Questions to think about:

1. What does it mean to you to love someone?

2. When things get bad, how can you stay strong and preserve your self-respect?

3. When have you witnessed someone put forth a lot of effort to improve a relationship?

4. What makes you stay hopeful when love is put to the test?

Love isn't about how easy life is; it's about how we love when things get tough. Every challenge brings us closer together, helps us learn more, and makes the things that are really important stronger.

5. What does "enduring love" mean to you right now?

6. How do you keep your ability to love all year long?

7. What is one thing about love that you want to remember every day after reading this?

Chapter: 5

The Sacrifices Love Makes
How love requires sacrifice for the benefit of others

Love is fundamentally non-selfish. It's not always about what we obtain; it's also about what we provide. Real love frequently entails giving up something for someone else, whether our pride, time, comfort, or even our needs. We don't have to change who we are to love someone, but we do have to think about them. In any outstanding love story, whether it's between lovers, friends, or family, there comes a time when sacrifice tests love. In those moments, love exposes how deep it is. It's not a loss to give up something; it's an investment. It's offering something of value to help someone else develop, heal, or feel appreciated, not because you have to.

When we contemplate sacrifice, we frequently think of large, dramatic things. But most sacrifices in love are small and go unnoticed. The mother sets up early every morning to take care of her kids, even when she is exhausted. It's the husband who works additional hours to aid the family or the friend who listens when they need help. These are tiny, ordinary sacrifices that mean a lot more than words. Love doesn't need to declare it's giving up something; it just does. And while these things may appear tiny, they can have a big impact. They transform relationships, help people trust each other, and remind us that love involves putting someone else's needs before our own without keeping track of who does what.

Love also means being patient. It's letting go when you want to move on, forgiving when it's simpler to harbor a grudge, and choosing peace when your pride wants to fight. That's the hardest part, because letting go of something usually costs something. It costs comfort. It takes time and work. But it provides you with something far more: peace of mind, progress, and connection. You discover that when you love someone, sacrifice isn't about losing; it's about making a choice. It's like saying, "I'll give up something for you." Giving often leads to a deeper understanding, more respect, and a bond that can't be broken.

Chapter: 5

Love takes up things because it wants to, not because it has to. It doesn't anticipate praise or remuneration; it gives because it feels it benefits others. Love transforms from being selfish to being unselfish as it grows. We begin to realize that the greatest joy comes from seeing others happy, not just ourselves. This phenomenon is something that parents know very well. They will sometimes put their wants aside to think about their children's future. Love grows when it learns to serve, as shown by people who stay up all night to help each other, spouses who sacrifice for peace, or even strangers who are kind without asking for anything in return.

Sometimes, loving means letting go. Sometimes, the kindest thing we can do is give up what we want so that someone else can find their way. It could mean letting someone you love pursue their dreams, even if it means being apart, or forgiving someone who never said sorry just to make your own heart feel better. One of the hardest things to do is let go, since it involves giving up control. But love that lets go doesn't hold on; it has faith. It believes that what is supposed to happen will always happen at the proper time. That kind of sacrifice doesn't weaken love; it strengthens it. It teaches us how to love without fear or possessiveness.

There is also a spiritual side to giving up something for love. It shows God's love, the kind that gives without expecting anything in return. Many religions assert the connection between love and sacrifice, emphasizing that the best way to demonstrate love is to do good for others. Loving at a cost makes us part of something bigger. We learn to be humble, courteous, and graceful. Giving isn't simply for other people; it changes us, too. Every sacrifice makes us better at loving, helps us see things from different points of view, and opens our hearts more. Love isn't just a sensation anymore; it's a way of life.

Chapter: 5

People come together in partnerships when they are willing to give up something. Love implies being willing to meet in the middle since people are different. It involves putting your pride aside long enough to understand how someone else feels. It could include choosing to listen rather than quarrel or to help your partner attain their goals, even if it makes you feel negative. Sacrifice doesn't take away who you are; it respects who you are with others. It states, "I care more about our relationship than I do about being right." That kind of humility makes love grow deeper. Never giving up weakens a love, but a love that is willing to adapt learns to withstand life's challenges.

There is also the loss of time. In our hectic, fast-paced society, giving someone time is one of the best things we can do. Being present, sharing a meal, or simply being there demonstrates love more effectively than words. We don't always know how strong being there is. You are making a sacrifice that says, "You matter," when you are entirely there for someone and don't let anything else stand in the way. You don't always need to do large things to show your love; it grows when you pay attention to each other during those tiny, planned occasions. When we choose to offer someone our time, we are saying, "You are worth my time and effort." People trust and become close to each other when they make sacrifices like that.

It takes strength to make sacrifices. Loving deeply means being open to pain, which can be painful. Even if they don't mean to, people will let us down, get us wrong, or harm us. But love that lasts learns to endure suffering without getting mad. It's the decision to remain loving even when love has been tested. Giving up anything teaches us how to be strong and provide without expecting anything in return, or love without expecting anything in return. It's challenging, but it's worth it. Love tested by giving up something becomes indestructible. It's not foolish or weak; it's brave and strong, since love is still the best thing we can give.

Chapter: 5

The best thing about love that hurts is that it changes both the giver and the receiver. The giver learns humility and kindness, while the receiver learns gratitude and compassion. Giving up something makes you develop. It teaches us to appreciate what other people do for us and encourages us to give back. Families are forceful in this period. Parents sacrifice for their kids, who learn to do the same for others. This ongoing act of love sustains generations. When we live like this, love becomes more than simply a word; it becomes something that lasts. And that legacy tells us that when we give up something, it's not the end; it's the start of something better.

Love doesn't necessarily entail giving up anything. Occasionally, it's a prayer for someone who injured you without saying anything. It's giving someone a second chance, even when it doesn't seem right. Occasionally, you just have to stay even when you want to leave so badly. All sacrifices come from the same place: being selfless. When you really love someone, you say, "I care about your health and happiness, even if it costs me something." And that cost is what makes love so great. Without sacrifice, love is not deep. It makes love deeper, more real, and more valuable for all time. It becomes a love that alters hearts and lives.

The most important thing about love in the end is not what it receives but what it provides. When we give up things for love, we don't lose them; we plant seeds of faith. They become trust, kindness, and strong bonds that last. When you love someone, you care about the good it will do, not the cost. Sacrificial love turns walls into bridges, heals wounds that words once hurt, and illuminates the way when hope seems lost. It is difficult, but it is heavenly. One act of kindness at a time, love that relinquishes for the sake of others not only endures but also has a profound impact on the world around it.

Chapter: 5

The Sacrifices Love Makes
Personal stories of sacrifice in the name of love

People talk a lot about love in songs, movies, and books, yet screens don't always portray the best examples. They live quietly, making small sacrifices every day that most people don't notice. These stories aren't about people who are perfect and do brave things. They are about everyday individuals who choose love even when it costs them a lot of time, money, or work. The purest love is giving up what you care about for another's happiness or growth. Love is what keeps things going in every narrative of sacrifice. It could be time, dreams, comfort, or even pride.

One of these stories is about a couple who had been married for almost thirty years. When the wife became ill and could no longer work, the husband became her full-time caregiver. He would rise early each day, prepare meals for her, assist her with her bathing, and remain with her throughout the night when she could not sleep. He had a difficult time. He wanted to retire early and travel, but he was okay with putting those plans on hold. He answered, "I meant it when I promised to love her in sickness and in health," when someone questioned him on how he could be so patient. He didn't give up because he had to; he did it because he loved her. His love wasn't loud, but it was intense. He showed that love doesn't go when things get tough; it stays, serves, and lasts through every hard day.

There's also the story of a single mother who worked two jobs, so her kids would always have food. She saved every dime for their school and didn't buy new clothes or go out at night too often. Her kids didn't find out how much mom had given up until years later. One day, her son stated, "Mom, I understand what you gave up for us now that I'm older." You didn't simply raise us; you carried us. She cried not because she was worn out, but because she was grateful. She didn't want attention for her sacrifice; she wanted affection. She demonstrated her belief in your worth by working extended hours, sacrificing sleep, and constantly worrying. Love is powerful because it provides without asking anything in return.

Chapter: 5

Another remarkable narrative concerns a youthful couple who were forced to endure their separation. The spouse relocated to the battlefield for a few years, abandoning his wife and their newborn child. The wife was compelled to assume the duties of both mother and father, as the husband withdrew from the initial milestones. They depended on prayers, letters, and phone conversations. Upon his return, they both expressed, "Love sustained us." Their narrative was not about the ease of their circumstances; rather, it was about their perseverance. They discovered that genuine love is not diminished by time; rather, it is strengthened by sacrifice. Every tear, every night spent alone, and every instant spent waiting demonstrated that love can endure even when individuals are physically separated. Occasionally, the sacrifices that love makes are not about time or distance; they are about letting go.

A father once recounted the tale of his daughter's departure from home to pursue her aspiration of becoming a doctor in a foreign country. Although he was proud, the mere thought of her being so far away caused him much pain. He had always safeguarded her, but this time, love demanded setting her free so she could become the person she was meant to be. "I was aware that loving her entailed not restraining her," he stated. Although his sacrifice was diminutive, it was of paramount significance. It was the act of abandoning, prioritizing her development over his well-being. At times, devotion requires relinquishing others, even if it leaves you with empty arms. That is the type of affection that provides you with the fortitude you need, rather than hindering your progress.

Additionally, there is the narrative of Sarah and Lena, who have maintained a lifelong friendship. Sarah relocated across the country to be with Lena after learning that she had cancer. She relinquished her employment, residence, and objectives. She provided her companion with care, entertained her, and listened to her for months. Sarah stated, "I did not even consider it." Loving appears, and that is precisely what it does. Sarah stated that she never regretted a single moment, even after Lena's passing. She whispered, "It was painful, but I would do it again in a heartbeat." Her narrative serves as a reminder that love is not contingent upon the duration of our relationship; rather, it is contingent upon the extent of our compassion during their presence. It transforms love into a legacy; sacrifice makes love meaningful.

Chapter: 5

Love also demonstrates its strength by making sacrifices when circumstances are adverse. A significant number of individuals jeopardize their own safety to assist their loved ones during natural disasters or other emergencies. During a tempest, an elderly neighbor found herself stranded in her flooded home, prompting one man to recall spending hours searching for her. He responded, "I was unable to simply sit and wait, as she was alone." Sacrificial love is akin to that; it operates independently. It simply provides without considering the cost. The true nature of love is revealed during those circumstances: it is unwavering, selfless, and courageous. It is a reminder that our willingness to sacrifice for one another is what defines us as humans.

The narrative of redemption is a quieter account of sacrifice that is not frequently recounted. Despite years of emotional distance and broken promises, a woman recounted how she had forgiven her spouse. "Forgiveness was my method of expressing my affection for him," she stated. "Not because he deserved it, but because I was unable to tolerate the anger any longer." It was an act of affection, not weakness, for her to forgive. A sacrifice of pride, anger, and ego was made to achieve harmony and healing. Love occasionally requires us to relinquish our right to anger to repair the damage we have caused. While forgiveness does not alleviate suffering, it does create an opportunity for reconciliation, which is also a form of sacrifice.

This is followed by the narrative of an elderly couple who have been married for over fifty years. The husband's wife became his unwavering support as Alzheimer's disease began to erode his memory. She entertained him with anecdotes from their youth and displayed photographs of their children, and, despite his ignorance of her identity, he held her hand. "He may forget who I am, but I will never forget who he is," she stated. Every day, she cherished him as if he were still capable of remembering. She made a sacrifice that was not only physical but also emotional, spiritual, and profound. The act of loving someone through loss, decline, and uncertainty is the essence of love. True devotion is exemplified by a love that endures beyond memory and is eternal.

Chapter: 5

Occasionally, sacrifice requires suspending one's own aspirations to assist another. Once, a young man declined an exceptional employment opportunity in a foreign country because his younger brother needed his presence at home. The passing of their parents made it impossible to leave their sibling alone. I was aware that I could reestablish my profession at a later date, but I would never be able to reclaim the time I spent assisting him. Many years later, his sibling achieved success and frequently expressed gratitude to him for his assistance. "You believed in me when I did not believe in myself," he stated. The older brother smiled and stated, "Love will continue to believe in you until you are able to believe again." The impact of his sacrifice on two lives is a testament to the enduring nature of love.

Love's sacrifices are not always substantial; they are often minute and daily. It is the spouse who stays up to comfort their partner after a bad day, the child who cares for their aging parents, or the friend who listens when the world seems silenced. These instances are not frequently reported in the media; however, they demonstrate the tremendous power of love. Usually, sacrifice appears to be a person, but occasionally it resembles a hero. When angry, one chooses patience; when scared, compassion; and when scared, faith. Although you have the option to depart, it indicates that you are present. The love that makes sacrifices does not seek attention; it simply chooses to care repeatedly.

Ultimately, every story about sacrifice teaches one key lesson: love that is reciprocated grows stronger. Real happiness comes from caring for others, not from the pursuit of comfort, as individuals who love profoundly understand. No matter how substantial or insignificant, each sacrifice enhances the significance of our existence. Such sacrifice teaches us that love is not contingent upon our possessions, but rather on the amount we give. The act of sacrificing something for another person demonstrates our commitment to a cause greater than our own. The most significant vocation, the most valuable gift, and the most enduring thing is love. The sacrifices we made for love will continue to resonate long after we are gone, even when everything else fades away.

Chapter: 5

The Sacrifices Love Makes
The rewards of sacrificial love

S acrificial love is one of the most potent forces in existence. It transcends sentiments and demonstrates the true essence of genuine affection. When we opt to donate, even if it results in a financial burden, we generate blessings that surpass our limited perceptions. The rewards of sacrificial affection are not always immediate, but they are always enduring. A love that sacrifices something does not seek praise or recognition; it simply gives because it has faith in the other person. However, the act of giving results in an extraordinary transformation: we undergo changes. Our awareness of what truly matters increases, and we become more resilient and compassionate. In unexpected ways, sacrificial love can return to us, such as through a deeper sense of satisfaction, thankfulness, and serenity. Sacrificial love's initial advantage is that it provides you with tranquility. When we act without expecting anything in return, we relinquish the burden of selfishness, which frequently hinders us. Knowing you've done something beneficial for someone else, even if no one else knows, brings a quiet joy. Love that gives does not require recognition to experience pleasure; it derives pleasure from the act itself. Think of a parent who is dedicated to their family, not for recognition, but because they adore them. You can't buy the peace that comes from knowing you have a purpose. Your heart is at peace when you act out of love. The quality of your sleep improves. Breathing may become easier for you. You experience a sense of belonging to a force that surpasses your limitations.

Relationships are fortified by love that is willing to sacrifice something for another to an unparalleled extent. You fortify your relationship with someone by contributing to them because you are concerned about their well-being. It cultivates loyalty, trust, and appreciation. Others may forget what you say, but they will never forget the good you did for them. Giving, such as staying up late to comfort someone, putting your plans on hold to assist, or forgiving even when it hurts, establishes a robust foundation that can withstand any challenge. In the long term, that type of affection instills a sense of security and belonging. Every time relinquish something, you contribute another thread to the robust fabric of connection, and the love you share expands

Chapter: 5

Growth, personal, emotional, and even spiritual, is another advantage of sacrificial love. We grow more compassionate, understanding, and grounded when we relinquish an object of our affection. We develop the ability to view life from the perspective of empathy rather than entitlement. Sacrificing love instills humility in us; it demonstrates that life is not solely about obtaining but also about contributing. Deep love enhances our character. We acquire a greater sense of thankfulness for our possessions and develop a greater sense of compassion for others. People who are the most generous are frequently the happiest, and their happiness is not an accident. They recognize that they are happiest when they are providing, rather than receiving. We become more balanced and better individuals as a result of the sacrifices love demands.

Sacrificial devotion also provides a spiritual benefit: a sense of alignment with God. Numerous religions and philosophies inextricably link love and sacrifice. The most profound form of love is selfless love, as it provides without anticipating anything in return. We are connected to something sacred through this form of affection. We are brought closer to God, our purpose, and the essence of humanity as a result. You soon realize that love is not merely an emotion; it is a vocation. Serve without concern for potential losses in order to cultivate greater faith. That faith transforms rough circumstances into opportunities and even pain into a reason to live. A love that is willing to sacrifice something for another person transforms not only the relationship but also the heart that provides it. The fact that both individuals are grateful for sacrificial love is one of its most wonderful qualities.

The giver expresses gratitude for the opportunity to make a positive impact, while the recipient provides thanks for the profound affection they have received. This mutual gratitude establishes a cycle of benevolence. Doing a kind deed for another person can inspire you to reciprocate the gesture. This leads to heightened awareness of others' needs, a greater willingness to assist, and greater gratitude for the positive aspects of one's existence. Thankfulness fosters the development of affection. It imbues ordinary situations with a magical quality. In those cases, both parties are reminded that love is never wasted, even if it costs a lot. Although it does not conform to our expectations, it consistently recovers.

Chapter: 5

The strength that is derived from it is also a result of sacrificial affection. When you opt to love despite the challenges, you develop greater resilience. In the face of adversity, one develops the ability to remain resolute and maintain faith amid fading hope. Through sacrifice, one is encouraged to persist. This serves as a reminder that love is resilient enough to endure even the most severe of circumstances. You discover that you are capable of accomplishing more than you initially anticipated when you voluntarily contribute. Love is not a source of weakness; rather, it functions as a source of strength. Individuals who possess a profound affection for one another are aware that the difficult moments, during which they were required to relinquish something, exercise patience, and have faith, are the reasons for the strength of their relationship. Your strength serves as a silent testament to the power of love to triumph over dread.

Knowing that your love has positively affected another's life is also very rewarding. Everyone, whether a friend, a child, or a companion, is affected by your sacrifices. The extent to which your compassion impacts others may remain unknown to you; however, love consistently sows seeds that take root in their hearts. Your support may have altered an individual's trajectory, or your forgiveness may have facilitated their recovery. Loving sacrifices have an impact on individuals whom you may never encounter. Every act of kindness you perform for another person contributes to improving the world. Such behavior illustrates that love is not solely confined to one individual; it continues to develop.

Sometimes, the most valuable recompense is introspection, as it allows one to recognize that their sacrifices were worthwhile. Things that you relinquished, such as time, pride, or comfort, appear to be less significant than the benefits you received in return. Love has made you more humble, brave, gentle, and strong. By now, you are aware that even the most difficult sacrifices have concealed advantages. They instructed you on the essential qualities of intelligence, fortitude, and kindness. Any love that sacrifices something becomes a legacy, a narrative lived and passed down. It conveys the message to the world that "I made the best effort I could, and it was sufficient." This thought provokes feelings of gratitude and serves as a reminder that no act of love is ever rendered in vain.

Chapter: 5

Through selfless love, we create a stronger bond with ourselves and others. It eliminates selfishness and acts as a barometer for what is really important. The act of giving reveals our ideals, resilience, and ability to care for others. Our purpose in life is to help, care for, and support others, as love teaches us. Often, we discover our purpose by letting go of things. It becomes apparent that love is not about obtaining everything one desires; rather, it is about experiencing pleasure in helping another person achieve their goals. Love is limitless when it is truly altruistic. At this point, it begins to permeate not only your relationships but also every aspect of your existence.

One additional advantage of sacrificial love is that it can be reflected upon with tranquility. With time, it reveals the true significance of our sacrifices. At first, what caused you pain may ultimately serve as a source of gratitude. One can observe the manner in which those circumstances altered your narrative, fortified your faith, and expanded your heart. Loving can transform surrendering into tranquility. You were able to achieve something greater as a result of the difficult times, the tears you shed, and the decisions you made for others. In retrospect, it will become apparent that the rewards of affection are typically intangible; they are tangible. No amount of worldly accomplishment can bring you the joy that selfless affection does.

The advantages of selfless affection are immeasurable. They cannot be purchased, counted, or thoroughly explicated; they can only be experienced. All that is beneficial, pure, and eternal is connected to us through sacrificial love, which gives our lives significance. When we love beyond our own selves, we achieve happiness that endures longer than suffering, tranquility that surpasses comprehension, and satisfaction that transcends time. In the most concrete sense, love that surrenders something is not a loss; it is a victory. This serves as a reminder that donating possessions, rather than retaining them, yields the most rewarding experiences in life. When we love sacrificially, we not only influence others but also reach our highest selves.

Chapter: 5

Love is one of the most powerful forces that may push us to do things, but it often asks something in return, like our time, our comfort, or even our pride. Think back to the instances when you had to give up something for someone you care about. You may have given up on a dream, put off a goal, or stayed when it would have been easier to leave. These instances illustrate how deep love really is. If we don't give anything up, love stays shallow. But when we do, love grows stronger, richer, and more important.

Reflection Questions:

1. What does "sacrifice" mean to you personally in the context of love?

2. Have you ever made a sacrifice for someone you love? How did it change your relationship?

3. When you think of love in your own life, what moments required you to put another person's needs above your own?

4. What emotions—joy, fear, frustration—did you feel in those moments of sacrifice, and what did they teach you about love?

Love isn't always exciting; sometimes it's calm, patient, and difficult to see. But those are the periods that make partnerships what they are.

Reflection Questions:

1. What story of love and sacrifice has inspired you the most in your life or in someone else's?

2. How did that story shape your understanding of what love really means?

3. Have you ever felt unappreciated for the sacrifices you made? How did you handle those feelings?

4. What do you think love looks like when it asks for perseverance and patience instead of comfort and ease?

Chapter: 5

The benefits of sacrificial love may not be apparent initially, but they reveal themselves over time. Giving freely fosters personal growth, peace, and a sense of fulfillment that money cannot buy. Each sacrifice strengthens us by teaching us to care for others, developing our trust, and giving our lives purpose. Love based on mutual exchange always returns in kind.

Reflection Questions:

1. What inner rewards have you experienced from loving someone sacrificially?
2. How has giving shaped your emotional or spiritual growth?
3. Do you believe love that sacrifices always finds a way to come back to you? Why or why not?
4. How can you remind yourself that acts of sacrifice are not losses but seeds that grow into lasting joy and peace?

Sacrificial love is lovely because it alters both the giver and the receiver. When we choose to love even when it's hard, we find a greater sense of purpose.

Reflection Questions:

1. What relationships in your life could benefit from a renewed spirit of selflessness?
2. How can you show sacrificial love in small, consistent ways each day?
3. What lessons from this chapter will you carry forward into how you love others?
4. In your own words, what does it mean to say, "The greatest love is the one that gives"?

Chapter: 6

The Importance of Trust in Love
How trust strengthens the bonds of love

T rust is what makes every wonderful love tale amazing. Love is weak and unstable without it, like a house constructed on sand that moves. But love may last through time, distance, and even harsh circumstances when trust is strong. Trust means, "I believe in you," even when it's challenging to trust in you. It can breathe and grow without fear of being stopped. You can't pretend to trust someone, and you can't rush it. You have to be honest, consistent, and courteous to get it. When things go wrong, people don't always say "I love you," but they do trust each other a lot. Even if you don't fully comprehend their actions, you must have faith in their intentions if you truly love them.

Trust begins tiny in any relationship. It gets bigger with each promise and every act of honesty. We develop trust when we keep our promises, listen without judging, or show up when we say we will. But it's a weak item that breaks quickly and is difficult to repair once it does. That's why you need to keep it safe. When two people trust each other, they can be open and honest without worrying about the other's reaction. Love doesn't need to wear armor in that area. It can simply exist. Trust doesn't mean someone is perfect; it means believing in their intentions even when their actions don't match. It entails expressing, "I understand your heart," and genuinely meaning it.

Trust also makes love less limited. Without trust, relationships can resemble prisons, requiring constant vigilance and a lack of trust. But love can flourish gently when there is trust. You don't have to constantly ask questions or be in charge. Just relax and realize that you're both working for the same goal. That freedom makes love stronger because it offers you strength instead of fear. You give someone freedom instead of chains when you trust them. You let them be themselves without contemplating what other people would say. And, oddly, it's that freedom that makes love stronger. Love doesn't flourish where fear governs; it thrives where trust rules.

Chapter: 6

One of the best things about trust is that it helps you feel protected inside. You can tell someone the truth without worrying that they won't believe you. You can discuss your fears, hopes, and dreams without worrying that someone will use them against you. Relationships grow deeper when people are that transparent. Real love isn't about needing to be told you're loved all the time; it's about having calm assurance. When two people trust each other, words don't mean as much since they already know what the other person means. You feel protected with this kind of bond even when you're not communicating. You know they care about you even when they're not with you. That's what trust does: it connects souls in a manner that words can't.

Additionally, trust makes love endure even in the face of adversity. Every relationship will experience feelings of distance at some point due to stress or misunderstandings. Those situations can make you angry or afraid if you don't trust them. But love endures because of faith. It serves as a reminder that a disagreement does not ruin a relationship and that a bad day does not make all the good ones disappear. Your perspective on love is altered by trust. Additionally, it states, "This is not enough to break us." When both partners understand that honesty is the foundation of a relationship, they can resolve conflicts without ending it. Because it maintains stability even when emotions change, trust is incredibly potent. It helps love get back on track, but it doesn't make things better.

Trust also makes love stronger by making things more stable. It's not only the giant things that show affection; it's the tiny things that happen every day that make you feel protected over time. When people believe they can trust you, they start to relax in a relationship. They stop thinking that anything horrible will happen and start believing that your partnership is strong. That feeling of trust makes relationships go from weak to powerful. It's not the enormous things that indicate you trust someone; it's the tiny things. You can trust someone who delivers texts on time, honors promises, and shows up simply to listen. In the end, those moments add up to an underlying truth: "You can count on me."

Chapter: 6

Our level of self-confidence shows in the degree to which we trust other people. Our inability to trust others is frequently rooted in our fear. Becoming abandoned, disappointed, or wounded is our greatest fear. Love fights that fear by challenging us to believe and take chances once more. To establish trust, we must overcome our concerns and find ways to remain open-minded despite our fears. It means being transparent rather than controlling everything. In love, we trust not only the other person but also ourselves. Learning to trust reduces the need to overanalyze situations and take unnecessary precautions. We open ourselves up to the beauty and imperfections of love. Then love begins to transform us; it mends the parts of us that were wounded by a lack of trust.

Believing in love also encompasses a more metaphysical aspect. Having faith in one another and in a power greater than ourselves is a lesson we learn from this. When we trust, we acknowledge that there are certain things beyond our control, yet we choose to believe in spite of that. That act of faith strengthens both the person and their relationship. Love is about commitment, not about making promises. The benefit of trusting is tranquility. When times become tough, knowing that love is there is the most comforting feeling in the world. Being trustworthy isn't about being perfect; it's about having excellent intentions at all times. Trust-based love endures through all challenges, as each partner ensures the other's heart is safe in the face of uncertainty.

There will be moments when trust is challenged. Things will change, you will feel dissatisfied, and doubt will creep in. It means love can grow stronger in that time. When you trust each other, it's not that you won't make errors; it's that you're both prepared to rectify them when they happen. Restoring trust in a relationship is painful but necessary. It becomes natural to be truthful, modest, and patient. Forgiveness and a fresh start strengthen love. Understanding has replaced idealism as the foundation. You are well aware that trust is not a given; rather, it is a garden that requires constant attention. When you forgive and have faith, you plant a new seed that will grow into love.

Chapter: 6

One of the greatest benefits of trust is the emotional freedom it provides. The only way to love someone deeply is to trust them implicitly. Your focus on building connections frees you from worrying about betrayal. You can love and be loved freely when you have such freedom. When you let go of your fear of loss, you may fully experience love in the present. Rather than protecting your heart like a stronghold, trust allows you to open it up like a home. Believing in another person's strength rather than their weakness is something you are well aware of. One of the loveliest forms of love is the ability to trust again despite past hurts.

Trust also deepens satisfaction. Having a relationship built on trust is simpler, calmer, and more fulfilling. No longer do people have to hold back their laughter, their love, or their honesty. Loving relationships flourish when partners can trust one another. No matter the topic, you'll always feel comfortable opening up, and any difficulty will always seem manageable. Such love does more than survive; it flourishes. It adds a soothing rhythm to existence. Stability persists even in the face of ambiguity. Despite disagreements, mutual regard remains. Love that is based on trust provides a secure haven for both partners when they feel overwhelmed by the world.

Love, after all, lasts for as long as trust does. You can't see it, but it binds two spirits through every season. Doubt kills love, but it strengthens it when it's there. When people trust one another, connections are robust and long-lasting rather than fragile and fleeting. It allows two people to go through life side by side, secure in the knowledge that their hearts are firmly planted in grace, honesty, and fidelity. Trust is the essence of love; it is love that strengthens love. Furthermore, love built on trust is unbreakable, no matter how much time passes.

Chapter: 6

The Importance of Trust in Love
Rebuilding trust after it's broken

When those you trust fail you, it might feel like everything is falling apart. My love, which was powerful and unwavering before, is now uncertain and feeble. Healing wounds from betrayal, dishonesty, broken promises, or pure indifference is difficult, if not impossible. However, trust can actually be rebuilt. Success is possible for those who dedicate themselves to making it happen, despite the challenges and time required. We should work toward healing as a community rather than trying to make the pain go away. Making small steps toward greater openness, honesty, and vulnerability is necessary. Despite the loss of trust, love can persist if both lovers are resilient enough to accept the hurt and choose to forgive rather than seek revenge.

Recognizing the wrongdoing is the initial stage in restoring confidence. If you avoid dealing with it, you will never improve. To confess, "I was wrong," and to acknowledge that one has betrayed another's confidence requires both bravery and humility. Even if it's painful to hear, the truth is the key to improvement. The victim has to be heard; therefore, don't keep quiet. They must feel safe enough to express their emotions, anger, grief, disappointment, without fear of judgment. Additionally, the offender should listen to the victim's story without becoming defensive. Healing begins with the truth, and being open to it is the first step in finding it. The pain will only increase if you hurry to forgive or choose to ignore what happened. Since being complete is more important than being comfortable, genuine love confronts the wrongs head-on.

Consistency follows logically from honesty. While words might spark action, only deeds can restore trust. Restoring trust requires just one day, one commitment, and one decision. Being truthful, honoring minor commitments, and being present when you say you are will be key. The betrayer must be patient because they can't control how long it takes to recover. Rebuilding does not imply weakness; rather, it means choosing optimism over wrath, and the damaged person must learn this. No matter how modest, every sincere attempt contributes to the new love foundation. It's the kind of labor that lingers for a very long time.

Chapter: 6

Healing a shattered heart requires the same patience, tenderness, and constancy as healing a broken trust. On some days, it will feel like you're going nowhere, and on other days, old hurts will resurface. You're not alone. There is no set timeline for when a person will heal. It fluctuates; some days bring calm and clarity, while others bring uncertainty. Resolute commitment is paramount. Embracing the present moment, no matter how challenging, is essential when love decides to start over. Rather than trying to put the past behind them, the one who betrayed trust should accept responsibility by making a difference going forward. After making a promise to change, the best way to regain people's trust is to really do it.

An integral aspect of this procedure is communication. Truthful dialogue brings people together, but being silent makes things worse. Let the other person know how they can help you recover by discussing what went wrong and what needs to change. Not as punishment, but to safeguard the heart that is relearning to trust, it is vital to set clear boundaries. Boundaries create safety, and when love feels safe again, it can develop. By mutually agreeing to follow these guidelines, the two parties create an environment that fosters trust. Instead of returning to the previous state, rebuilding entails creating something fresh, more mature, and with a greater sense of purpose.

You can't force forgiveness, but it's crucial on this path. An apology is not the same as telling someone, "It's okay." For example, saying, "This won't define us forever," can be helpful. It's making the conscious decision to let go of resentment and move forward without dwelling on the past. Forgiving someone does not imply ignoring their wrongdoing. They are being offered an opportunity to recover. Don't worry if it takes some time. Love is lovely since it doesn't demand perfection but rather growth. With each new blossom of forgiveness, trust sprouts again, a fragile leaf at a time.

Chapter: 6

Being transparent and honest is also crucial for reestablishing trust. Love cannot grow in darkness; it needs light to do so. That includes being open about your thoughts, feelings, and anxieties. If trust has been broken due to lies, secrecy, or betrayal, being open and honest is the way to restore it. While it might seem challenging initially, maintaining honesty fosters a sense of comfort. Checking in, telling someone what you want to do, and being responsible are all methods to express love and say, "You can trust me again." It is not about monitoring or regulating; it is about making people feel comfortable. These small gestures of transparency gradually develop trust and remind both hearts that honesty is still possible.

Patience is another crucial aspect in rebuilding trust. You cannot hasten the healing process. It's fine if the injured individual still has concerns from time to time. Patience responds, "I understand you need time." It allows the other person to regain their sense of safety without feeling pressured. Patient love understands that trust takes time to bloom, just like a flower breaking through hard soil. It requires time, attention, and tenderness. If you have injured someone, understand that your readiness to wait with grace is part of your apology. And if you're learning to trust again, allow yourself to recover at your own speed. Healing is not a race; rather, it is a rhythm.

To rebuild trust, you must also relearn how to love without fear. After being betrayed, it's natural to desire to shield your heart and erect walls so high that no one can hurt you again. However, the same walls that keep pain out also keep love out. The idea is to improve rather than toughen up. To love again requires guts, the type that says, "I know what it's like to be hurt, but I choose to believe again." That is why trust is so powerful: it is not dumb; it is courageous. When you choose to love again after being harmed, you demonstrate the greatest sort of strength.

Chapter: 6

When trust is restored, love becomes stronger. Overcoming a challenging circumstance has strengthened the bond. While the injured person learns to be strong and graceful, they also learn to be responsible and kind. Such growth gives the suffering a reason to exist, but it does not make it go away. It transforms suffering into insight. Restored trust shows that forgiveness is not the end of dignity, but rather the start of peace, that love can heal, and that atonement is possible.

One of the most beneficial aspects of rebuilding trust is that it draws people closer together. When people are honest and open again, their hearts begin to connect on a more profound level. A love that has endured fire is unique. It's more considerate, gentler, and deliberate. The cracks where agony used to be are now where light enters. The weird thing about healing is that what damaged you in the past now makes you stronger. Rebuilding trust does not change the past; rather, it alters our perception of it. It transforms the narrative from "we broke up" to "we got back together."

Repairing trust after it has been destroyed is about discovering the true strength of love, not merely saving a relationship. It's about demonstrating that love is more than just words and emotions; it's about doing things, being kind, and never giving up. When trust is reestablished, it is indestructible because it has been tested and proven. It bears wounds, but they tell a story of courage, forgiveness, and trust. If love can restore people's trust in each other, it can overcome any obstacle. Because when two hearts resolve to start afresh, not as flawless persons, but as new souls, they demonstrate to the world that genuine, patient, healing love always returns home.

Chapter: 6

The Importance of Trust in Love
The role of honesty in love that lasts

Everlasting love is based on honesty. Lack of trust will cause even the strongest relationships to fail. The basis of enduring love is honesty rather than constant perfection. A sincere, stable friendship forms when two people decide to be honest with each other. Since love thrives in openness rather than concealment, you cannot truly experience love without being honest. This is the essence of sincerity: "You can see all of me, the good, the bad, and the growing, and I still choose to love you, and I want you to love me as I am." Stability is fostered by people's trust, which is earned by such honesty. It's about being honest about mistakes at all times, not about making them.

Honesty brings light into a relationship that could otherwise be gloomy. It clears up any confusion before it escalates into wrath. When you talk honestly, you are not only offering someone facts; you are also showing them your heart. You are stating, "I care about you enough to be honest with you." Even if it is painful, the truth is always preferable to lying or remaining silent. Being dishonest not only hides the truth but also alienates others. As small lies mount up over time, love starts to seem shaky. But love becomes a true partnership when honesty becomes a habit. There's no need to speculate about your position because everything is obvious. You have the freedom to love deeply and fearlessly because of that openness.

Being honest also contributes to genuine love growth. People can discuss their concerns honestly rather than pretending they do not exist. Pretending may make things tranquil for a short time, but being truthful makes things peaceful for a long time. Honesty does not imply meanness. It entails being clear, kind, and honest at the same time. True love does not avoid difficult conversations; rather, it welcomes them because it prioritizes connection over comfort. When you express the truth with love, you are not attempting to hurt anyone; rather, you are trying to help them. And when you're honest with each other, even when things are difficult, your relationship grows stronger because it's built on respect rather than lies.

Chapter: 6

One of the most crucial aspects of honesty in love is making people feel emotionally comfortable. You may feel at ease around someone who will always tell you the truth. You don't have to read between the lines or question what they're up to; you simply trust. That safety allows love to exist. When people are unable to be honest, they begin to hide. They choose their words carefully, guard their hearts, and tread lightly around the truth. That is not love; rather, it is survival. When you love someone, you may be yourself without fear of rejection or judgment. It allows both parties to speak freely, knowing that being honest will always be welcomed with kindness rather than judgment.

Honesty also contributes to the longevity of love. Honesty keeps love alive even when life can grow complicated, routines can change, and emotions can wane. If two people promise to be honest with each other, they may manage change jointly. "This is where I am" or "This is what I need" can help them sort it out. Love remains receptive to new experiences when it is honest. Good relationships are maintained by people who are honest with each other. They talk about their disappointments, fears, and even worries without feeling bad about it. People's love is strengthened when they are open and honest with each other. On the surface, maintaining a calm exterior may seem to mean acting as though nothing is wrong, yet love is sustained by honesty.

Honesty also makes people more responsible. We all make mistakes in love, but confessing them makes the connection stronger, not weaker. Being open and honest about your faults demonstrates humility. You show that your love is mature enough to recognize when it is insufficient. People will trust you more if you acknowledge, "I was wrong," or "I could have handled that better," rather than making excuses. When two people are honest with each other, they can confront their flaws together rather than individually. It converts issues into opportunities to learn and grow. When love is honest, even the most difficult situations can be used to make things stronger than before.

90

Chapter: 6

Being honest fosters long-term love by making you feel more connected to one another. Intimacy is more than simply being physically close; it is also about being emotionally close through honesty. When you share your thoughts, fears, and dreams with your spouse, you open your mind to them. That frailty forms an unbreakable bond. Many people believe that being too honest will drive love away, but this is not the case. Honesty does not scare away love; rather, it strengthens it. Unconditional love occurs when you realize that someone sees your shortcomings but still desires to be with you. When you are honest, love becomes genuine. It eliminates the masks, acting, and pretending, leaving only genuine connection.

But it takes bravery to be honest. It's not always straightforward to be honest, particularly when doing so could result in conflict or disappointment. But dishonest love is brittle and unpredictable. Lying to spare someone's feelings can hurt them more. While the truth may cause temporary pain, lies will cause lifelong harm. Since enduring love is based on respect and understanding for one another, it can handle the truth. Being honest means caring enough to present the facts in a way that is helpful rather than hurtful; it does not mean being unkind. Courageous honesty fosters loving communication and strengthens character in both relationships.

In long-term partnerships, honesty means being forthright about how you feel. Love isn't static; it evolves along with life. Being open about what you need, how you feel, and how worried you are stops the distance from widening. We believe our spouse understands what we are thinking or feeling, yet they cannot read our minds. That vacuum is filled by honesty. It reads, "This is where I am." Let's figure this issue out together. When you're honest with each other, that's what keeps love alive through life's ups and downs. Love not only endures but also blossoms when two people are truthful with one another.

Chapter: 6

In love, honesty is like a mirror: it reflects our true selves and helps us evolve. Speaking the truth to our partner means speaking the truth to ourselves. It's easy to hide behind quiet or denial, but stating the truth allows us to confront our fears and flaws. That type of development is what love provides. When both parties are honest, the relationship is a safe environment to develop. People do not perceive mistakes as failures; rather, they see them as learning opportunities. Real love emphasizes honesty above perfection. It conveys the message: "Let's be honest, even when it's hard." That kind of truth strengthens the link and the people who share it.

Love and honesty are ultimately synonymous. You can't claim to love someone and then lie to them, and you can't expect to be genuinely loved if you hide who you are. Love that lasts is built on telling the truth gently, accepting it with humility, and practicing it every day. It is about being honest even when it is simpler to remain silent. Honesty leads to peaceful relationships over time. There is no reason to pretend, and there is no danger of being discovered. This provides a peaceful assurance that love is founded on truth. That calm allows love to blossom in its most pure form: a connection founded on truth rather than deception.

Finally, being honest is the most respectful thing you can do for love. It concludes: "You are important enough to deserve the truth." When love is genuine, it not only endures but also develops. It becomes unbreakable because love keeps it alive while truth keeps it anchored. Being honest entails more than simply speaking the truth; it also entails living it. It's about ensuring that your words, deeds, and heart are all in sync so that love never doubts your integrity. Time, change, and distance are not a threat to honest love. It remains strong because it understands that truth will always be its greatest asset. That is the kind of love that endures, even when it is imperfect.

Chapter: 6

Trust is at the heart of every long-lasting relationship. Love struggles to breathe without it. When trust is present, love becomes a source of calm, understanding, and safety. It allows two people to be honest with each other without fear of being turned down.

Reflection Questions:

1. How do you define trust in your relationships, and what does it look like in action?

2. What moments have taught you the importance of building and protecting trust?

3. When someone places their trust in you, how do you honor and maintain it?

4. Have there been times when fear or insecurity made it difficult for you to trust others? How did you handle that?

When trust is broken, it does not imply that love has failed; rather, it invites love to expand. Rebuilding trust requires time, humility, and patience. Who or what encouraged you to believe again? These thoughts can help you comprehend the connection between healing and trust.

Reflection Questions:

1. Have you ever had to rebuild trust after it was broken? What steps helped you in that process?

2. What makes forgiveness difficult, and what makes it possible?

3. How can honesty and transparency help restore trust where it has been damaged?

4. What can you do differently in your future relationships to protect trust before it breaks?

Chapter: 6

Honesty and trust are inseparable. You need both of them. Being honest creates a safe environment for love to blossom because there are no secrets. Being honest does not imply stating everything that comes to mind; it entails being courteous and truthful. It entails being honest even when it is difficult. Honesty plays a simple yet crucial role in maintaining long-term love by fostering authenticity.

Reflection Questions:

1. For you, what does it mean to be "honest in love"?
2. How can honesty strengthen trust between two people?
3. Why do you think people sometimes hide the truth in relationships, and how can that be changed?
4. How can you practice honesty without being harsh or insensitive?

By virtue of honesty and forgiveness, trust cannot be ruptured. That is what ensures that love endures rather than disintegrates. The objective is not to achieve perfection in the relationship; rather, it is to establish a foundation where truth, patience, and forgiveness are interwoven to foster harmony. While concluding this chapter, contemplate the significance of trust in your daily existence.

Reflection Questions:

1. What daily habits can you practice to strengthen trust and honesty in your relationships?
2. When love feels shaken, how can you rebuild trust step by step?
3. Which do you think is harder—trusting others or being trustworthy yourself? Why?
4. After reading this chapter, what truth about trust do you want to carry with you into every relationship you build?

Chapter: 7

Love and Communication
Open communication is the key to understanding in relationships

L ove that doesn't communicate is akin to a song that lacks a melody: it exists, but it is not in harmony. Communication maintains healthy, connected, and vibrant relationships. Communication enables two hearts to understand each other's demands, fears, and desires. We grant love a voice by engaging in candid and transparent communication with one another. Frequently, relationships terminate not due to the waning of affection, but rather due to the cessation of communication. During conversations, bridges are constructed, while barriers are constructed by silence. In addition to engaging in more conversation, it is imperative to listen attentively and communicate candidly. By allowing for candid dialogue, love can develop without becoming conflicted or perplexed. Planning is the foundation of open communication. You can express your affection for your partner. Conversing is effortless; genuine communication, however, requires empathy and respect. It signifies, "I am interested in comprehending your perspective, rather than merely responding to it." The objective is not to emerge victorious in an argument; rather, it is to comprehend an angle of view. As both individuals feel secure enough to be themselves without fear of rejection or judgment, their love develops. You begin to develop greater trust, share more, and establish a more profound connection when you recognize that your voice is significant. The beauty of open communication is that it transforms ordinary conversations into moments of emotional intimacy.

People sometimes don't talk because they think love should come with intuitive understanding. We assume that they are already aware of my intentions. Love, however, is not the act of reading minds; it is the act of sharing souls. There is no one who can comprehend what you failed to articulate. To develop the ability to communicate candidly with one another, one must give up one's dignity and embrace transparency. This means expressing, "This is how I feel," even when it is challenging. Love is better with honesty. Opening up allows for a resurgence of comprehension in your relationship. Though it is not always effortless, open communication is the means by which love regains its vitality.

Chapter: 7

Open communication also trains us to listen attentively, rather than merely hearing words. Listening to respond and listening to comprehend are vastly different. You stop considering how to safeguard yourself and instead focus on establishing connections with others when you listen with your heart. You leave space for your partner to disclose the truth. Listening to a loved one with empathy is one of the best things you can do for them. It states, "You hold significant value for me." Misunderstandings are eliminated, and affection is fortified through this type of attentive listening. In every relationship, one person should speak while the other listens quietly, not to fix problems, but to understand them.

Nevertheless, tone, cadence, and body language are also critical components of communication. Speaking style can occasionally be more significant than the content of one's statement. The language of love is gentle, even when one disagrees. When individuals are in a state of distress, words can readily translate into weapons. This is the reason it is crucial to pause, take a deep breath, and choose compassion before speaking. Talking to someone in a gentle manner does not diminish the strength of your argument; rather, it fortifies your love. You can share the truth without causing harm to the individual you care about. Respectful communication fosters healing, while abusive language causes division. All words possess the capacity to either construct or deconstruct; therefore, it is better to construct.

Open communication is also characterized by transparency. Secrets and half-truths do not foster the development of affection. Withholding even minor details from others can make them question your credibility. "Openness" does not necessitate disclosing all of one's thoughts; rather, it involves being forthright about what is significant. It is equivalent to expressing, "This is my current location and the necessities I require." Openness fosters trust, and love remains robust in its presence. The two companions become teammates rather than adversaries when they can communicate without fear. Love is not perfect; it is a partnership based on truth.

Chapter: 7

The avoidance of problems, not disagreements, is what destroys love. If you are having a problem, voice it instead of keeping your anger inside. There is less room for anger or presumptions as you communicate more. Respectful conflict resolution can strengthen rather than weaken a relationship. These painful conversations reveal the maturity of love. However, it is always possible to choose to grasp, even if one does not always concur. Talking to each other might help two people who are ready to settle a dispute, rather than place blame on each other, develop a closer friendship. Addressing issues constructively is another aspect of open communication.

Proper open communication necessitates that both parties feel comfortable expressing their emotions. Consistency, empathy, and the absence of judgment toward others are the factors that ensure one's safety. Being aware that love will persist regardless of one's disagreement is the essence of it. Individuals are inclined to expose themselves when they feel secure. They share their fears, needs, and aspirations without hesitation. If you and your partner feel insecure when talking, try listening more, avoid criticism, and remind each other that you're on the same team. It is not the desire to prevail in an argument when one is in love; rather, it is the preservation of the bond that unites them.

Occasionally, the most challenging aspect of conversing with someone is shedding old behaviors. You may have been raised in an environment where emotions were suppressed or where being frank resulted in complications. However, affection mandates that you cease engaging in those activities. It is not a matter of perfection; rather, it is about consistently demonstrating honesty and kindness in all interactions with others. Messing up is permissible as long as one persists. Daily dedication to fostering a deeper understanding of one another is crucial. Practice, perseverance, and love can improve speaking with others.

Chapter: 7

Talking honestly with each other helps you feel closer, which is what keeps love alive. Talking honestly with someone else about your ideas, hopes, and difficulties creates a profound emotional bond that no amount of surface-level affection can match. When you talk about everything with someone you love, it seems genuine. It turns into a collaboration when both parties have a sense of being seen, appreciated, and acknowledged. When you talk to each other frequently, that kind of relationship never fades and gets stronger. Being open and honest can coexist peacefully in love.

Talking honestly with each other also helps you understand things better. You won't misunderstand each other anymore if you discuss and listen to each other honestly. You begin to regard your partner as a friend rather than an enemy. Talking things over clears up any confusion and saves people from making wrong assumptions that hurt. It's not about being right; it's about being honest. When you choose to converse openly, you choose to be close to someone instead of far away and to comprehend instead of being quiet. That choice turns love into something strong instead of weak. It serves as a reminder to both hearts that love is the most accurate source of truth.

In reality, talking to each other is what keeps love strong, no matter how far apart you are. It states, "I will keep talking to you, I will keep listening to you, and I will keep picking you." Love lasts when it learns to be honest with each other. The truth is that love doesn't fade because feelings fade; it fades when individuals don't get along. Continue chatting, then. Listen some more. Keep coming back with words that help, not hurt. When you talk honestly with each other, you establish a love that lasts and grows.

Chapter: 7

Love and Communication
Expressing love through words and actions

We don't just say we love someone; we show it. When we say and do things that demonstrate we love somebody, we make our feelings real. We all want to be loved, but we also want to know that we are loved. At that point, it's crucial to talk to each other and do things that make sense. Words remind us that we are recognized, respected, and valued, and actions indicate that those words are true. Some people demonstrate love by doing nice things for others, while others do it by touching, helping, or spending time with them. But at its core, expressing is what turns feelings into connections. Love might become an assumption without it. Saying "I love you" every day is like watering a plant; it keeps it alive, growing, and full of life.

Words like "I love you," "I appreciate you," and "I'm proud of you" can mean a lot. They may look small, but they mean a lot and bring people together. When you say nice things to your partner, family, or friends, they will remember that they matter. But words can mean more than just love letters. They can also express support, appreciation, and agreement. It's like saying, "I see what you're doing, and it means something to me." Usually, the best way to convey love isn't a grandiose speech, but simple, everyday reminders that say, "You're not alone." "You are important here."

But just saying things isn't enough. What they say and what they do must match. Love becomes real and lasting when what you say and do match up. You may feel empty when you speak but don't act, or hazy when you act but don't speak. Relationships operate best when there is a satisfying balance between the two. If you care for someone, demonstrate it through your conduct when others are not present: attentively listening to them and offering your support. You can say "true love" with your hands or your heart. When both languages are proficient, love is a living, breathing energy that creates lifelong bonds.

Chapter: 7

Everyone loves in their own way. Some people require kind words to open their hearts, while others need kind acts, physical touch, or service. Mastering the ability to communicate fluently in your partner's or even your friend's "language" is one of the most rewarding aspects of love. Devoting time to understanding someone's desire for love demonstrates your profound concern for them. Your partner might not need to hear you praise them all the time, but they'll feel immensely loved when you do something nice for them. Alternatively, your child may need to hear you say, "I'm proud of you," to feel secure. When you show love in a way that the other person understands best, it grows stronger.

When done deliberately, actions can reveal a lot about love. You can show someone you love them in ways that are louder than words, like cooking a meal, running an errand, or offering to help without being asked. They say, "I see what you need, and I'm here for you." People don't always notice the little things that show love. It's not simply huge things. It's been there when it's hard. It involves maintaining attentiveness, fulfilling commitments, and focusing on matters that are significant to the other individual. Those things show that I should spend time with you. Small, consistent gestures of affection create deep trust and a sense of belonging that one powerful gesture can't replace.

But actions are just as essential as words. It's always delightful to hear someone declare they love you. Verbal affirmation enhances connection by making things more evident. When you tell someone how much they mean to you, you dispel their doubts and make them feel safe. Life is busy, and we often assume that the people we love already know how we feel. But love has to be reminded to flourish. A brief message, a kind comment, or a meaningful note might make someone's day. When you plant words with honesty, they blossom into safety, hope, and confidence.

Chapter: 7

You also have to be honest and open to demonstrate love. Expressing your emotions can often be challenging, particularly if you have experienced past wounds or fear rejection. But being honest is what makes love real. When you open your heart with words or acts, you take a magnificent risk. You provide someone the chance to see who you really are. That honesty makes relationships stronger and more authentic. You might think it's safer to keep your sentiments to yourself, but it usually makes you feel more alone. Real connection occurs when we open up and show affection. It states, "I care about you," without contemplating how the other person will react. When you are open and honest with other people, your relationships go from normal to outstanding.

Sometimes, demonstrating love involves not attempting to solve problems and instead learning to listen. It's about being there for someone, being patient, and being understanding. When you listen without criticizing, you say, "Your voice matters." When you forgive, you display love that places peace before pride. These subtle ways of demonstrating affection can say more than words. They demonstrate that love extends beyond our emotions and encompasses our responses when those emotions face challenges. Love doesn't grow by being perfect; it grows when you work on it on purpose. Being present for someone over and over again when it counts is frequently the best way to demonstrate you care.

It's also vital to remember that love expressed through activities should come from a genuine place, not from duty or performance. We do not genuinely love someone when our actions are driven by feelings of guilt or external pressure. But when we do things because we are honest, they are real and warm. It doesn't matter if you embrace, send a letter, or spend time together; what matters is the thought behind it. When you honestly say you love someone, it flows naturally. It feels simple because it comes from the heart. And the more we exhibit love in a real way, the easier it is for other people to trust us and accept it.

Chapter: 7

You need to balance what you say with what you do to demonstrate affection. People claim they love someone, but they don't always show it. Some people do everything correctly but never tell you how they feel. The best relationships are those that strike a balance between the two. Say "I love you" a lot, but also show it. Do small acts that make life simple for someone else. You can show thanks by being polite, attentive, and speaking well. And if you do anything out of love, make sure your words back it up. When you put them all together, they produce a connection that feels whole, stable, and very satisfying.

Another lovely thing about showing love is that it spreads like ripples. When you show love to someone, they will automatically start to exhibit love back. When you are kind, other people are kind too. When you are gentle, others learn to be gentle. The way you display love affects not only the person you love but also the mood of those around you. A kind remark, a thoughtful act, or a moment of understanding can all help mend hearts and restore confidence in love. A little act of love can make a big difference in someone else's life.

In the end, the most important thing is to be there for someone when they need you. Being there for the people who matter and being truthful with them is what it's all about. It signifies "I see you, I'm here, and I care." You don't always need to do enormous things or offer long speeches to convey love. You simply need to show it, say it, and live it. The more love we give, the more we receive. We don't just offer love; we also become love. We don't just say "I love you" when our words and actions show love; we are love in action.

Chapter: 7

Love and Communication
How miscommunication can erode love

Miscommunication is one of love's quietest killers. It doesn't end relationships all at once; it does so gently, one word at a time. If you don't talk things out, a tiny fight can make you feel distant from each other. To grow, love needs to be connected, but to grow, connection needs to be understood. When people don't articulate what they mean or how they feel, even the strongest relationships can start to feel weak. What hurts isn't necessarily what is spoken; it's what is left unsaid or, even worse, what is inferred. Many relationships don't end because the love fades; they end because the communicating ceases. Love needs to be clear, because without it, even the strongest bond starts to break down.

The difficulty with misunderstanding is that it often lurks behind good intentions. You may say something intended to preserve someone's feelings, but they might interpret it as a lack of concern. You might also stay quiet to prevent a quarrel, but the other person will think you would rather not be with them if you do. In love, words matter more than just what they say. They also have feelings, tones, and goals. Things get confusing when those layers aren't in the appropriate order. Now, "I need some space" means "I don't love you anymore," and "I'm fine" means "I feel ignored." When things aren't obvious, people start to make assumptions instead of trying to understand, and that's when love starts to fade.

People can misunderstand each other even when they aren't talking. People lose touch with each other when they stop talking. You would think that silence symbolizes tranquility, but it can also make people angry. Love isn't about avoiding tough conversations; it's about being honest and kind when you have to have them. Couples who cease communicating, asking, and listening to one another slowly become emotionally distant. That's when small mistakes start to feel like enormous betrayals. When people stop communicating, love falls apart. It doesn't fall apart when they stop caring. And when that happens, it becomes far more challenging to repair the connection.

Chapter: 7

One of the primary ways miscommunication damages love is by making people feel distant from each other. People who don't understand one another anymore often feel they aren't being seen or heard. You might still live together or share a room, but emotionally, you're quite far away. When people cease talking to each other, love loses its warmth. What used to make us laugh now makes us angry, and what used to be a conversation is now a fight. Trust falls out when people don't understand each other. Over time, the fissures grow bigger, and love starts to seem more like perplexity than comfort. It is simple to misinterpret someone's intentions, to assume the worst, or to become discouraged when faced with confusion.

Pride and making assumptions about one another might also make it harder to comprehend each other. We stop asking questions occasionally because we think we already know what the other person is thinking. We also cease talking about it since we think that how we demonstrate love should be evident. The truth is that love needs to be put into words. One person's idea of love might not be the same as another person's. If your partner says, "You never listen," they truly mean, "I don't feel valued." "You don't care" could signify "I feel disconnected" to someone else. When we don't pay attention or make things plain, those emotional cues become buried, and misunderstanding spreads like a shadow over everything else.

The problem of miscommunication is that it affects the tale that love tells. People in relationships stop being friends and start being enemies. Instead of getting back together, every talk turns into a quarrel over who's right. And the longer the miscommunication goes on, the harder it is to remember that you're all working toward the same goal. Even while love isn't disappearing, tiny things like not texting back, getting the tone wrong, or taking too long to react can start to feel like proof that it is. Miscommunication can turn good into bad, not due to a lack of love, but because the love's message isn't getting through.

Chapter: 7

Emotional disengagement is another subtle way that miscommunication can destroy love. When people feel that they aren't being understood again and again, they start to drift away. They don't do it because they're mad; they do it because they're tired. It's exhausting to keep explaining yourself or to feel like your words never come through. Love becomes more delicate as time goes on. People don't communicate as much, discuss as much, or feel as much. After the silence, there is no serenity; there is only distance. The connection begins to fade like an untended flame when one person stops trying to communicate. It's sad, but true: love doesn't die when there are no feelings; it dies when people don't talk to one another.

Miscommunication also makes it challenging for people who love each other to see each other. Every thought that isn't spoken and every word that isn't comprehended adds to the problem. After a while, love can't get over those boundaries. One person can say, "They don't care," while the other might say, "I don't know how to fix this." Both are hurting, but neither thinks the other is listening. People who seek the same things—closeness, attention, and love—don't always understand each other, which is ironic. But the messages become muddled, and instead of bringing them closer together, they drive each other apart.

To keep love from fading due to misunderstandings, both parties need to commit to honesty and kindness. It's not about being perfect; it's about being there for someone. Listen to what others say more than what you say. Don't assume things; ask questions instead. Choose to be kind instead of defensive. "Help me understand what you mean" can occasionally save a relationship. You must reach the other person's heart, not just say what you want. When you communicate with someone with empathy, you help them understand rather than confuse them, and love starts to heal where it was once wounded.

Chapter: 7

You must be patient and humble in order to move past a misunderstanding. You must be modest to admit that you were wrong. You must have patience to correct others when they are in error. However, love is worth the work. If two people are prepared to listen with open hearts, even the most formidable barriers can be broken down. A misunderstanding doesn't have to mean the end of a relationship; it could be a turning point. Determining what went wrong can sometimes strengthen love. Don't let your pride get in the way of your love. You may state, "I made a mistake" rather than "I should have asked instead of assuming." Every sincere statement you make strengthens the bond.

Another method to clear up misunderstandings is to always be honest. Couples typically split up because they stop being honest with each other about their feelings. They don't say, "I'm hurt." They say, "I'm fine," instead. Instead of saying they're worried, they act remote. But love can't make the hidden things better. When you are honest, even when it's painful, it brings trust back into the conversation. Being honest clears the air and allows love a chance to flourish afresh. When communication becomes clear, love finds its rhythm again. Because it chose truth over silence, the voice that used to hurt can now be the voice that provides peace.

Love doesn't have to end because of a misunderstanding; it may teach love. It reminds us that relationships take work, that talking and listening are both vital, and that sometimes it's better to communicate than to stay quiet when hearts are moving away. Love wasn't meant to be perfect; it was designed to evolve through understanding. When words become mixed up or feelings get crossed, don't jump to conclusions. Instead, take a step back and choose clarity. Love doesn't merely last when people are honest and truthful with each other; it becomes unbreakable.

Chapter: 7

When two people can be honest with each other, listen to each other without judgment, and respond with kindness and love, love is easier to comprehend and keep. But people don't just talk to each other; they have to choose to do so and trust each other. Even when it's difficult, it's being honest about how you feel. It's about learning to listen without judging or cutting people off. Think about how the way you talk to people right now influences your relationships. Do you speak so that others can understand you, or do you listen carefully so that you can comprehend? The manner in which you communicate with one another reflects the depth of your love, as love that cannot be expressed will eventually fade.

Reflection Questions:

1. What does "open communication" mean to you personally, and how does it show up in your relationships?

2. When was the last time you felt truly heard by someone? What made that moment special or meaningful?

3. Do you find it easier to speak honestly or to listen deeply? Why do you think that is?

4. What steps could you take to create a safer, more open space for communication in your relationship?

You can't just feel love; you have to say it and show it. We show we care by saying and doing things that show we love someone.

Reflection Questions:

1. What are some ways you naturally express love — through words, actions, or both?

2. Do you think the people you love clearly recognize your expressions of love? Why or why not?

3. How can you make your words and actions more aligned with how your loved ones best receive love?

4. What small, meaningful actions could you start doing today to communicate love more intentionally?

Chapter: 7

A lack of understanding between people is one of the most prevalent reasons that love fades. It usually starts with small mistakes that grow into bigger ones. When people stop talking to each other, love starts to wane. When things grow complicated, hurt typically follows. Being aware is the most important thing to do right now. If you observe tension, refrain from making hasty assumptions. Ask questions first. If something doesn't feel right, talk about it before it becomes worse.

Reflection Questions:

1. Have you ever lost connection with someone because of miscommunication? What do you wish you'd done differently?
2. When conflict arises, do you tend to talk things out or withdraw? How has that affected your relationships?
3. How can you practice more empathy in your communication — especially when emotions run high?
4. What does forgiveness look like when miscommunication causes hurt in a relationship?

Love and talking to each other go together. One person speaks for the other. When people talk to each other honestly, with patience, and with a goal in mind, their love grows stronger and more secure.

Reflection Questions:

1. What does "healthy communication" look like to you in a lasting relationship?
2. How do you usually express love when words fail you — and what might you improve?
3. What lesson about communication from this chapter resonates most deeply with you?
4. If love could speak through you more clearly, what would it want to say?

Chapter: 8

Love and Respect
Respecting boundaries and individuality in relationships

The most crucial factors in any long-lasting relationship are love and respect. Love builds connections, and respect keeps love alive. Respect implies treating someone else's thoughts, dreams, and personal space with the same care that you would treat your own. You know that your beloved is a whole person with their own personality, not just a reflection of you. When we respect boundaries, we allow love to breathe. Even if the individual means well, love can become domineering or suffocating without respect. "I love you for who you are, not who I want you to be," is a sincere compliment. And that's what makes love last: the freedom to grow together, not under each other's shadow.

Boundaries are not walls; they are means to get to know each other better in a healthy relationship. They show where one person finishes and the other starts. Boundaries let both people be true to themselves while still being emotionally close to each other. When people respect each other's space, love feels safe. There is no need to be concerned about being excessive, misunderstood, or becoming overwhelmed in the relationship. You know that your partner respects your space and requirements. Setting limitations isn't selfish; it's a way to show love that keeps both individuals in line. It says, "I care about us enough to tell you what I want." When both spouses accept those restrictions, the relationship develops more strongly and peacefully.

The way we communicate with one another is another way we show respect. The way we say things is just as important as what we say. Speaking properly, listening intently, and exercising patience when you disagree are all components of being polite. Despite its passion, disrespectful love is fragile; it burns fiercely but does not last. Respect-based love, however, endures because it is based on mutual trust and understanding. It translates to "I still love you, even though we don't agree." Respect like that transforms love from a fleeting emotion into a lasting relationship. Even when they disagree on issues, it keeps their hearts in sync.

Chapter: 8

To honor each person's uniqueness in a relationship, you shouldn't try to eliminate differences; instead, you should cherish them. Everyone has their ideals, experiences, and way of seeing the world. Sometimes, such differences might be challenging for us, but they are also what keep partnerships fascinating and alive. Healthy love doesn't desire everyone to be the same; it loves those who are different. It's fine if you and your partner have different hobbies, emotional needs, or ways of communicating. The most essential thing is to learn how to appreciate such differences without trying to alter each other. Real love doesn't say, "Be like me." It reads, "I see you." I accept you. And I'm willing to learn more about you.

Boundaries also help us honor ourselves. When you know your limits and tell people, you teach them how to treat you. For love to last, you need to respect yourself. When you constantly sacrifice your comfort or identity to maintain harmony, it can lead to feelings of anger. Part of respecting boundaries is knowing when to say yes and when to say no. You need to have faith that love will persist through both. You can be alone, do what you choose, or just be silent. A respectful relationship realizes that being alone isn't a sign of rejection; it's a way to recover. The more you cherish what makes you special, the more you can love.

It's also vital to remember that you can respect someone without agreeing with them. Even if you don't entirely understand or agree with someone's choices, ideas, or feelings, you can nevertheless respect them. Acceptance is frequently where the strongest love shows up. When we let others be themselves, we create trust. You don't have to be responsible for someone to feel secure with them. You just need to believe that their differences enhance your connection. The goal isn't to become one person, but to stay who they are while walking together as two people who chose to be together.

Chapter: 8

Disrespect can creep into relationships in small ways, such as interrupting, disregarding what others say, making judgments about their choices, or making guesses about what they want. These minor flaws might grow over time, weakening the basis of love. Being aware is an aspect of respect. It's about waiting a moment before you speak, putting other people's needs before your own, and listening instead of reacting. Love comes easily and naturally when both parties feel heard and cherished. You don't have to fight for affirmation since it's already there in the relationship. Respect is what makes love feel safe and normal. It builds a bond based on trust between the two people, not control.

Respecting limits also means learning how to control your emotions. In every relationship, one person sometimes wants to be alone while the other wants to be close. When love is strong, it can handle both things without fear. Giving your partner space shows you trust them, not that you don't want to be with them. It says, "I know we can still be close even when we're not together." You must possess wisdom to understand that separation can enhance your love for someone. Distance doesn't end relationships; reliance does. Love thrives when it can breathe. Each individual matures in their own way, and this personal growth adds additional depth and vigor to the connection.

Love and respect combined create emotional equality. There is no one in control, and no one leaves. Both people have needs and a say, and it's their job to maintain the connection. The balance begins to shift when one person feels ignored or powerful. Being fair is beneficial for love. It's the back-and-forth between two people who care about each other's peace as much as their own. When respect is the basis of the connection, compromise is easier because it's no longer about winning; it's about keeping the connection strong. Respect has a silent power: it keeps love strong even when sentiments shift.

Chapter: 8

Respecting individuality also means helping people grow. It is fortunate that the individual you cherish today will not be the same person they will be in the future. People's dreams, priorities, and goals vary over time. Respectful love is lovely because it doesn't fear progress; it embraces it. It reads, "I love you enough to let you grow." It's beneficial to support your partner's achievement, even if it means giving up some power. If you both make time for personal improvement, your relationship will be better and more rewarding. Love that values each person's uniqueness doesn't shrink when things change; it grows.

Boundaries grow as couples do. Things that seemed fine at first might need to be altered later. The most essential thing is to continue communicating. Talk to one another. Think about what feels right and what doesn't. Respect evolves with time. As life changes, so do our requirements. Couples who stay together learn to love each other no matter the season. They never underestimate each other, constantly striving to learn from one another. They understand that respect isn't something you receive once; it's something you do every day.

In the end, love and respect are the same thing. Your affection will wane if you love someone but don't respect them. Your respect will wane if you don't love someone. They work together to build a partnership founded on trust, justice, and kindness. Respect gives love its shape, and love gives respect its warmth. Respecting someone's limits, listening to them, and enjoying who they are creates a safe, free relationship. That kind of love endures: it does not seek to dominate or compete; rather, it affirms daily, "I love you as you are, and I respect who you are becoming."

Chapter: 8

Love and Respect
Why mutual respect is essential to lasting love

L ove and respect are not two different things; they are the same thing, like heart and breath. Love makes a relationship warm, but respect makes it strong. If there is no respect between the two people, even the strongest love can start to fall apart. Respect is what stops love from turning into wrath, domination, or pride. It's the unspoken promise between two individuals that says, "I care about you as much as I care about myself." When there is respect, both people can love each other without fear. You don't have to worry about being criticized, disregarded, or made to feel tiny. But love tends to feel one-sided when respect goes away. It becomes harder to be seen, heard, and valued. Respect is not a choice; it is the foundation that prevents love from disintegrating.

To respect each other, you have to see each other as people. It's not thinking of your spouse as an extension of yourself but as a person with their own thoughts, feelings, and decisions. It involves listening to what someone says, treating them as an equal, and being kind even when you disagree. There will always be disagreements in a partnership, but respect keeps those differences from turning into splits. If you fail to show respect to someone, you can still damage the relationship, even if you love them. Love says, "I care about you," but respect says, "I'll treat you with respect even when we don't agree." When both spouses adhere to that principle, love transforms into a harmonious relationship rather than a struggle for power.

Respect is also what makes love last. Respect endures through challenging times, shifting emotions, and changing seasons. When you care about your partner, you safeguard their heart even when yours suffers. You don't talk to hurt; you talk to become better. You don't use quiet to hurt someone; you use it to give them time to calm down. That kind of growth keeps love alive even when things become tough. It's true that passion can start a relationship, but respect is what keeps it going. It changes short-term love into a long-term relationship. When two individuals really care about each other, they don't just fall in love once; they fall in love over and over again.

113

Chapter: 8

Respecting each other also makes you feel protected, which is important for love to last. When people feel valued, they can be themselves without fear of rejection or ridicule. They don't have to worry about being judged when they talk about their concerns, dreams, and doubts. People feel connected to one another when they are safe like that. You can't be open or close to someone if you don't respect them. When you listen carefully or answer kindly, you strengthen that safety. Respectful places make love stronger. It allows both individuals to be human, which means they can make mistakes, apologize, and improve together.

On the other hand, love steadily dies when there is no respect. When one partner's comments become careless or controlling, or when they don't care about the other's feelings, the emotional gap widens. It doesn't have to be loud; it can be subtle, like rolling your eyes, crossing lines, or making minor jabs that create bruises that aren't visible. Disrespect slowly breaks down trust and love, leaving only silence and defensiveness. That's why you need to be purposeful about respect. Avoid rudeness; choose to be nice, even when you're really mad. Love gets stronger when you respect it. Love can handle stress, arguments, and changes without losing its core stability.

Respect for each other keeps love fair. In a respectful partnership, no one is better than anybody else. Both voices matter. Both points of view are significant. There is no conflict for control because both individuals recognize that love and leadership are shared. You don't control someone when you appreciate them; you work together. You speak, listen, and decide things together. That kind of equilibrium lets everything operate together. People feel like they can do their best. In relationships where both people are equal, loyalty comes naturally. You don't have to ask for it. Respect leads to trust, and trust leads to love that grows stronger.

Chapter: 8

Another reason mutual respect is vital for love that lasts is that it prevents each individual from becoming the same. Love should not alter your true self; rather, it should enhance and refine the best version of who you are. When there is respect, both people may do what they want, make friends, and grow without feeling negative or frustrated. You don't have to make yourself smaller to make someone else feel safe. Respect means "I want you to be the best you can be, even if it means I have to change with you." In a relationship, when both people respect each other, love stays strong. Everyone brings something new to the relationship based on their experiences and how they see things. It's like taking care of two trees that are close to each other and are both healthy. Their roots cross, but they still grow in their own manner.

Respect also teaches you how to be responsible. When you really care about your partner, you are responsible for what you do. You do not manipulate your emotions to achieve your desires, assign blame to others, or engage in manipulative tactics. You own up to your mistakes and try to make things right instead. One of the most caring things you can do is hold someone accountable. It says, "I care about you enough to keep your trust." When couples respect each other, they can work through their challenges without hurting each other. It turns the question from "Who's right?" to "How can we make this work?" That little shift in your perspective can spare a relationship a lot of misery. It turns arguments into opportunities to learn.

One of the best things about mutual respect is that it helps you enjoy things more. When you respect someone, you focus on their positive qualities rather than their negative aspects. You admire how strong they are, how positive their character is, and how diligently they work. In a place where people are polite, gratitude naturally arises. You express gratitude more frequently, not out of obligation, but because you sincerely intend it. End it. And that thankfulness grows into love. Couples that constantly thank each other for their efforts tend to stay joyful and close. Respect teaches us that love isn't about being perfect; it's about finding worth in things that aren't perfect.

Chapter: 8

Respecting each other also builds trust. When both parties perceive honest, fair, and caring treatment, they can unwind and enjoy each other's company. You don't have to be careful or constantly ask for proof. When you respect someone, you know they won't injure you deliberately with what they say or do. That safety is what lets love grow. Trust and respect are linked: the more you respect someone, the more they trust you, and the easier it is to keep respecting them. They work together to form a sturdy framework that makes love feel safe and steady.

You also have to be humble to love someone. This means being able to acknowledge, "I don't know everything," and recognizing that your partner's opinion matters as well. You can give up your pride and strike a deal because you are humble. Without it, love becomes harder and harder to handle. But it's simpler to talk to, forgive, and love each other when both individuals are modest. It's not about being perfect; it's about both individuals working diligently. You listen before reacting, apologize when needed, and are kind to your partner, even when things are tense.

Respect for each other ultimately ensures the longevity of love. It keeps love grounded when desire fades, and it lifts it up when things become tough. Love is compassionate, consistent, and long-lasting when there is respect. It reminds both people that love isn't about having someone; it's about working together. When you respect the person you love, you make a place where both of your hearts can develop. You build a friendship that lasts and grows stronger over time. Love without respect may shine for a while, but love with respect lasts forever.

Chapter: 8

Love and Respect
How to nurture respect within love

Respect must be worked on, defended, and maintained over time. Talking to, listening to, and responding to the person you love makes your love stronger. Many people believe that love is all a relationship needs to last, yet love fades when there is no respect. Respect is what keeps love strong and steady. It's how two people can stay close without getting in each other's way, argue without losing trust, and grow as individuals while still growing together. To build respect, you need to choose to acknowledge your partner's humanity every day, even in small ways.

Deliberate listening is the first way to demonstrate love and respect. People often listen primarily to formulate a response rather than to truly understand. One way to express love is to listen well. It tells the other person, "I care about you enough to stop and listen to everything you have to say." When you give someone your whole attention without any distractions, interruptions, or assumptions, you show them a lot of respect. People feel comfortable and connected when you listen like that. Even if you don't agree, the fact that you are willing to listen indicates you care. In fact, when both parties feel heard, many disputes end. It's not about curing someone when you listen; it's about getting to know them.

You can also build respect by valuing your partner's opinion, even when it differs from your own. You can live together even if you don't agree on everything. Appreciative-based love learns to say, "I might not agree with you completely, but I still respect what you think." That kind of maturity makes relationships last. It prevents conflicts from becoming excessive. People are more likely to talk and establish common ground when they sense their perspectives count. Respect is all about being kind, not being right. It's important to remember that your purpose is to bring people together, not to win.

Chapter: 8

Maintaining your partner's dignity, even in moments of anger, is a sign of love. Words can bring people together or tear them apart. When you are angry, it becomes effortless to utter words that deeply wound and leave scars that love alone cannot readily mend. Taking your time to choose your words properly is a sign of respect. Instead of yelling or mocking, talk to them to heal, not hurt. When you dispute with respect, you show that the problem is the issue, not the person. That's how love stays strong even when things go wrong. Anger may fluctuate, but your response to it will determine whether your respect levels rise or fall.

Doing things to show you care is another way to earn respect. Even if it's just a small bit, noticing your partner's hard work makes them appear more important to you. Saying "thank you" is more than just being nice; it's a way to show you care. When you say "thank you," you express "I see you, and I appreciate what you do." Saying thank you for their hard work, patience, or support keeps the relationship warm and even. People do better when they know that others care about and respect them. It's not the huge things that keep love alive; it's the little things that remind both people that they are loved and seen every day.

Setting limits also helps people learn to respect each other. Everyone has limits on their bodies, minds, and emotions, and those limits should be respected. Respectful love knows that saying "no" doesn't imply you would rather not be with someone; it indicates you care about yourself. When both individuals can articulate what they want, trust grows organically. Setting boundaries makes love stronger by making things clear and safe. If you think your limits don't matter, you can't feel safe in love. Respecting limits is one of the best ways to show someone you care. It states, "I care about your peace as much as I care about our relationship."

Chapter: 8

To build respect in love, you need to let each other be who they are. Love doesn't mean losing who you are; it means growing together. When you encourage your partner's aspirations, interests, and independence, you show that you value who they are outside of the partnership. That support helps you grow as a person, making your partnership stronger. Supporting your partner's individuality could include encouraging them at work, giving them time to unwind, or just being interested in what makes them fulfilled. Respectful love acknowledges both "us" and "you."

It's also vital to be honest with each other if you want to retain respect. Being honest makes people trust you, and trust keeps respect. Discussing uncomfortable topics, even if they upset you, strengthens your bond. It's not always easy to be honest, especially when the truth can hurt or disappoint someone. But being honest and kind develops trust. Your partner should never have to wonder if you're being honest. Respect comes when everyone is honest. It communicates to both parties, "You can rely on me to speak the truth, even when it's challenging."

Another crucial part of teaching respect is being humble. When both people are willing to say they're sorry, forgive each other, and accept their mistakes, love grows. Ego and respect don't get along. When you're proud, you aren't concerned about other people. But being humble makes it simple to love. It gives both people the chance to say, "I was wrong" or "I could have done better." Those simple sentences can be quite useful. If you are humble in your relationship, it will be easier for your partner to be humble as well. Over time, humility builds a culture of understanding where respect can flourish on its own.

Chapter: 8

Another crucial aspect of respect is being consistent. You cannot demonstrate respect intermittently; it must be conveyed consistently at all times. To be dependable, you need to show up on time, maintain your word, and follow through on your promises. Respect is based on trust. When what you say and do match, your spouse feels they can trust you. That regularity makes you feel safe emotionally, which is important for love to blossom. It's the little, everyday gestures of honesty that keep a relationship strong long after the thrill has gone off.

Empathy also makes you more respectful of other people. You can better understand your partner's feelings and experiences by putting yourself in their shoes. People are less mean and more patient when they have empathy. It helps you comprehend how people felt when they did things in the past. Your connection will be closer when your partner shows empathy. Love without empathy can seem superficial, but love with empathy can seem deep. It means, "I care about how you feel, even if I don't fully get it." Empathy turns simple respect into compassion, the highest form of love.

In the end, building respect within love involves being kind, humble, and understanding every day. It's about speaking softly, genuinely listening, and taking care of the heart that someone has given you. Respect is something you do every day for the rest of your life to keep love strong and pure. When two individuals vow to respect each other's dignity, they build a partnership that works for both. Respect is the gentle beat that goes through every wonderful love tale. No matter how many storms come and go, it stays alive because of its steady heartbeat.

Chapter: 8

Love and respect are inseparable; one can't do well without the other. Respect provides love with a structure that keeps it healthy, balanced, and kind. When we respect the person we love, we make both of our hearts feel safe and loved. Respecting someone doesn't imply agreeing with everything they say or do. It is understood that they have the freedom to think, feel, and choose differently. It concerns the ability to listen without interruption, to set boundaries without feeling guilty, and to love without exerting control.

Reflection Questions:

1. What does respect look like to you in a loving relationship? How do you personally define it?
2. Can you recall a time when you felt deeply respected by someone? How did that moment impact your connection with them?
3. When have you found it hardest to show respect in love? What caused the tension, and what could have been done differently?
4. In your opinion, how do love and respect work together to create emotional safety between two people?

Respecting someone's differences and their personal space is one of the most compassionate things you can do when loving someone.

Reflection Questions:

1. How comfortable are you with setting boundaries in your relationships? What emotions come up when you do?
2. Have you ever felt your boundaries weren't respected? How did that experience change your view of love or trust?
3. What boundaries do you think are essential for maintaining peace and balance in a relationship?
4. How can you show respect for your partner's individuality without feeling like you're losing your own identity?

Chapter: 8

Respect for one another is essential to a lasting relationship. It transforms desire into an objective and love into a relationship. The relationship shifts from rivalry to equality when both parties feel appreciated and seen. Should appreciate others, acknowledge their differences, be truthful, and give up attempting to be correct. It entails being considerate of your spouse's opinions and feelings, even if they diverge from your own. Love becomes a conscious decision when it is treated with respect. Every day, the decision is made to construct rather than destroy.

Reflection Questions:

1. What daily habits or gestures help you show respect to those you love?

2. How do you respond when you feel disrespected? Do you react defensively, or do you communicate your feelings calmly?

3. What would change in your relationship if respect became as intentional as affection?

4. How can mutual respect help two people grow closer, even during disagreements or challenges?

Building respect and love over a lifetime involves humility, tolerance, and sensitivity. It's about placing understanding above pride, compassion above criticism, and being present instead of being proud.

Reflection Questions:

1. What are three small ways you can begin nurturing more respect in your closest relationship today?

2. How does empathy help you show respect, even when you're hurt or frustrated?

3. What role does forgiveness play in rebuilding or maintaining respect after conflict?

4. If love could speak through your actions, how would it show your partner that you truly respect them?

Chapter: 9

Love as a Choice, Not Just a Feeling
Understanding love as a daily decision

Many people perceive love as a sensation, akin to a warm surge of emotions or a glimmer that illuminates the heart. But feelings don't stay around for long. Similar to waves, love fluctuates, rising to a peak and then falling to a low point. Love that lasts through difficult times, and time isn't solely about how you feel. It depends on what you want. When you choose to love someone, you pledge to be kind, patient, and understanding even when things seem tough or dull. Choices keep the story moving, even though feelings initiate it. When we stop waiting for love to happen and start living it every day, it grows stronger.

If love is just a feeling, it can change based on your mood, the situation, or your chemistry with someone. But love grows stronger when we understand that we may choose it. It's the choice to stay, even though it would be easier to go. It's nice to show kindness even when you're furious. Forgiveness is possible even after being injured. We may choose love every day by the way we talk, behave, and think. It's wonderful because this kind of love isn't an accident; it's on purpose. It represents a commitment to caring for, understanding, and growing alongside another person throughout all stages of life.

Choosing love every day doesn't mean disregarding your feelings; it means taking charge of them. Feelings are wonderful guides, but they don't always know where to go. Some days you feel close to someone, while other days you feel distant. That's not strange. Choosing to love fills up the gaps that sensations can't. Love doesn't change because of every argument, disappointment, or moment of uncertainty when it's a choice. It has a goal. When you love someone, you say, "I'm here for you, not just because it feels beneficial, but because you deserve it." That's what makes love last longer than a fleeting passion.

Chapter: 9

Recognizing that love is a choice you make every day means knowing that relationships need work. Many believe that love is easy if it's "meant to be," but that's false. It's not about being perfect; it's about sticking with it. Long-lasting love is. You choose to be pleasant every day, even when you're exhausted. When things go wrong, you choose to be patient. It's nice to forgive your partner when they do something wrong, knowing that you will need their forgiveness someday. Love doesn't grow because it's easy; it grows because it's steady. When love isn't enough to keep a relationship going, the choice to love is what keeps it going.

Picking love even when it's difficult is a sign that you're an adult. When we feel things, we can act right away, like when we talk, blame, or leave. But choice teaches us to pause and reflect on what we want to do. When we choose to love someone, we don't let anger tell us what to do. We do things based on what we believe, not how we feel. We learn to apologize more quickly, listen longer, and forgive more quickly. It's not as vital to win debates as it is to retain the relationship. Our proximity is affected by what we say, how we act, and where we focus. When choosing love, it's crucial to know your heart's direction.

Choosing to love doesn't make difficulties go away; it alters how you confront them. Feelings alone can't keep a relationship going when things get rough; they fluctuate with the situation. But love stays strong when you have a choice. It reminds us that being devoted doesn't mean being perfect; it means being there. It states, "I'm going to stay involved, care, and believe in what we're building, even when things are hard." That's what gives love strength. It's the choice to come with faith rather than fear, grace rather than anger, and understanding rather than pride. Every deliberate act you perform to express love contributes cumulatively to something greater: a love that never fails.

Chapter: 9

When we see love as a choice, we realize it's about giving, not getting. Feelings inquire, "What benefits do I gain?" whereas choice questions, "How can I strengthen this relationship?" Love isn't about waiting for inspiration; it's about choosing to spend. You may need to prioritize your feelings over your personal desires or to exert effort rather than choose the convenient path. It's recognizing that every little thing you do out of love is a seed that strengthens the bond. A kind word or a touch after a disagreement can completely transform the mood. On purpose, you may make love grow.

This doesn't mean that love should feel like a machine or be pushed. We don't avoid the spark when it dies; we revive it. When you choose love, you often do little things deliberately, like listening when you're busy, saying "I'm sorry" when you don't want to, or thanking someone for something you used to take for granted. These decisions bring relationships back to life. They remind us that love isn't something you acquire; it's something you build. People who stay together don't have to confront problems all the time. They just keep choosing love even when they do.

When we choose to love someone, we also let go of unreasonable expectations. You cease striving for perfection when you recognize that love is an action, not merely a sentiment. You cease believing that every day will be full of fireworks and butterflies. Instead, you learn to appreciate the peaceful times, like when you laugh after a fight, share silence, or just have someone stay with you. That's what love as a decision looks like: it's strong, stable, and grown-up. It's not pretty, but it's true. And in a society where people often confuse excitement with profundity, choosing love every day is a daring and wonderful act.

Chapter: 9

The best thing about choosing love is that it changes you as well. Choosing to love on purpose makes you more patient, humble, and understanding. You start to understand that love isn't only about the other person; it's also about who you are becoming. Choosing love affects who you are. It teaches you to put understanding above judgment, loyalty above passing feelings, and peace above pride. You become stronger emotionally by learning to love even when it's challenging. That's when love becomes something holy, something that brings out the best in you.

Choosing love doesn't mean neglecting your needs or letting someone mistreat you. Proper love values balance and chooses honesty, respect for each other, and setting limits. It's not faith without thinking; it's a collaboration. It indicates, "I love you, but I also love myself enough to be honest about what I need." That kind of love doesn't make you weaker; it makes you stronger. It helps both people grow as individuals and as a pair. When love is based on healthy decisions rather than fleeting emotions, it becomes stronger, safer, and more genuine.

Love as a choice is being devoted to more than just someone else; it means being engaged in loving properly. You have to choose to provide, forgive, and understand every day. You can still choose to love, even though your sentiments will change. It isn't always easy, but it's always worth it. It's not about being perfect; it's about sticking with it. When you choose love every day, you're not just keeping a relationship running; you're also keeping your heart open to what love was always supposed to be: faithful, lasting, and wonderfully planned.

Chapter: 9

Love as a Choice, Not Just a Feeling
How to choose love even when it's hard

It's not difficult to choose love when it's easy. When you're pleased and everything is going well, it's easy to love. The real test of love comes when things get tough, when you're upset, fatigued, let down, or not understood. At that point, love goes from being an emotion to a promise. When challenges arise, choosing love necessitates recalling your initial motivations and maintaining a positive outlook. It means not giving up even when it would be easy to do so. It's the choice to be compassionate rather than angry, to want peace rather than retribution, and to see your spouse as someone who is trying their best rather than an enemy. People who keep selecting each other are what make love last.

It's normal to feel irritated or worn out when things aren't going well in your relationship. You can feel different things from one day to the next. You can feel angry or distant one day and full of affection the next. That's when your choice to love is more important than being right. Choosing love during those moments doesn't mean pretending everything is fine; rather, it means deciding to make things better. It's about pausing before you act, listening to what others have to say before you judge, and trying to understand rather than jumping to conclusions. It's not grandiose gestures that show love that lasts through terrible times; it's modest, everyday actions of patience, forgiveness, and humility.

It's also vital to remember that choosing love when it's challenging isn't a sign of weakness; it's a sign of strength. It's brave to love someone even when they're hurting, to forgive someone even when you're hurting, and to keep your heart open when you want to close it. Many people assume that leaving is a sign of strength, but sometimes the best thing to do is stay and heal together. When you choose love, you don't ignore your limits; instead, you promise to grow as a person and as a partnership. It's like saying, "We may not know everything, but I'm willing to fight for what we have." When things are rough, real love doesn't give up; it grows stronger, more intelligent, and more stable.

Chapter: 9

You have to adjust the way you look at things to choose love when it's challenging. You may notice what's wrong, but love helps you see what's still right. Every relationship has issues, but the person who loves you is usually trying to love you in their own way. When you stop being frustrated and start being grateful, everything changes. You may add, "I appreciate the times you do listen," instead of "You never listen." You contemplate what you've made together instead of what you don't have. Being thankful makes the heart softer and helps it recover faster. When you choose to see the beneficial in things, even when they are painful, love finds a way to breathe again.

Another crucial part of choosing love when things are challenging is being patient. Love isn't a race; it's a long trip. One individual may go quicker than the other at times. Your partner may take longer to change or display love in a different way than you do. At those moments, being patient means being kind. It's choosing to trust that love is still there, even if it doesn't look like you thought it would. Patience doesn't disregard problems; it just lets them be worked out without getting frustrated. When you choose love with patience, you tell your partner, "You're worth waiting for, and our relationship is worth the time it takes to heal."

When it's difficult to choose love, forgiveness is also vital. There are flaws in every relationship, and no one is flawless. Forgiving someone doesn't make the hurt go away; it frees your heart from its grip. When you forgive, you choose freedom over wrath. You do not necessarily need to forgive someone only once; there are instances when forgiveness must be extended daily. But every time you choose it, you allow love a chance to flourish again. Forgiveness does not obliterate the past; it transforms it. It changes pain into knowledge and fury into understanding. Letting someone go is one of the nicest ways to show love.

Chapter: 9

Communicating with one another is another strategy for overcoming difficult situations together. Pride, silence, and prejudices can prevent two people from communicating with one another. But being honest can be beneficial. Choosing love means you are willing to confront challenging issues, not to place blame but to look for solutions. It entails politely voicing your opinions and listening without getting defensive. It may be necessary to say, "I'm sorry," recognize, "I was wrong," or say, "I hurt you." But sometimes, after a quarrel, it's preferable to just sit silently and wait for the situation to calm down before speaking again. When ego is replaced by empathy and honesty by fury, love blossoms; when compassion guides a conversation, even difficult ones can be healing.

Remembering that both individuals are growing is another way to choose love when it's challenging. You will sometimes mess up, act childish, and not get it. But love helps you grow instead of expecting you to be flawless. It's choosing to see your spouse with optimism instead of condemnation. When you recall that you required grace and tolerance from others on your journey, it's simpler to provide them to others. Love that endures through difficult times does not need to be perfect; it learns to grow, adapt, and persist with understanding.

It's also crucial to know oneself when you choose love. It's simple to see what's wrong with your lover, but love requires you to look at yourself first. Consider this: Am I making things calmer or more tense? Am I doing your actions out of love or pride? Am I offering what I want to receive in return? When you take responsibility for your role, things start to shift. When both individuals are prepared to adapt instead of blame, love deepens. You may opt to prioritize establishing a connection over asserting your correctness and to set aside your ego. That is what renders love so powerful: it unites you and transforms you at the same time.

Chapter: 9

You also need faith when you choose love, even when it's challenging. You need to believe in the process, the person you love, and the strength of commitment. There will be moments when nothing appears to work, when you feel alone or like no one understands you, and when every interaction seems difficult. During those times, picking love is a leap of faith. It says, "This is challenging, but I believe in us." Faith doesn't deny what's real; it merely believes that love can come back. Every strong relationship has been through challenging times; that's what makes it strong. Choosing love makes both hearts stronger and trust deeper when things are challenging.

Choosing love can entail giving up control at times. It means understanding that you can't cure everything or change something when you want to. You have to let go of your need for perfection and trust the process to love someone. When you quit trying to control what happens, love becomes calmer. It's not about giving up; it's about giving in to understanding. When you choose love, you don't worry as much about being right as you do about being close. It's the option to keep your heart open, even though it would be easier to close it.

In the end, the key to a long-lasting relationship is to choose love even when it's challenging. It's the choice to come back with grace, to forgive again, and to keep believing in the beauty of what you're making. You have to choose to love someone; it's not easy. Every time you choose love over pain, you prove that your bond is stronger than your battle. And as you keep making that choice—day after day, moment after moment—you discover that the worst moments often bring out the deepest sort of love: the kind that lasts, changes, and never gives up.

Chapter: 9

Love as a Choice, Not Just a Feeling
The role of commitment in love that never fails

L ove lasts when people are committed. It's what makes love last when things become tough and feelings alter. It's wonderful to have feelings, but they're not necessarily right. Your attitude, the weather, and the scenario all affect them. But you choose to be dedicated with your head and heart. It indicates, "I'm in this, even when things are tough." In a society where people typically prioritize convenience above consistency, sincere love is what makes commitment stand out. It's not about how wonderful things are; it's about how willing you are to stay when things go wrong. When you make a promise, love goes from a transient spark to an unbreakable flame.

When you pledge to love someone, you create a bond that cannot be sustained by feelings alone. Commitment gives your relationship purpose and direction. It reminds you of why you are together. When storms strike, when they don't agree, or when life becomes boring, it keeps two people together. Passion is not permanent; it will die if you don't nurture it. Real love isn't about always being in love; it's about always choosing to love. It's getting up every day and deciding to be loyal, helpful, and kind, even after the fun is over. That's why love lasts: it's based on a promise, not a feeling.

Being dedicated also makes you feel safe. When both parties know they are sincerely devoted, trust builds. You don't worry about being left behind in tough times anymore, because your commitment shows that the link is strong. It tells your lover, "I'm here for you." That safety makes you feel safe enough to be emotionally close to someone. If you don't commit to a relationship, it can feel like it's about to end at any moment. But if both people are committed, they can be sure that love will stay even when they don't agree. That's what makes love last: it doesn't change readily over time.

Chapter: 9

A firm belief in love is akin to the foundation of a house: it remains invisible, yet it sustains everything. For a building to last, it needs a sturdy base. The foundation is dedication. It doesn't look good or make you feel anything, but it's strong. It's made up of hundreds of modest sacrifices, pledges kept in silence, and moments of patience that no one else sees. If love is built on dedication, it may persist through tough times, misunderstandings, and even the passage of time. It states, "We might trip, but we won't break up." Being committed doesn't mean you'll be flawless; it means you'll keep trying.

Commitment also strengthens love by providing it with a goal. It functions like a compass, keeping your relationship on the right path toward progress rather than letting it drift. When you're devoted, you choose things that benefit the relationship rather than harm it. When you disagree, you think more carefully, act more thoughtfully, and are kinder. Rather than viewing yourself and your spouse as rivals, you learn to view them as a cohesive team. Love matures as it changes from "me" to "us." When you make a commitment, you align your priorities with the goal of love: to build something enduring and meaningful together.

It's easy to make a promise while things are going well, but real dedication is revealed when things are challenging. It's when you still choose love after being hurt. It's when you keep coming back, even when you don't feel like you're worth it. When you stay loyal to someone even when no one else does, those instances reveal how deep love is. Being dedicated doesn't imply being perfect; it means being the same all the time. It doesn't state, "I'll stay as long as I'm happy." It adds, "I'll stay because this love is worth the work." Such strength provides love with roots deep enough to endure life's challenges.

Chapter: 9

Commitment is also very crucial for emotional growth. It takes time, forgiveness, and strength to get through it. If you don't know how to put aside your pride, make sacrifices, and look past short-term concerns, you can't really care about someone. It demonstrates that love is about faith, not about winning or losing. When two people are really in love, they don't see it as a contract anymore; they see it as a promise. It's not about how well you do or what you do; it's about a sacred vow to be there for each other, to grow, and to maintain a belief in each other, even when your feelings change. A love that never fails is always built on commitment, not demand.

Commitment also makes love unselfish. When you get what you want, it's easy to love, but commitment is loving even when you have to give more than you get. It tells you to put someone else's needs ahead of your own, without losing yourself in the process. You should offer your time, energy, and effort freely because the relationship is more important than your short-term comfort. That's what makes commitment so strong: it translates love into service, sacrifice, and stability. The finest relationships are those in which both parties are willing to work to keep love alive, not those without problems.

Staying faithful is one of the best benefits of dedication. Being faithful in every aspect—not just physically—is a daily choice you make. Faithfulness is what makes love real and strong. It's simple to say "I love you," but being faithful over time proves it. It's choosing not to allow pride, boredom, or temptation to ruin everything you've worked diligently to build. Being faithful and being committed are two aspects of the same concept. They maintain a robust love by not letting it fade away due to neglect or preoccupation. A relationship that lasts and grows happens when both people choose to be faithful.

Chapter: 9

Commitment also teaches you how to keep going. Every long-term relationship will test your strength, like when you run out of feelings, don't understand each other, or face outside demands. But being committed can help you recall why you started. It says, "This is worth fighting for." Being persistent doesn't imply ignoring difficulties; it means facing them with love as your guide. It's about choosing to speak up rather than run away, to work diligently rather than harbor a grudge, and to be compassionate rather than furious. That strength is what turns a normal love into an incredible relationship. Couples who stay together aren't lucky; they work at it. No matter what, they keep selecting each other.

Another great thing about commitment is that it frees you instead of putting constraints on you. At first, commitment may appear like a limit, but it actually frees the heart from doubt. When both people are fully dedicated, they don't have to worry about losing each other. They can relax and know that love is safe and steady instead. That safety lets you be yourself. You can just be; you don't have to compete, pretend, or prove yourself. You understand that love will not diminish when circumstances deteriorate if you commit to remaining with someone. The promise of "you are safe with me" is what allows love to endure indefinitely.

Ultimately, the most crucial promise of love is commitment. It links emotions to behaviors, desires to objectives, and beliefs to emotions. It turns "I love you" into "I'm always here." Without commitment, love is weak and can be quickly broken by feelings or situations. But love is unshakable when you are dedicated to it. It can withstand any challenge and emerge triumphant. Love is strong, deep, and long-lasting when you are committed to it. It's not about being perfect; it's about being present. Never-failing love isn't the kind that always feels easy; it's the kind that never ends. That's what makes commitment so beautiful: it keeps love alive forever.

Chapter: 9

Love is more than a sensation; it's a choice we make again and again. Your feelings can fluctuate depending on how you feel or how long it's been. But choosing love implies being consistent. You must choose to show up, care, and be gracious daily, even if you don't feel as strongly. Love grows stronger when you do it on purpose.

Reflection Questions:

1. What does "choosing love daily" mean to you personally? How do you practice that choice in your relationships?

2. Have there been moments when you didn't *feel* loving, but chose to act lovingly anyway? What did that experience teach you?

3. What are some small, practical ways you can show love intentionally each day, even in ordinary moments?

4. How does seeing love as a decision rather than a feeling change the way you view commitment and connection?

It demonstrates how strong your heart is when you choose love even when it's difficult. It's easy to love while things are going well, but love becomes stronger when things are challenging. It could mean forgiving when it's hard, talking when it's easier to be quiet, or staying when it's easier to leave.

Reflection Questions:

1. When love felt hard in your life, what helped you hold on instead of giving up?

2. How do you remind yourself of your "why" when emotions start to fade or frustration sets in?

3. What role does forgiveness play in your ability to keep choosing love through difficult seasons?

4. How do you balance choosing love with maintaining healthy boundaries for yourself?

Chapter: 9

Commitment is a gentle power that keeps love alive. It's the promise to stay and keep working when things get tough. Being committed doesn't mean you can't move on; it means you feel protected. It says, "I'm here for the long haul, not just the favorable times." This kind of love doesn't end when feelings change; it grows stronger and deeper. It's the difference between temporary affection and lasting devotion.

Reflection Questions:

1. What does commitment mean to you, and how do you demonstrate it in your relationships?
2. Why do you think lasting love requires commitment instead of relying only on emotion?
3. How has commitment—yours or someone else's—helped a relationship survive challenges or change?
4. How can you practice loyalty, patience, and faithfulness even when the excitement fades?

Three things make up love that never fails: daily choices, lasting patience, and unyielding commitment. You are in charge of love's growth when you see it as a choice. You make things more complicated when you choose love, but you also make them easier to be closer to.

Reflection Questions:

1. What have you learned from past experiences about what real, lasting love requires?
2. What do you think it means to love someone "on purpose" rather than "by accident"?
3. How do daily choices—both big and small—shape the strength of your love story?
4. In what ways can you commit to loving more intentionally from this day forward?

Chapter: 10

Love and Faith
How faith sustains love through uncertainties

L ove and faith work together to make each other stronger. Faith tells us why we should keep going, and love offers us something to hold on to. When life is uncertain and partnerships are going through difficult patches, faith is what keeps love from wandering away. Faith steps in when things don't make sense. It's simple to love when things are clear. The quiet voice that says, "Hold on, there's still hope," is what keeps you going even when things seem dismal. Faith doesn't make things easier; it helps you get through them without giving up. When you're in love, faith turns fear into trust and concern into patience.

There are times in every relationship when you doubt it, when the future appears unclear, and when the present seems heavy. You can experience difficulties with money, distance, misunderstandings, or unaddressed grief. Faith is more than simply a belief; it's a choice to maintain believing in each other during those moments. "I don't know how the future will turn out, but I believe in us," says Faith. That type of faith provides the power to persevere through hard times without falling apart. It's what keeps you going when your sentiments would have made you fall.

Believing in love is not only good for your soul, but it's also good for you. You trust that the individual you cherish will continue to improve progressively, even if such progress requires a considerable amount of time. It's trusting that forgiveness can heal what words have damaged and that being patient can bring two hurting hearts together. Faith makes love want to come back. Without it, love is weak and can be broken by fear or disappointment. But love is strong when you have faith. It bends but doesn't break, and it battles but doesn't give up. Faith keeps the light going when the room grows dark.

Chapter: 10

Faith is beautiful because it shifts the focus from control to trust. It's normal to want to control things when you're in love, like fixing problems, knowing what will happen next, and avoiding pain. But love that is only about control goes old very quickly. Faith helps you carry that weight. It teaches you to believe that love can last even when you don't yet understand it. It means stating, "I don't know what's going to happen next, but I believe that something good can still come from this." That type of faith makes love tranquil, even when things are out of control. Faith provides the heart with serenity by taking away anxiety and replacing it with confidence.

Faith also helps you keep love alive by reminding you that good things take time. Sometimes love feels strong and certain, while at other times it may feel distant and uncertain. But faith responds, "This is just a moment, not the whole story." It reminds you that silence can mask progress, and healing takes time. Love doesn't hasten; it waits with faith. It doesn't let short-term feelings get in the way of long-term ambitions. When both people choose to walk by faith, they stop expecting everything to be perfect and start being grateful for progress.

There is certainly something compelling about believing in a love guided by divine timing. Sometimes faith involves letting go of your plans and trusting that love will unfold as it should. You have to believe that when doors close, it's not the end; it's just a new way to go. Love and faith together help you stay balanced. Love makes you accomplish things, and faith teaches you to let go. When you bring them together, you discover tranquility in the process. You stop trying to control everything and start trusting that the love that was meant for you will always find its way back to you, even when things are unclear.

Chapter: 10

Faith helps love last during challenging times by making you stronger. It provides love and the courage to endure through the moments when it's difficult to talk to each other or when one person is having a challenging time but not saying anything. "This isn't forever; it's just a test," Faith explains. And when people take examinations together, their relationships improve. Faith doesn't make pain go away, but it does give it a purpose. It indicates that love is about your willingness to endure difficult times, not how easy things are. Every lasting relationship is due to one person deciding love was worth the effort, even when feelings weren't enough.

Faith also helps you be kind to your partner. You help them grow rather than criticize them when you focus on their strengths rather than their weaknesses. Faith helps you believe that people can change, that damaged hearts can mend, and that you can get over the gap. It makes love deeper. Anyone can love while things are good, but a faith-filled love chooses to stay hopeful even when things don't look good. It says, "I see where we are, but I believe in where we're going." You can transform fear into confidence simply by believing in yourself.

And sometimes, having faith means believing that love can mend what has been broken. When people become angry, don't meet expectations, or old scars come back, it can be detrimental to their relationship. But faith says that if two people are ready to work on it, nothing is too broken to repair. It keeps hope alive until mending can happen. When all else appears uncertain, faith offers love a reason to stay. It provides love, a reason to keep coming back, trying, and hoping that what is meant to last will. Love can't be shattered because it isn't simply based on feelings; it's also built on faith.

Chapter: 10

Faith not only keeps love alive; it strengthens it. It makes the link stronger by turning fear into trust. When you believe that love serves a greater purpose, you cease to panic when circumstances become difficult. You don't say, "What if we fail?" anymore; you say, "What if such an outcome makes us stronger?" That little modification makes a huge difference. Faith lets you see obstacles as possibilities to learn and grow. It turns anguish into working together. It brings people together when they don't know what's going to happen. When you love someone out of faith, you no longer regard challenges as marks of weakness. You regard them as proof that your love is getting stronger.

Faith also lets love become grace. It reminds you that no one loves perfectly and that we're all still learning. Occasionally, you have to forgive someone; other times, you have to ask for forgiveness. Having faith makes you humble enough to forgive. It states, "We are both human, but we can still love better tomorrow." Faith-based love is tolerant of defects because it realizes that people need time to grow. People can make errors without hurting their relationship. This type of love endures not because it avoids challenges, but because it maintains its faith in them.

Eventually, faith sustains love by preserving hope. When you know that love is guided by something bigger than fear or circumstance, you stop doubting its power. You know that love doesn't have to be perfect; it simply has to last. When life's circumstances seem out of control, faith can help you stay calm. It adds softly, "This isn't the end; it's just a step along the way." Faithless love builds up too quickly, while love with faith stays strong. It faces the uncertainty with power and grace. What makes love genuinely unshakable is that it believes even when it can't see the road forward.

Chapter: 10

Love and Faith
The spiritual aspect of love that endures

Love extends beyond feelings, personality, or physical connection. At its core, lasting love has a spiritual aspect that is incredibly strong but invisible. This spiritual part is what keeps love going even when reasoning says it should have perished. It's the calm power that comes up when both people feel empty, the inner tranquility that says, "There is more here than what we see." Spiritual love is not based on what is happening around you; it is based on something deeper and more sacred. This love does not require constant demonstration or ideal circumstances. Instead, it draws its vitality from two people having faith, hope, and a common goal. When love becomes spiritual, it is harder to shatter because it is held together by more than just feelings.

One of the loveliest things about spiritual love is that it may bring two people together even though they are very different. Emotional love can cause problems, but spiritual love sees the whole picture. It asks, "What is the purpose of this connection?" and "How can we grow together through this?" It makes every moment more humble, gentle, and graceful. It reminds us that love isn't just about making one another feel better; it's also about making each other better people. Spiritual love can help you learn to be patient, forgive, and open your heart. It knows that love isn't simply what happens between two people; it's also what happens inside them as they grow.

Spiritual love provides couples with a meaningful purpose in their relationship. You begin to believe that your connection wasn't an accident and that you were destined to meet, heal together, and learn things from each other that you couldn't have learned on your own. This sense of divine timing gives love a power that nothing can break. When you believe your connection has a purpose beyond the present, it's easier to endure tough times, distance, or uncertainty. When love is spiritual, it seems to have a purpose. It changes from an event to a journey. When two people feel this calling, their link becomes indestructible, even when things seem to be moving in circles.

Chapter: 10

Spiritual love lasts because it seeks to learn about the other person rather than control them. Instead of forcing the connection to conform, spiritual love allows it to thrive. It recognizes that individuals change and embraces that transition with grace. This love is gentle; it doesn't require perfection or constant reassurance. Instead, it makes both hearts patient, trusting, and willing to accept things as they are. You don't panic when things are unclear because your love is based on spiritual principles. You think this link can deal with change. You think that the lessons you're learning, good or bad, are making your love stronger and more grown-up.

Forgiving is another vital component of spiritual love. Spiritual love understands that everyone makes mistakes and lets individuals be imperfect. Not because it is weak, but because it knows that love can only carry on through forgiveness. When two people are spiritually connected, forgiveness doesn't mean disregarding sorrow. Instead, it means choosing healing over bitterness. It's important to see the individual, not just the mistake. It is the understanding that love need not be perfect; it simply must be genuine. Forgiveness is not about absolving someone of their responsibility. It's about protecting the sacred link between you.

Love for God also makes you feel grateful. When you love the little things like laughing together, talking honestly, and being together in silence, you start to see your relationship as something special. You stop taking your relationship for granted when you realize how much it means to you. Being thankful makes love stronger by shifting your attention from what you don't have to what you do have. Spiritual love doesn't say, "What am I missing?" It says, "What have I been given?" instead. This way of thinking strengthens the relationship and reduces stress. It helps you see your relationship as a blessing instead of a chore. And when you practice being thankful every day, love becomes easier, lighter, and lasts longer.

Chapter: 10

The spiritual side of love is also shown by how two people support each other's growth. Spiritual love doesn't weigh you down; it raises you up. It doesn't mind change; it welcomes it. Even if they are walking together, each heart is on its journey. When you love someone spiritually, their growth pleases you rather than terrifies you. You support their dreams, help them become better, and celebrate their successes. Your love shouldn't keep them locked up; it should set them free. When you love someone spiritually, you don't simply love who they are now; you love who they are becoming.

This kind of love also makes you more intelligent. It understands when to hang on and when to let go. It knows when your spouse needs to talk and when they should be quiet. Spiritual love doesn't merely hear with its ears; it hears with its heart. It becomes simpler to understand what your spouse is trying to convey when they can't find the perfect words. A growing gut feeling and a shared way of discussing emotions help both individuals navigate challenges without feeling alone. Spiritual love clears up uncertainty and calms fear.

One of the best things about spiritual love is that it makes individuals faithful in every way: physically, emotionally, and spiritually. It keeps your heart solid even when doubts or temptations try to drag you away. When love is spiritual, you don't look for reasons to leave; you look for reasons to stay. You don't run away from your difficulties; you learn from them. You don't allow fear to tell you what to do; you let faith show you the way. This type of loyalty builds a strong foundation for love that time can't break. It becomes a love that lasts even when things are hard.

Chapter: 10

Spiritual love can also make you feel at peace in a way that conventional love can't. You can relax knowing that you're not the only one in the relationship. It implies having faith that something bigger than you is looking out for you, guiding your steps, safeguarding your heart, and helping you navigate through challenging times. This piece provides you with strength when things become difficult. You don't freak out; you have faith. You don't doubt; you remember why you're connected. When love is spiritual, you stop viewing challenges as grounds to quit and start seeing them as possibilities to get closer.

Spiritual love endures because it can begin again. It doesn't rely on recollections of the past; it discovers fresh justifications to remain in the present. It seeks to marvel at the everyday things that happen. I like being together for no reason. When love is spiritually alive, every day is a chance to come to know each other again. This replenishment keeps the flame of love and dedication alive. It helps both people remember why they fell in love in the first place. It's not by chance that spiritual love stays strong; it's because it keeps moving deeper.

The spiritual side of love is what makes it last forever. It helps it navigate through tough times, changes, and pain. Love that is spiritual never really goes away. It changes, grows, and continues to guide both hearts long after the first feelings fade. It's a love with a purpose, strengthened by faith, and kept alive by something bigger than the two individuals in it. There is no stopping your love once it becomes a spiritual entity. Spiritual love doesn't depend on what's going on; it depends on a connection, a sense of purpose, and a trust that won't let fear win.

Chapter: 10

Love and Faith
Stories of love built on faith

Faith holds some of the strongest love stories together. These are the calm, constant relationships that can weather storms, distance, and moments of doubt. One of these stories is about Daniel and Meidah, who are a couple. They began dating when they were both still sad about their last breakups. They loved each other a lot, yet their fear often got in the way of their enjoyment. They didn't run away from each other; instead, they opted to have confidence that they could heal and that their connection was meant to be. One of them might feel awful some nights, while the other would hold on and say, "We'll get through this." And they did. Their love didn't grow since everything seemed easy. It grew because they believed things could get better, even if they couldn't see it now.

Their faith helped them heal much. When trust was low, they decided to remain patient. They chose to comprehend when it was difficult to talk to one another. They learned, prayed, and cried together. When one spouse was weak, the other would uphold the connection with unwavering hope. Their love grew stronger over time because one person would lift the other up when they were feeling down. They did little things every night, like saying kind things to one another or reminding each other of what they were thankful for, to help them stay strong in their faith. These behaviors didn't solve problems, but they did create a deep tie based on faith. Today, their partnership demonstrates that love does not need to be perfect to be powerful; it only requires two hearts willing to believe in something greater than fear.

Their story reveals that the best relationships are not those without troubles; they are those guided by faith. Daniel and Meidah were able to look past their short-term feelings and focus on their long-term ambitions because of their faith. They realized that faith doesn't promise an effortless life; it gives you strength. If you look at their journey, you'll understand that love based on faith is never only between two people. It's about two people who believe their relationship has significance, direction, and a future worth fighting for.

145

Chapter: 10

Another inspiring story is about a couple named Sam and Elise. Many people assumed their long-distance relationship would end after three years. They lived in different states, had full-time careers, and had considerably different schedules. They didn't live near each other, yet they trusted each other. Occasionally, I felt lonely or like talking to people took too long and was too stressful. But every night they remembered what they had promised from the start: "We'll trust this process until we can build a life together." That vow served as their steadfast foundation. They didn't need to hear that everything will be okay all the time. They trusted each other's plans, their future, and the timing of their trip.

Sam and Elise made things stable by believing in their love even when circumstances didn't seem perfect. They were able to overcome their doubts through their faith. They were honest with each other, discussed serious things, and never let distance make them think love wasn't possible. There were weeks that were harder than others. They sometimes questioned their timing, their patience, and the sacrifices they were making. But instead of giving up, they kept the idea of the life they were constructing in their heads. When they were finally close enough to stand next to each other, both decided that it was faith, not convenience, that had brought them to this stage in their relationship.

Their narrative shows us that faith doesn't just cover the gap; it connects it. When love seems to be challenged, faith fills in the gaps. It reminds us that real love is more than just being physically near to someone; it also needs emotional trust and spiritual connection. Sam and Elise showed that religion can keep two individuals together even when they are far apart. Their narrative offers hope to many who believe that their problems are too big to tackle, as long as they have faith that anything is possible.

Chapter: 10

There is also a compelling narrative about a couple, Grace and Nathan, who had to endure one of the hardest things a relationship can face: being sick. Jonathan's diagnosis of a debilitating illness transformed their relationship completely and abruptly. Things are different now. The jobs changed. Things were different. But their trust never wavered. Grace says she was afraid at first. She wasn't sure if their relationship could survive the stress of going to the doctor so often, having money problems, and feeling fatigued all the time. She chose faith over fear, nonetheless. They thought that love would bring them through. Belief that strength will come one day at a time. Belief that pain could have a purpose.

Nathan sometimes worried he didn't deserve Grace because he was afraid his condition might get worse and make her leave. But she chose love over fear, kindness over ease, and staying with him over being comfortable. She really believed in her faith. When he wanted to give up, she stood by him, cheered him on, and reminded him how much he was worth. And Nathan loved her back in a way that disease couldn't touch. Their beliefs transformed how they thought about love, strengthening their bond. They learned that love isn't exhibited by how easy things are; it's shown by how much you care. Their tale shows that love founded on faith doesn't break down when things become tough; instead, it becomes stronger.

These days, they discuss their relationship with gratitude rather than anger, even though they still have problems. They believe their love is more real, meaningful, and spiritual than ever. Their tale shows that faith doesn't constantly change situations, but it will help you navigate through them. Love founded on faith is like a shelter that can withstand storms without tumbling down. Grace and Jonathan's tale now inspires others because it shows how love can be beautiful when it doesn't give up.

Chapter: 10

Finally, there's the story of Nadia and Paul, two friends who fell in love and got married. They began their trip as close friends, honest, trusting, and appreciative of each other. They didn't think it would blossom into love, but faith eventually pulled them together. When they eventually told each other how they felt, they were both afraid. They were scared that doing so might hurt their friendship, something they valued. But they didn't let fear decide; they trusted God. They assumed that the things that kept them friends could also help them start a new chapter in their love lives. Their switch wasn't ideal; they had instances when they felt awkward, unsure, and insecure. But when they were doubtful, they would tell each other, "Let's trust this, even though it scares us."

Their faith not only brought them together but also strengthened their relationship. They still employed the same qualities that had made their friendship strong: talking to each other, being honest, and always being there for each other. They thought their love had a reason to expand, and it did. They learned that trust doesn't always mean knowing for sure; sometimes it means being brave enough to take the first step. Today, they say their love is peaceful and steady, as if it is being guided rather than driven. They believe that their faith allowed them to recognize that the right person was always present; they just needed faith to see it.

The love tales of Daniel and Meidah, Sam and Elise, Grace and Nathan, and Nadia and Paul all prove that faith-based love lasts. It lasts through fear, distance, pain, and not knowing what will happen next, since it is built on something more substantial than feelings. It comes from having hope, a goal, and the belief that what you share is worth fighting for. Love and faith can create a bond that time and problems cannot break. Faith-founded love not only endures but also transforms, heals, restores, and inspires.

Chapter: 10

Faith alters our perception of love. It provides you with strength when your feelings are weak, when life becomes unpredictable, and when partnerships face challenges neither party expected. Faith keeps love going by reminding us that uncertainty is part of the journey, not the end. There may have been times in your life when faith took you beyond what you could have understood.

Reflection Questions:

1. When you think about uncertainty in relationships, what role has faith played in helping you stay grounded?

2. Have you ever experienced a moment where you didn't know what was ahead but chose to trust anyway? What did that decision reveal about your heart?

3. How does faith influence the way you respond to challenges, misunderstandings, or emotional distance?

4. In what ways do you rely on faith to strengthen your love when circumstances feel overwhelming or unclear?

Love has a spiritual side that extends beyond romantic sentiments or emotional ties. It's the element of love that makes you feel safe, led, and essential. It helps you see your partner as a lifelong companion, not just someone you care about.

Reflection Questions:

1. What does "spiritual love" mean to you personally? How does it differ from emotional or physical love?

2. Have you ever felt that a relationship or connection in your life had a deeper purpose or divine timing? What made it feel that way?

3. What spiritual values (forgiveness, compassion, patience, grace) show up in the way you love others?

4. How might embracing the spiritual dimension of love change the way you show up in your relationships?

Chapter: 10

Faith-based love is strong because it won't give up. It is grounded in hope rather than perfection and endures through challenging times. The stories you read, as well as those of Daniel and Meidah, Sam and Elise, Grace and Nathan, Nadia and Paul, and others, illustrate that love founded on faith can remain strong even amid distance, illness, fear, and doubt. These stories aren't ideal fairy tales; they're about love, strength, and patience.

Reflection Questions:

1. Which story from this chapter resonated with you the most, and why?
2. How do these stories challenge or inspire your understanding of what faithful love looks like?
3. Do you believe faith has the power to heal, strengthen, or restore a relationship? What personal experiences shape your answer?
4. If you were to write your own story of love built on faith, what chapters would it include? What moments would stand out?

This chapter wants you to think of love as more than just an emotion. Think of it as something holy that you should defend, believe in, and care for with purpose. Faith gives love wings when life attempts to drag it down. It turns wounds into wisdom, tests into testimonies, and times of doubt into opportunities to become closer to people.

Reflection Questions:

1. What does it mean to you to love someone with faith—heart, mind, and spirit?
2. In which areas of your relationships do you feel you need more faith—and why?
3. What commitments or changes could help you build a more faith-driven, enduring love?
4. How does faith reshape your definition of love, not just as something you feel, but as something you believe in?

Chapter: 11

Love and Vulnerability
The importance of being vulnerable in love

People often misinterpret vulnerability in love. Many people assume it means being weak, letting someone damage you, or being open. But being open and honest is what makes love blossom. It's the willingness to expose yourself, including your worries, dreams, disappointments, and hopes, rather than hide behind masks or pretend to be flawless. If you choose to be vulnerable, you choose to be real. You are stating, "This is who I am." I trust you with the truth about me. Love doesn't grow on the outside; it grows in the truth. To be honest, you have to be open. Love stays shallow, far away, and weak without it.

Being open in love means letting someone into parts of your life you generally keep to yourself. It's about being honest with them about your feelings, telling them when you're terrified or talking about memories you don't often share. Being open makes it easier to connect with other people because it replaces showing off with being honest. Letting someone see your flaws and insecurities allows them to love you for who you are. Being in a relationship makes you feel entirely noticed and welcomed, which is one of the finest things about it. Although vulnerability can be challenging, it can transform your life.

Being vulnerable is vital because it helps individuals feel emotionally close to each other, and that intimacy lasts. If you are honest with your partner, they will be honest with you too. The relationship ceases being a performance and becomes a secure space. It's simpler to talk to each other, arguments are less serious, and love lasts longer. When you're vulnerable, you say, "I trust you enough to be imperfect." It reminds both parties that love doesn't have to be flawless; it simply has to be present. It's a hint that being honest doesn't mean you could lose love; it means you can acquire a deeper, more meaningful version of it.

Chapter: 11

Vulnerability is powerful because it breaks down the boundaries that fear sets up. People would rather not open up because they fear being turned down, judged, or misunderstood. But love can't get through to a heart that is closed off. Letting your guard down, even if it scares you, is what it means to choose vulnerability. You choose to show someone your human side. You decide to be connected instead of safe. Being open doesn't imply showing everything at once. It means you open up carefully, deliberately, and with honesty. Every time you show your vulnerable side, you build trust, which lets love grow.

Being open and honest can sometimes be forceful. It takes courage to express things like "I'm scared of losing you," "I don't know," or "I'm hurting." It takes courage to ask for help, say you're sorry, or confess that things are challenging. Being open doesn't mean looking weak; it means being honest. When both individuals possess the courage to express their true feelings rather than pretending everything is fine, love blossoms. When partners are open and honest with each other, they learn how to soothe, support, and grow up together. Relationships filled with misunderstandings and unspoken expectations arise when people aren't open to each other. When you feel weak, your partners offer understanding, intimacy, and clarity.

Being open to love also helps you learn how to accept it. Many people appreciate being the strong, dependable one, but they don't like allowing someone else to take care of them. When you are vulnerable, you transition from independence to interdependence. The result is a healthy equilibrium where both people help one another. Letting someone comfort you strengthens your bond with them. It changes from a performance to a partnership. You may be helpful, recover together, and feel safe emotionally if you are open and honest. You don't have to carry love alone any longer; you can give it to someone else.

Chapter: 11

Knowing how to ask for what you need is a necessary part of being open. Many relationships fail, even when there is love, because people fail to communicate their needs. Using statements like "I need to feel connected," "I need comfort when I'm stressed," or "I feel closest to you when we talk openly" will help you feel less alone. Sharing your wants with your partner enhances understanding and is not intrusive. Vulnerable communication decreases anger, lessens assumptions, and fosters trust. When both people are at ease talking about their wants, the relationship becomes more peaceful, compassionate, and fulfilling.

Being vulnerable is also crucial during a fight. When things get tight, it's easy to get angry, defensive, or distant. However, if you express your feelings honestly, you might say, "I feel hurt," "I'm afraid you'll stop loving me," or "I didn't intend to push you away." These open-ended questions make the discourse less tense. They want people to understand them rather than fight back. They tell both people that even though they don't get along, they both want to stay in touch. When you're vulnerable, conflict turns from a fight into a chance to learn more about each other. It builds bridges instead of walls.

Being open and honest with each other is another wonderful aspect of vulnerability. It creates shared experiences that strengthen the relationship. When you talk to your spouse about your past, your concerns, or your dreams, you let them see the real you. These times produce strong memories that will stay with you for a long time. When you are open, love can reach the deepest depths of your spirit. It instills in you a genuine sense of understanding, and receiving love from someone who profoundly understands you is unparalleled. Love is divine and one-of-a-kind when you let yourself be vulnerable.

Chapter: 11

Being open in love also entails letting go of the sense that you are in charge. You can't know how someone will respond to your honesty, and that uncertainty is what makes being open so brave. But love is letting go. You have to believe that your partner will take care of your heart, even when you reveal to them the delicate portions. Being vulnerable is letting go of fear and choosing to be with other people. It serves as a reminder that love does not simply occur; it requires nurturing and care. You allow yourself to be vulnerable because you believe that the individual before you is worthy. That leap of faith is what makes the connection stronger than any love that is only skin deep.

Being open means being your true self instead of trying to be who you think others want you to be. It involves discussing your likes, dislikes, challenges, and joys. It is being able to mourn, laugh, and convey love without holding back. You allow your spouse to be authentic when you truly are. This honesty between the two people makes them feel close to each other. It takes away the pressure to accomplish something or pretend. It gives the partnership a comfortable place for both of you to rest your hearts without worrying. Love provides a secure environment for honesty, fostering mutual growth for both individuals.

In the end, honesty and transparency are what keep love alive. It builds trust between people, brings them closer together, and helps them work together as a team. Being open makes it possible to interact with others on a deeper level and get closer to them. It turns normal relationships into something special since you can only be totally loved if you let yourself be fully seen. When you say, "I trust you with my heart," you are willing to be hurt. And that trust is what makes love powerful enough to last, grow, and thrive for a lifetime.

Chapter: 11

Love and Vulnerability
How vulnerability deepens connection

Vulnerability is the way to connect deeply with someone; it is the bridge that links two hearts together in one emotional universe. If you don't let yourself, be vulnerable, love stays on the surface, safe, polite, and predictable. When you allow your spouse to see the true you, you show them your anxieties, shortcomings, dreams, and realities. You permit them to admire you for your authentic self, rather than solely the persona you project. Being open with someone is what brings you closer to them. When vulnerability is involved, love goes from being casual to being deep. It helps people be honest, close, and trust each other in a way that nothing else can.

Your spouse will understand your heart better if you tell them about things, you generally keep to yourself, such as your concerns, uncertainties, and wounds from childhood. Now, I understand why you reacted the way you did. You know better what you need. It's easier to understand your sensitivity than it is to understand it. Being vulnerable doesn't mean telling everyone everything or crying all the time. It involves deciding to show your spouse the elements of yourself that will help them understand you better. Being open about how you feel makes your hearts softer and brings you closer together in a way that words can't fully describe. It makes the relationship a secure space for both people to be themselves and relax.

The power of being vulnerable comes from the fact that it creates trust over time. When you explain to your partner and they understand instead of judging you, the relationship develops stronger. Your heart says, "It's okay to be seen here," after that. When both partners are honest and open with one other, the relationship becomes a secure place where being real is more essential than being flawless. The bond grows stronger as trust builds. Vulnerability is the subtle relationship that says, "I'm always here for you." This kind of emotional honesty is what turns ordinary love into something special.

Chapter: 11

Being vulnerable makes relationships stronger by breaking down the walls that fear forms. People often use sarcasm, silence, stoicism, and distance to avoid feeling pain. But the same walls that protect individuals also keep them apart. Being open and honest slowly tears down those boundaries. You can improve your communication by saying, "I felt hurt," rather than acting indifferent. It's gutsy of you to say "I miss you" instead of waiting for the other person to say it first. Instead of pretending you don't care, admitting "I'm scared of losing you" is a powerful moment of truth. Being vulnerable means you don't have to guess anymore; instead, you can be honest, which helps connections grow in clarity instead of confusion.

Discussing your inner life with someone might actually bring you two closer together. Talking about your feelings brings you closer and becomes part of your story. You could cry on their shoulder after a hard day, tell them about a phobia you've never told anybody about, or reveal a shortcoming you're trying to fix. These times aren't just emotional; they're sacred. You can't fake the intimacy they make. When you're open and honest, you say, "I trust you with my truth," and that trust is what keeps the relationship going when things get hard. Emotional connection gets stronger, more honest, and more stable.

Being vulnerable also strengthens ties since it makes individuals want to help others. If you open your heart first, it will be easier for your spouse to do the same. Because you're honest, they can be themselves. You are brave, so they are too. They get softer when you are. This opening up to each other starts a lovely cycle of understanding and kindness. You stop connecting on the surface and start connecting on a deeper level. The partnership becomes a place where both hearts feel welcome, accepted, and loved just as they are. Conversations grow deeper, and moments become more precious.

Chapter: 11

Being vulnerable also helps you understand how you feel about the other person. Telling your partner how you feel helps you both understand what's really going on. This information keeps misunderstandings from getting worse. Being vulnerable makes things clearer, rather than leaving you to guess how the other person feels. You learn how to state things like "I need more reassurance," "I'm feeling overwhelmed today," or "I feel disconnected." These honest disclosures let individuals discuss things in a way that brings them closer together instead of pulling them apart. When you're vulnerable, communication is honest and open, rather than defensive or distant.

Being vulnerable also makes love more personal and human, which helps lovers connect on a deeper level. You could feel protected when you keep your sentiments to yourself, but you also feel alone. By allowing your guard down, you provide your spouse the opportunity to show kindness, empathy, and emotional support. Letting your partner see your weakness allows them to care for you meaningfully. They want to be there for you, not because you want them to. When people are honest about their feelings, they develop a compelling link. It provides people with a sense of connection, both emotionally and spiritually.

Being vulnerable also makes connections stronger since it makes you feel closer to someone emotionally than physically. It is possible to share a bed with someone and yet still feel as though you are on entirely different planets. Being open and honest fills that gap. It creates an intimacy that doesn't need contact; it needs truth. When you open your heart, even a simple glance or a quiet moment together can carry significant meaning. When two individuals are open and honest with one another, silence can be a source of comfort instead of discomfort. It turns ordinary things into memories and ordinary conversations into opportunities to get to know each other better. Emotional closeness is the most crucial component of the relationship.

Chapter: 11

Being open and honest with others makes you feel more connected to them, especially when things are challenging. When things get hard—when stress levels rise, misunderstandings arise, or feelings run high—the best way to stay close is to be open and honest with each other. It takes guts to say things like, "I need you right now," "I feel distant, and I don't want to," or "I'm scared we're growing apart." But when you are honest with yourself, you don't build up emotional walls. When the heart wants to shut down, being exposed keeps it open. It keeps the bond strong even when things try to break it. Financial difficulties can make love stronger instead of weaker.

Being forthright and truthful makes the partnership feel less like a show and more like a partnership. Once the desire to hide your actual sentiments is gone, you and your partner may find that you can be honest with one another. It's not necessary to hide your issues, seem harsh, or try to outdo or impress other people. The partnership allows you to unwind and rejuvenate while also providing a sense of security. When both hearts feel safe, loved, and free, the connection grows stronger. One of the most intimate things that may happen to you is to be completely known and loved.

Truthfully, being open makes you feel more connected because it enables love to touch the deepest pieces of who you are. It converts love from something outside us to something within us. It grows inside the heart, not simply around it. Vulnerability says, "I want to be honest with you, even when it's hard, because I think our connection is worth it." That choice makes love richer, deeper, and more significant than anything that closed hearts could ever feel. Love isn't weaker when you're vulnerable; it's stronger. It turns two people into one strong partnership built on trust, understanding, and emotional strength. And that's the kind of bond that lasts.

Chapter: 11

Love and Vulnerability
Overcoming the fear of being hurt in love

For many individuals, overcoming the fear of injury in love is one of the most complex emotional struggles. It's very acceptable to want to keep your heart safe. Love involves welcoming individuals into your life whom you have not seen for an extended period, possibly even decades. But the truth is that fear pushes people apart, whereas honesty brings people together. When fear is in charge, you start to think that something catastrophic will happen before it does. You think too much and hold back so much that love can't get through. To get over this fear, you don't have to pretend you're not worried. You just have to learn how to keep going even when you're scared. It implies steadily choosing to become close to others rather than keeping oneself safe.

Most individuals are fearful of being wounded because of past experiences, such as being betrayed, left behind, misunderstood, or taken for granted. The heart remembers pain very well. But you can feel better when you realize your past doesn't have to shape your future. Every time you start a new relationship, it's a new chapter, a new character, and a new journey. When you bring past scars into a new relationship, it's like anticipating rain every day after enduring a storm. You must know that love is challenging, but it also brings rewards that fear would never let you experience before you can get over your worries. Letting go of fear does not mean forgetting the past; it means deciding not to allow the past to control your present.

Accepting vulnerability shows that love doesn't need to be perfect, just brave. You recognize that sustaining an injury is not the conclusion; it is merely a component of the developmental process. Even in strong relationships, there will be times when you don't understand each other, when you're let down, and when you have emotional ups and downs. But if you choose love, you can't run away from your difficulties. You have to confront them. When you remember that love is worth the danger, fear loses its power. You choose things based on hope, not trauma. And when you reach that point, your heart opens in ways that make your relationships stronger than you ever dreamed they could be.

Chapter: 11

Learning to trust again is one of the first steps you can take to overcome your fear of injury. It's challenging to trust others, especially if someone in your past broke it. But trust is also something you learn over time, not something that happens all at once. When you choose to trust someone new, you are not declaring, "You will never hurt me." Instead, you say, "I trust you to grow with me." You build trust by being honest, keeping your word, and communicating. You create trust by being there for someone, listening to them, saying you're sorry, forgiving them, and choosing to be with them every day. When trust grows, it's easier to overcome fear.

Another crucial step in overcoming fear is understanding that being open doesn't mean you'll be harmed; it just means you'll be authentic. Many individuals believe that being vulnerable entails being hurt. But the truth is that pretending to be strong all the time harms you just as much. Emotional walls don't keep grief out; they restrict people from being close to each other. Being open and honest with your partner helps them understand you, support you, and love you more fully. It helps you realize that love isn't about letting someone harm you; it's about giving them a chance to repair the parts of your heart you didn't even know needed mending.

It's also crucial to remember that fear makes things seem worse than they are. When you're afraid, you think that every argument is a harbinger of trouble. Fear makes you think you're either too much or not enough. Fear convinces you that if you tell your lover how you feel, they will leave you. However, those feelings are not genuine; they are merely psychological illusions. It is easier to face your anxieties when you are honest with yourself about them. When you use logic, love, and open communication to face your fears, they start to lose their grip on your heart. You go from "What if the situation hurts?" to "What if this is the best thing that ever happened to me?" This shift alone can change your feelings about love.

Chapter: 11

Another great way to overcome your fear of hurt is to be honest about your feelings. When you express things like "Sometimes I get scared" or "Sometimes I feel insecure," you and your partner are more likely to connect than to fight in quiet. Being emotionally honest with your partner lets them know what bothers you, helps you heal, and calms you down when you need it. You don't try to hide your fear; instead, you show it. It's easier to cope with dread once you see it. People aren't terrified of love itself; they're afraid of what occurred when they loved the wrong person or at the wrong time. Being honest about how you feel helps you keep your past and present separate.

Being kind to yourself is another crucial way to overcome fear. Many people are too hard on themselves and blame their sentiments, their vulnerability, or their trust for the agony they experienced in the past. But getting hurt doesn't mean you're weak; it indicates you have the strength to love. Don't be hard on yourself for being sensitive; it's a sign of strength. It signifies your heart is alive, able, and ready to go. Being nice to yourself gives you space to heal. You begin to let go of the expectation of being flawless and instead view your emotional journey as an opportunity to grow stronger, become wiser, and be more receptive to love.

You need to recognize that love is a shared duty if you want to stop being afraid of getting harmed. You don't have to deal with all of the emotional stress on your own. When two individuals agree to talk to each other, help each other, and work through challenges with understanding, fear isn't as awful. When both hearts work together, you realize you don't have to be afraid. Love changes from something dangerous or unexpected to something safe, planned, and caring. When love feels like working together rather than a test, your fear fades, and your connection grows stronger.

Chapter: 11

To get over fear, you also need to learn to stop wanting to be in charge of everything. You can choose your actions, honesty, kindness, and work ethic, but not others' actions or feelings. And just knowing the truth can make you nervous. But giving up control doesn't imply letting fate decide everything. It implies having faith that you can face whatever comes your way. It signifies that you don't think other people should decide how much you are worth. The dread of getting injured loses much of its power when you stop trying to control what happens and just be yourself.

Taking tiny emotional risks is one of the best things you can do for your health. You don't have to tell everything at once. Start simply by telling someone what you need, sharing a memory, or being honest about a worry. Every little thing you do weakens the barriers you've constructed around your feelings. Over time, these small risks accumulate to yield significant improvements, such as increased trust, greater closeness, and greater emotional power. You get stronger when you show yourself that being open and honest doesn't hurt you. Every time you feel scared, you demonstrate that you are stronger than your fear.

You don't have to get rid of all risk to stop being afraid of getting wounded. You just have to think that the danger is worth it because real love is so beautiful. Fear may try to tell you that being guarded keeps you safe, but it also inhibits you from establishing deep connections, emotional closeness, and long-lasting relationships. Being vulnerable means being bold, hopeful, and willing to grow. It involves choosing to believe that love is possible rather than focusing on past hurt. When you face your fears, you open the door to a connection that feeds your heart, grows your spirit, and provides you with the type of love you were always destined to have.

Chapter: 11

Being vulnerable is one of the best things you can do for love, yet it often feels the most dangerous. It urges you to be honest about who you are, including your raw feelings, the things that make you feel weak, the wounds that have molded you, and the hopes you have for someone to understand. Being vulnerable lets your spouse see a side of you that most others don't, which brings you closer to them.

Reflection Questions — The Importance of Being Vulnerable in Love:

1. What does vulnerability mean to you, personally? How do you currently show it—or avoid showing it—in your relationships?
2. When have you felt most deeply connected to someone because of a vulnerable moment (yours or theirs)? What made that moment meaningful?
3. What parts of yourself do you struggle to share with someone you love? Why do those areas feel hard to reveal?
4. How does hiding your emotions affect the closeness in your relationships? What changes when you choose to open up?
5. If you viewed vulnerability as a strength instead of a weakness, how would that change the way you show love?

Being vulnerable not only helps you show your feelings, but it also makes connections deeper than anything else can. It breaks down emotional barriers, lowers expectations, and builds trust one truth at a time.

Reflection Questions — How Vulnerability Deepens Connection:

1. How comfortable are you with sharing your true emotions, even when they're messy or imperfect?
2. When have you witnessed vulnerability strengthening a relationship in your life? What did that moment teach you?
3. What would deeper emotional intimacy look like for you? What role would vulnerability play in building it?
4. How do you respond when someone opens up to you? Does your

Chapter: 11

One of the most important emotional barriers to love is the fear of getting harmed. It might make you aloof, guarded, or too cautious, even in relationships where love is real. Fear doesn't mean there's something wrong with you; it means your heart remembers pain. This chapter wants you to think about that fear, not to judge it, but to understand it.

Reflection Questions — Overcoming the Fear of Being Hurt in Love:

1. What past experiences contributed to your fear of being hurt? How have they shaped the way you love today?
2. When fear shows up in your relationships, how do you typically react—withdrawal, defensiveness, overthinking, pretending, or something else?
3. What small step could you take to challenge the fear that keeps your heart guarded?
4. How would your relationships change if you trusted that love can be safe, nurturing, and healing?
5. What does choosing courage in love look like for you right now, emotionally, mentally, or spiritually?

This chapter makes a strong point: being vulnerable isn't just about showing your heart; it's also about liberating it. Love can't blossom behind walls, and connection can't grow stronger without openness. Being vulnerable is what makes two people partners, comrades, and soulmates.

Final Reflection Questions:

1. What does a "safe relationship" look like for you? How can you help create that safety for yourself and your partner?
2. What truths about yourself are you finally ready to share with someone you love?
3. What would loving without fear, loving with openness, honesty, and courage, look like in your life today?
4. What commitments can you make to nurture vulnerability within your relationships moving forward?

Chapter: 12

Love Beyond Romantic Relationships
How love transcends romantic connections

L ove is more than just romance, yet many people think of it only that way, unaware of how much it shapes everything else in their lives. Romantic love is wonderful, but it's only one aspect of a much wider picture. Love is more than just being in a romantic relationship. It changes how you care for yourself, defend your family, treat your friends, and even treat strangers. When you stop seeing love as a relationship status and start seeing it as a universal power, it shapes your decisions, makes you more open-minded, and transforms who you are. Love is more than just being together or being passionate; it's also about caring for others, being connected, and being human.

Knowing that love is more than romance may help you value the people who truly hold you together: the friend who checks on you daily, the sibling who has seen you grow, and the mentor who believed in you before you did. These kinds of love tend to last longer than most romantic relationships, but people don't often celebrate them as much. But these relationships can help you through the most challenging times. They provide you mental safety nets that romance alone can't match. If you approach love from a different perspective, you'll discover that you already possess a significant amount of it; it's just that it doesn't always manifest itself in a romantic manner.

Love beyond romance also shows you that connection can exist anywhere there is real care, not simply between partners. Love is shown by the instructor who helps you realize your goals, the neighbor who looks after your house, and the coworker who makes you feel better when you're having a difficult day. When you understand this, you start to live with more gratitude. You don't see love as something that happens only once in a while; you see it as something that constantly happens. You feel less alone, under less pressure to find romantic validation, and more open to the many beautiful opportunities to interact with others that are all around you every day now that you see things differently.

165

Chapter: 12

Friendship is one of the strongest ways that love goes beyond romance. Friendship is a form of love that doesn't require titles, gifts, or extravagant gestures. It only needs honesty, loyalty, and being there. Your friends are the first to hear your dreams and help you when things go wrong. They adore you no matter what, with no conditions or expectations. Friendship teaches you how to talk to people, trust them, forgive them, and always be there for them. These are things that will benefit you in all of your other relationships. When you cherish your friends, you are not merely creating memories; you are cultivating a type of love capable of lasting a lifetime.

Love goes beyond romance in families as well. Love from your family makes you feel like you belong in a way that love from a romantic partner can't. It can happen at birth, through adoption, or by choice. A parent's love teaches you how to let go, a sibling's love teaches you how to be loyal, and an elder's love teaches you how to be smart. These sorts of love help you discover who you are before you ever enter into a romantic relationship. They show you how to love genuinely, handle problems, and forgive again and again. The love of your family gives you a strong emotional base on which to build. Even when family ties are challenging or imperfect, they teach us essential skills in being strong and caring for others without expecting anything in return.

Love is more than just romance; it's how you connect with your community. Giving someone a hand without expecting anything in return, assisting families in need in your neighborhood, mentoring young people, or just being polite to a stranger are all examples of love in its purest form. Loving your community expands your heart and reminds you that you're part of something bigger. When you choose to give someone outside of your small circle your time, understanding, or support, you are practicing a love that makes the world a better place. People may have hope, come together, and get others to do the same with this sort of love.

Chapter: 12

Love for yourself is another outstanding quality of love, aside from romantic connections. It's not selfish to love yourself; it's vital. You rely on others to fill emotional voids that only you can address. Self-love helps you learn to set appropriate boundaries, maintain your peace, and recognize your worth. When you engage in positive self-talk, prioritize your health, and offer yourself a break during challenging times, you experience a unique form of love that no one else can provide. This love for yourself is what makes all of your other relationships grow. When you feel positive about yourself, you make healthier connections and are more real.

Love can also be more than just romantic; it can also involve mentoring and guiding. A mentor, coach, or leader who believes in someone's potential can help them find love that changes their life. These partnerships are built on goals, not emotions. Your mentor is not obligated to do this; they do so out of genuine concern for your well-being. Mentorship is a form of love that motivates you to achieve your objectives, challenges your boundaries, and aids in your personal growth. It reminds you that love isn't always sweet or soft; it may sometimes be direct, harsh, and focused on helping you grow.

Helping others is another way to display love that extends beyond romance. Every time you help someone, show compassion, or do something pleasant for them, you exhibit a love that extends beyond your needs. This broader love tells you that you don't need to be near someone to connect with them; you simply need to be a person. Helping, supporting, or encouraging people makes your heart broader. You discover that love doesn't run out; it expands the more you offer it. This universal love cultivates a sense of connection with people and places you've never met before. You have never previously been acquainted. It makes you a beacon of light and optimism in the world.

Chapter: 12

Love is more than romance if it stays the same when a relationship changes. You don't always expect life to alter in ways that affect your friends, family, and mentors. But love is still there. The affection of individuals who aren't present still affects you. You will never forget what they taught you, how they helped you, and how much they believed in you. Love is not just proximity; it's also how you remember, grow, and change each other. Love, in all its manifestations, leaves a trace that lasts, even as romantic relationships come and go.

Love also helps you see the wonderful in everyone you meet, not just romantic partners. When you live with an open heart, you become more compassionate, patient, and understanding. You begin to realize that everyone has their own narrative to tell, one full of troubles, dreams, happiness, and dread. This insight makes you kinder and more compassionate to individuals every day. You show grace instead of judgment, understanding instead of criticism, and proximity instead of distance. When love serves as a perspective rather than a goal, your connections strengthen in all areas of your life.

Non-romantic love teaches you that you can feel connected, like you belong, and emotionally content without a romantic partner. Love is everywhere. It shows itself in friendships that feel like home, familial ties that keep you anchored, mentors who help you grow, communities that raise you up, and the quiet relationship you have with yourself. Seeing love in all its forms makes your life fuller, richer, and more meaningful. You no longer look for love; you live it. And this remains one of the most empowering realizations you can attain at any stage of your life.

Chapter: 12

Love Beyond Romantic Relationships
The power of love in friendships, family, and community

Society frequently puts sexual connections at the top of the list when it comes to love; therefore, love in friendships, family, and community is often disregarded. But the truth is that some of the strongest love we feel comes from those who are there for us without asking for anything in return. Friendship love is one of the purest forms of connection. It's not based on physical attraction or responsibility, but on trust, loyalty, shared experiences, and real care. Individuals appreciate you for your authentic self, not merely for the assistance you can provide. They select you during your moments of greatest strength and remain loyal during your times of greatest vulnerability. When you think of the occasions that helped you navigate through challenging situations, it's usually a friend's voice, presence, or words of support that helped you. Friendship is love that comes without being asked, listens without judgment, and helps without conditions.

In friendships, love comes up in the small things, like talking late at night, sharing jokes, and feeling understood without having to say anything. When you forget, your friends remind you how essential you are. They tell you to be honest when you need it, and they cheer you on when you win. This love teaches trust, honesty, and how to relate to others. It helps you feel less lonely and provides a sense of belonging that lasts even when circumstances become challenging. Love for friends is powerful since it's a decision. It's not founded on blood or love, but on loyalty, connection, and mutual respect.

Friends can assist you in discovering how to love in romantic situations. Friends teach you how to be polite, patient, and forgiving. They help you understand what you need emotionally, your boundaries, and what you're strongest at. If a buddy really loves you, they won't want to steal your romantic partner's place. Instead, they'll help you be a better partner. This is why friends are more than just great to have. They make you feel safe, responsible, and pleased. Friendships are more than just romantic interactions; they are places where you can be yourself and feel at home.

Chapter: 12

Family love is another key factor in our behavior and relationships. Family ties, whether they are biological, adopted, or chosen, teach us some of the most important things in life. Family love can be messy, imperfect, and challenging to understand, but it can also provide you with a sense of stability that nothing else can. A parent's love imparts the lessons of relinquishing attachment while ensuring their safety. A sibling's love encourages you to be loyal and to have a history with them. A grandparent's love teaches you about your background, patience, and intelligence. These interactions affect how you feel about love long before you start dating. Even with family issues, love, gentle or strong, affects your identity and ability to connect with others.

Family love is another sign of its power. Despite witnessing your worst and most flawed moments, family members remain by your side. They support you in difficult times, cheer you on, and are always there for you. Words don't always indicate how much you care about your family. You demonstrate your concern through acts such as preparing meals for them, offering guidance, or providing support during times of happiness or sadness. These things will stick with you for a long time. They show you that little things may be just as essential as large things in love. Being there for someone every day is sometimes the best way to demonstrate you care.

Family also helps you understand who you are. That's where you learn about what it means to belong, as well as about culture, values, and customs. When your family loves and supports you, it helps you grow with confidence. When you work on rebuilding or redefining relationships with family members who are having problems or who have broken up, you learn how to be strong, forgive, and be emotionally intelligent. Your family may be your greatest help or your most significant problem. The affection you receive from your family, even if you lose it, changes how you see the world. Your love for your family is the most important kind, and it will help you in all your relationships.

Chapter: 12

One of the best ways to connect with others is through community love. This love makes you feel like you're part of something bigger than you. Community love is when people look out for each other, when volunteers donate their time without asking anything in return, and when people work together to aid someone who is having a difficult time. This broader form of love shows us that people shouldn't have to be alone. We thrive when we experience a sense of belonging, recognition, and assistance. When their community loves them, people feel safer, more connected, and a part of something bigger. It is a love that lifts up not just one person, but even groups of people.

Communities are great places to find love when people are nice to each other and work together. Think about the times when people you didn't know provided money to families in need, helped rebuild after disasters, or comforted those who were grieving. Those who do these kind acts may never meet you, but they do it out of love and faith in humanity. The best part about community love is that it is typically powerful, altruistic, and without conditions. It shows you that love may be vital even if you don't touch it. Holding a door open, giving someone a pat on the back, or helping them carry their baggage are all tiny actions that can make the world a better place where love is omnipresent.

Community also fosters a sense of belonging in ways romantic love cannot. Being a part of a church, neighborhood, business, or social club that helps others might make you feel like you belong in the world. You can share your experiences, utilize your strengths, and request help whenever you need it. When you care about your community, you help develop networks of care that make life better, safer, and more meaningful. It reminds you that you're not the only one going through this; everyone else is, too. When people come together with love at the center, their communities become stronger, kinder, and more resilient.

Chapter: 12

Love is not just for romantic relationships; it is a part of every facet of life. Friendships, family, and community all show how powerful love can be. When you take care of these forms of love, your life becomes better and more balanced. Romantic relationships can't provide you with everything you need emotionally, and they weren't supposed to. You need friends who know you well, relatives who keep you grounded, and a community that helps you grow. These different ways of demonstrating love come together to build a network that makes you stronger in all three areas: emotionally, mentally, and spiritually. When you let more than one person love you, you learn that you are surrounded by love far more than you thought.

Love beyond romance also teaches that being with other people, not being alone, is what makes you happy. When you embrace love in all its manifestations, you do not require a single individual to be your entire universe. Instead, you develop a healthy network of relationships where love flows freely and abundantly. This makes you feel happier and more comfortable because your happiness doesn't depend on just one person; it rests on many essential relationships. Loving many people and receiving love from many places teaches you to be thankful, understanding, and balanced. Opening your heart makes your life more exciting.

Ultimately, love from friends, family, and the community can be as impactful as romantic love, if not more. It teaches you to be strong, kind, loyal, forgiving, generous, and united. These kinds of love will help you navigate moments when romance is missing, unclear, or changing. They improve your life in ways that last. When you see that love is more than romance, you appreciate how valuable every bond is that makes your life more meaningful, happy, and calm. Love is everywhere: in the friend who listens, the family member who helps, and the people in the community who work together. When you let all these kinds of love into your heart, it goes from being a sensation to a way of life.

Chapter: 12

Love Beyond Romantic Relationships
Learning to love others selflessly

Learning to love others without expecting anything in return is one of the best things you can do for your life. You need to stop focusing on what you can obtain and start contemplating what you can provide. When you love someone selflessly, you don't ignore your needs or lose yourself. You show them care without expecting anything in return. It is the kind of love that genuinely listens, offers assistance without solicitation, and remains present for you. A heart that realizes how wonderful it is to offer without expecting anything in return has selfless love. It doesn't have to be difficult. When you learn to love without expecting anything in return, your connections with friends, family, and the community grow more profound, more meaningful, and more fulfilling. This sort of love teaches you to be patient, humble, and kind, which makes you a better, kinder person.

One benefit of unselfish love is that it may help soothe the ego. The ego always wants to be correct, earn praise, or be served. But selfless love makes you consider the other person's feelings and worldview. It prompts you to consider questions such as, "What does this individual require at this moment?" or "How can I enhance this experience?" When you love someone without expecting anything in return, you stop assessing love by what you receive and start judging it by how happy and tranquil you make other people. This shift in thinking improves relationships since the focus shifts from what you want to what you can provide. Additionally, showing kindness always strengthens the connection between people.

Being there for someone is also part of learning to love them without conditions. Many people care about others from afar, but true unselfish love involves being there for them in person and in spirit. It means not using your phone while someone else is chatting with you. It means being present even when it is difficult. Being there to listen, even when you're exhausted, is what it means. That simple phrase makes people feel comfortable and like they are part of something.

Chapter: 12

A nother key component of learning to love others without expecting anything in return is to practice empathy. To be empathetic means to be able to perceive things from another person's perspective. It makes you stop and consider how someone else feels, rather than just yourself. Empathy improves relationships by making people less judgmental and more connected. When you cultivate empathy, you refrain from making hasty judgments or presuming the worst. You stop, think, and reflect instead. Selfless love, rooted in empathy, helps you be compassionate rather than critical. It helps you understand that everyone has a story that isn't visible, a conflict you may be unaware of, and emotions they might prefer to keep hidden at first.

You can also exhibit selfless love by doing things for others. You show that you care about someone by doing these small things every day. Acts of service include making dinner for a tired friend, doing errands for a family member, helping a coworker fulfill a tight deadline, or stepping in when someone needs extra help. These little things may not seem like much, yet they have a big effect on how someone feels. When people do things for others without expecting anything in return, it reminds others that they aren't the only ones with difficulties or duties. Additionally, it provides a sense of purpose because nothing feels better than knowing you have brightened someone's day or lightened their heart.

Another wonderful thing about unselfish love is that you can be happy for others without being jealous or comparing yourself to them. When you love someone and harbor no expectations, their accomplishments bring you genuine happiness. They are happy when you are happy. You want them to win, but you don't want what they have. You lift them up without being scared. This kind of love helps people build healthy, supportive relationships where progress is encouraged rather than feared. Learning to celebrate others with a pure heart fosters gratitude and reminds us that love is not a competition. Everyone has ample space to excel.

Chapter: 12

Another approach to demonstrate selfless love is to forgive someone. If you have never felt disappointment, bewilderment, or rage toward someone, you cannot fully love them. However, you may see the good in someone when you forgive them. Selfless love recognizes that relationships require forgiveness and that everyone has imperfections. Forgiving someone doesn't mean forgetting the pain; it means choosing to heal rather than being enraged. Forgiving someone without asking for anything in return protects the relationship from bitterness and lets love grow again. This does not suggest tolerating unacceptable conduct; it entails responding with kindness when appropriate and then proceeding with the insights gained.

Another way that selfless love shows up is through healthy boundaries. Many people assume that boundaries are selfish, but they're really a way to show love for yourself and keep the relationship secure. Setting limits means you want your relationship to be strong, healthy, and long-lasting. Selfless love recognizes that you cannot give to others if you are depleted. You can be there for other people if you take care of your mental and emotional health. Boundaries help you give your love freely, not because you're frustrated. Boundaries help you maintain fair and respectful relationships, allowing you to love from a place of strength rather than exhaustion.

Being there for people in need is a wonderful way to show selfless love. Love that isn't selfish sticks with someone who is sad. It makes room for a sad person. It assists someone who wants to quit. It stays the same even when things get tough. When you love someone without expecting anything in return, you're there for them in good times and bad. People who are feeling lost or overwhelmed can count on that type of love. It reminds them that they are not alone and that someone cares enough to be there for them, even when things are hard.

Chapter: 12

Loving someone selflessly implies offering them affection without trying to control or possess it. It means allowing others to grow and make their own choices, even if you disagree. Selfless love respects differences. It helps people become who they were meant to be, not who you want them to be. This kind of love makes you feel free instead of stressed. It says, "I care about you not because you meet my needs, but because you are a person who is worth my time." When you love someone this way, your relationships become better, more respectful, and more real.

Support is another crucial component of unselfish love. Encouragement is like oxygen to the soul. Saying kind words to someone gives them more self-assurance and hope. Encouragement doesn't have to cost money, but it can make someone's day—or even their life—better. Selfless love doesn't dominate, break, or injure people. Rather, they provide them with power, healing, and building. Long after the moment is finished, these words continue to send out affectionate vibrations. You may, for example, tell a friend that you have faith in them, tell a family member that they are strong, or provide a hand to someone in your community.

Learning to love others without expecting anything in return changes your life from the inside out. It makes you more caring, expands your heart, and deepens your sense of purpose. When you love someone without expecting anything in return, you don't lose yourself; you become the best version of yourself. It teaches you to give without expecting anything back, forgive deeply, always be present for others, and be honest when you celebrate. When you learn to love without expecting anything in return, you feel a level of calm and contentment that romance alone can't provide you. Selfless love improves all relationships, including those with friends, family, and the community. It also makes your life a mirror of the love you provide. It becomes a way of life, a way of thinking, and a legacy that lives on long after you're gone.

Chapter: 12

Love beyond romance has a way of widening your understanding of what real connection looks like. You can understand what a meaningful relationship is like through love that isn't romantic. You may see that you have many important people in your life, such as friends, relatives, and communities that pull you up. These types of love demonstrate that there are other sources of happiness beyond romantic attachment. The love that endures the longest is the kind that comes to you unconditionally.

Reflection Questions — How Love Transcends Romantic Connections:

1. When you think about love outside of romance, which relationships come to mind first, and why?

2. How have your friendships, family relationships, or community connections shaped your understanding of love?

3. How does seeing love as abundant (rather than limited) change the way you show up in your relationships?

One important idea in this chapter is how important friends, family, and community are to your mental health.

Reflection Questions — The Power of Love in Friendships, Family, and Community:

1. Which friendships have had the greatest impact on your life, and what made them meaningful?

2. In what ways have your family (biological, chosen, or both) shaped your ability to love and be loved?

3. How does your community, church, workplace, neighborhood, or social circle support your emotional or spiritual growth?

4. What relationships do you feel called to nurture more deeply, and why?

5. How does giving love to your community deepen your sense of connection and purpose?

Chapter: 12

This chapter also teaches us how to love people without expecting anything in return. You consider what you give more than what you receive when you experience this kind of love. Being patient, understanding, giving, and supporting others are all necessary for unselfish love. It asks that you pay attention, understand, and show concern without anticipating anything in return. Being compassionate from the heart and giving love without expecting anything in return is not about abandoning oneself. When done correctly, it strengthens all of your relationships.

Reflection Questions — Learning to Love Others Selflessly:

1. In your relationships, do you tend to give freely, or do you hold back until you feel safe? Why?
2. What does selfless love look like for you in everyday life?
3. How do you balance loving others generously while still protecting your emotional well-being?
4. When was the last time you offered love without expecting anything in return? How did it feel?
5. What areas of your life would benefit from practicing more selfless love?

Keep in mind that this chapter isn't just about seeing love in other people; it's also about realizing how much love you have inside you. Love is not just in the romantic parts of your tale; it is in every relationship that makes you who you are.

Final Reflection Questions:

1. What would your life feel like if you fully embraced love in all its forms, not just romantic, but relational, communal, and selfless?
2. How do you want to show up in the lives of the people you love this week, this month, and this year?
3. What would change in your relationships if you practiced more empathy, presence, and generosity?

Chapter: 13

Love as a Healing Force
How love heals emotional wounds

Words can't properly convey how love makes us feel. People often feel closed off, alone, or unsure of their worth after being betrayed, losing someone, being turned down, or going through something terrible. But love can slowly and gently make those harsh areas less painful. When someone loves you with compassion, respect, and real care, you feel safe enough to start mending. Love can't undo the past, but it can help you change how you feel about it. It helps people who are hurting, makes sense of things for people who are confused, and brings people together who are alone. Love does not complete you; instead, it supports you as you heal your broken pieces.

Injured people feel safe when loved, which many have never had. Emotional safety means you may discuss your worries without being judged, share your thoughts without being ignored, and expose your shortcomings without being turned away. When love makes you feel safe like that, you start to trust again. You find out that not everyone will hurt you in the same way. You learn that how you feel matters. You know you should be treated well. This kind of healing doesn't happen right away. It happens over time, with ongoing help, love, and presence. Love heals over time, and it does so deeply.

When you feel love that actually recognizes and values you, it helps to mend pieces of your identity that have been harmed by pain. People who are damaged emotionally often believe they are worthless or unloved. But love gently confronts those lies. When someone chooses to support, listen to, and stay with you through challenging times, you start to feel valuable. It's possible that you matter. You might be all you need. This transformation is one of the nicest things that can happen to a heart. It helps it heal. Love reveals to you who you really are: not broken or hurt, but human, valuable, and deserving of care.

Chapter: 13

Love can also help heal emotional wounds by bringing people together. When people are sad, they frequently feel that they are the only ones. They want to hide their sentiments, stay away from others, or pretend that everything is OK when it isn't. But love brings individuals together who were alone before. It makes you want to let someone in, even if you're terrified. It encourages you to express your feelings openly rather than suppressing them. You feel better knowing that you don't have to do everything by yourself. You feel like someone cares when they call, text, check in, sit with you, or just listen. And one of the best things you can do to get better is to feel like someone cares. Love reminds you that your feelings are important and that you should be listened to.

When you experience emotional flashbacks—unexpected waves of pain brought on by memories or anxieties—love can also help you heal. When you're with someone who understands how you feel, they can make you feel comfortable, calm, and stable. A warm hug, a gentle touch, or quiet words like "I'm here with you" can help your body calm down. Love helps you control your emotions. It shows your heart that there can be peace even in the midst of pain. You begin to replace your old emotional responses with ones that are better for you. You learn to calm down via breathing. You learn to lean in rather than push others away. Love can provide support when your emotions become overwhelming.

Love can also help you shift the way you think about things. Stories that make you feel awful, including "I'm not enough," "Everyone leaves," "No one understands me," or "I can't trust anyone," might hurt your feelings. But love offers you a new story. The stories start to alter when someone shows you care, commitment, and respect all the time. You discover that some people care for you. Love doesn't make you forget the past; it shows you that the past doesn't have to define the future. One of the best things about love is that it can change how you feel.

Chapter: 13

Love also facilitates healing by assisting you in rediscovering aspects of yourself that you previously lost due to emotional trauma. Emotional harm can cause people to lose touch with their interests, dreams, and sense of self. But when someone loves you in a healthy, supportive way, they often push you to reconnect with the pieces of yourself that you lost. They remind you of what you're excelling at, celebrate how far you've come, and encourage you to keep getting better. They help you perceive yourself in a better way. This sort of love helps you heal and provides you with the strength to take back the parts of your heart that trauma sought to stifle. Love can bring back happiness, creativity, confidence, and peace.

Accepting is another way that love can help heal. When someone loves you without attempting to alter, judge, or correct you, it fosters a sense of belonging. This feeling is what many damaged hearts seek. Acceptance means "You're safe here," "Your feelings are real," and "You don't have to act like you're someone else." That kind of acceptance makes shame less strong. Shame likes to be quiet and out of sight, but love breaks that silence by urging people to be honest. When you can speak your tale and not be condemned for it, shame loses its potency. Acceptance acts as a soothing balm that heals emotional wounds.

Love also heals by giving people something to look forward to. When you have emotional wounds, you could feel like things are permanent or that recovery is impossible. But love offers you a new hope: the idea that things can become better, that happiness can come back, and that the heart can be secure again. Love offers you a reason to get up in the morning and something to look forward to. It provides you with a glimpse of a future where pain doesn't control your feelings. Hope is like medicine for a heart that hurts. And love is usually the thing that administers that medicine.

Chapter: 13

One of the best things about love is that it can help you grow emotionally. When you are surrounded by love, whether it comes from a spouse, a friend, a family member, or even a supportive community, you can confront obstacles with courage instead of dread. You get stronger when you know that other people believe in you. This support system makes it easier for you to deal with your emotions. You don't stop; you reach out. You don't break; you bend. You don't stop; you try again. Love strengthens your emotional foundation, so your heart can endure life's troubles without breaking every time.

Love also teaches you how to control your feelings. Love that is good for you teaches you how to keep your emotions in check, such as not acting on impulse, not shutting down, and not being too terrified. When someone treats you like way, you start to act like a calm, nice, and consistent person. You learn to talk rather than be quiet. You learn to stop instead of panicking. You learn to act rather than react. Love transforms how you feel over time, gradually eliminating bad habits and replacing them with good ones. This emotional equilibrium is a key part of rehabilitation because it breaks old patterns and initiates new ones grounded in stability and care.

Love doesn't erase the past; it changes what can happen in the future to heal emotional wounds. Love lets you feel, trust, hope, and open your heart again without worry of what others may advise you to do. It reminds you that you deserve love, support, and close relationships. One of the most crucial things you may believe is that love can make you better. Your heart can mend after it hurts or breaks. Love lights up the darkest corners and helps you rebuild yourself from the inside out. And when you allow yourself to totally accept love, healing becomes not just possible, but certain.

Chapter: 13

Love as a Healing Force
Stories of recovery and healing through love

S tories of love healing demonstrate that genuine care can heal even the most severe emotional wounds. Nia tells a powerful story about a woman who believed she didn't deserve love because of something that happened to her as a child. By the time she was an adult, she had learned how to disguise her feelings and be on guard. Then she met a buddy named Norden, who was kind, patient, and understanding. He didn't ask her about her past or make her talk about it. He created a place for her to be herself without fear. Nia began to trust again as time went on. Not because someone asked her to, but because someone deserved it. Jordan's consistent kindness made her see that love didn't have to hurt or come with strings attached. His presence was the first step in her healing.

Nia learned she didn't have to act like someone else to be welcomed into their friendship as it evolved. She had never felt like someone cared about her just because she was a person. When she didn't believe in herself, Norden would tell her what she was good at, and he never made fun of her for being insecure. The walls she had put up because she was scared started to come down. Nia began to be more honest about her feelings. She would talk about her past, and occasionally she would cry; other times she would be unsure, but she would always be strong. Norden listened, not out of sympathy, but because he understood. That simple act of being heard helped her mend wounds she believed would never heal. Through this companionship, she learned that love could be calm, steady, and safe.

Nia's tale teaches that love doesn't heal through extravagant gestures; it heals by always being there for each other. A lot of the time, healing starts with one person who agrees to remain, listen, and help without expecting anything in return. Love gave her back her self-esteem, let her feel positive about herself again, and let her trust again. It didn't happen all at once; it happened in subtle ways of being pleasing. Her story is a lesson that love can repair things that people thought were broken for years. The right person doesn't always heal your wounds; sometimes, they help you find the fortitude you already possess to face it alone.

Chapter: 13

Peter is another positive illustration of how love can heal. After losing his work and a long-term relationship in the same year, he had a difficult time with acute depression. He had lost his confidence and his ambition, and the world felt too heavy to carry. Peter sealed himself off from everyone except his sister Maya, who wouldn't let him hide from his feelings. She visited him often, cooked for him, cleaned his apartment when he couldn't, and gently pushed him without ignoring how he felt. Some days, Peter didn't say anything, but Maya stayed nevertheless. Her determination sent him a message he desperately needed to hear: "You are not alone." Her presence became a lifeline.

Maya also helped Peter take little measures toward becoming healthier. She encouraged him to exercise in the morning, attend therapy, and remain in touch with friends who genuinely cared about him. For months, he made modest and uneven improvements. Some days he felt strong enough to laugh, while other days he could hardly get out of bed. Maya never changed her mind, though. She didn't say, "Get over it." She helped him get through it. Peter began to improve when he realized the difference between pushing and supporting. His sister's affection didn't make the agony go away, but it did help him cope. He began to gently and steadily rebuild his life with newfound confidence.

Peter's tale shows that love can heal when you are there for someone, patient, and kind. It takes time for depression to go away, and one kind thing won't make emotional wounds heal. However, love that is steadfast, genuine, and consistently present helps individuals regain their footing. Peter's love for Maya didn't save him; it brought him back to life. She was there for him so he could start over, try again, and believe in his future again. This story shows us that love doesn't solve things; it heals by being there for someone until they can get back up.

Chapter: 13

Charles's and Rosa's stories of healing are distinct. When they met, Rosa had just come out of a problematic relationship in which she felt dominated and put down all the time. She had emotional scars that made it challenging for her to trust others. Charles could tell she was unsure, so instead of demanding closeness right away, he gave her emotional space. He never asked her to get better immediately. Instead of being rough with her, he showed her what healthy love was. He told her the truth, didn't judge her, and respected her limits. Over time, Rosa understood that love didn't have to be insane. Love might be peaceful. Love might be stable. She had never really felt love before, although it could be kind.

Rosa's past trauma sometimes came back to her and made her shut down emotionally. She was scared that being honest would make her feel worse. But Charles kept assuring her that getting better wasn't a straight line. Every step forward was vital. He told her how much better she was doing, calmed her down, and made her feel comfortable enough to trust again. Rosa learned what set her off and told him what she needed from him. She could strengthen their relationship without worrying about what other people would say. He wasn't afraid of her wounds; instead, he recognized her strength, attractiveness, and resilience in overcoming them.

Rosa's healing through Charles's love illustrates that the right love doesn't hurry healing; it assists it. Her tale shows that wounded hearts may mend if you are patient, feel safe emotionally, and are honest with each other. Love is powerful because it is based on understanding, not perfection. Charles's warm, steadfast affection helped Rosa recover her self-esteem and understand what a healthy relationship is like. Their experience teaches that when love is sincere, healing is not only possible but also definite.

Chapter: 13

Celia, a grandma, offered another lovely story about how love can make things better. She loved her grandson Malik no matter what. Malik's parents had problems with drugs and alcohol; thus, he was lonely as a child. He struggled with feeling rejected and not being worthy enough throughout his youth. But Celia was there for him with open arms and an open heart. As she reared him, she was patient, knowledgeable, and loving. She attended all his school events, helped him with his homework late at night, and taught him ideals that would influence his life as an adult. Malik used to say that she didn't simply save him; she taught him what love is actually like. He learned from her affection that he was worthy of love, competent to accomplish, and deserving of stability.

Malik understood how much his grandmother's love had changed him as he grew up. She had healed scars that he couldn't even talk about when he was a kid. Her love helped him break the cycle of emotional abandonment that had persisted for a long time. Malik transitioned into a youth counseling role, leveraging his personal journey to support children facing similar challenges. His mending didn't erase the anguish of his childhood, but it did provide him a reason to live. Celia's love helped him heal, and it was also the reason he wanted to help other people heal.

Malik and Celia's tale teaches us that healing frequently comes from someone who loves you all the time, not just when things are going well. Love, whether it's from family, friends, or a romantic relationship, provides injured hearts the stability, understanding, and solace they need. Love heals because it provides people hope, helps them trust each other again, and reminds them that their past misery doesn't have to define their future. Healing through love isn't about healing what's broken; it's about helping someone regain their power, value, and ability to love again. Love cures us by showing us that we don't have to go through life by ourselves.

Chapter: 13

Love as a Healing Force
The role of love in overcoming trauma

Trauma can have impacts on people that are challenging to understand and even harder to heal. It leaves behind feelings like fear, humiliation, mistrust, worry, or a feeling of not being connected to oneself that persist long after the experience is gone. Many people try to get better on their own, but being alone doesn't usually help. You need to connect to get better. This moment is when love starts to become a powerful force. When someone truly loves, supports, and understands you, it gives you the strength to deal with emotional pain that once seemed insurmountable. Trauma takes away your safety, but love gives it back. When the heart feels safe, it begins to release the walls it has built to shield itself from years of pain.

Love helps people get over trauma by eventually helping them trust again. Trauma makes the mind stay alert, ready for disaster, and prepared for the worst. When a person receives consistent love, whether from a spouse, friend, family member, or even a supportive community, those terrifying thoughts start to fade. The neurological system slowly calms down. The heart begins to believe that not everyone is a threat. The mind begins to understand that not every situation is painful. Someone does not make that transition; it occurs because love allows new feelings to replace the old ones.

Love makes individuals feel like they matter, which is one of the finest ways to help them heal from trauma. Trauma survivors often feel unimportant, misunderstood, and uncared for. But when someone listens to understand, not merely to answer, it makes sentiments that have been ignored for too long become true. It's beneficial for them to see someone. It's beneficial for you to be heard. Being welcomed helps you get better. Love enables individuals to discuss their grief without feeling bad about it, and just that helps them let go of some of the emotional weight they've been carrying for years. Trauma separates people; love brings them back together. Love makes people communicate, but trauma keeps them mute. Love patiently and softly rebuilds trust, while trauma destroys it.

Chapter: 13

Love also helps people overcome past trauma by reminding them of who they are. When people go through challenging times, especially when they are young, they often lose aspects of themselves, such as their confidence, joy, innocence, or sense of deservingness. Love helps bring those parts back together. When someone is always there to help, love, and praise you, it helps you remember who you were before the trauma. Love tells someone, "You're still whole," even when they don't feel whole. Over time, this reassurance becomes a powerful force that transforms how you feel about yourself.

Another way love helps people heal from trauma is by helping them cope with their feelings. People who have been through trauma often become locked in a cycle of fear, fury, or panic. But love makes things better. The body starts to function differently when someone who cares provides grounding, soft words, a gentle touch, or just being there. The heart learns to calm down rather than be afraid. The mind learns to beg for aid instead of shutting down. This rule doesn't mean that the trauma never happens; it only means that the person learns better ways to cope with it. Love shows you how to stay calm when you were scared previously.

Love can also help people break negative habits that trauma might cause. People who have been through trauma often make the same mistakes in their relationships over and over again, such as picking partners who aren't emotionally available, avoiding intimacy, or pushing away people who care. But love that is gentle and persistent can break those old habits. It shows a better way to live. Love makes things orderly instead of chaotic. Love doesn't deceive others; it reveals the truth. Instead of terror, love offers comfort. This new partnership is a positive example of how to make better decisions going forward. Over time, the person learns that they deserve more than what trauma taught them to accept.

Chapter: 13

Love gives us many things we need to heal from trauma, like patience. There is no apparent way to get over trauma. Some days feel like progress, while others feel like regress. Love acknowledges that healing is not a linear process. When someone loves you, they are patient when you need space, understanding when you feel overwhelmed, and kind when you have problems trusting. This patience keeps the mending going. It reassures the hurt individual that they don't need to act, hurry, or pretend. They can heal at their own pace, knowing they won't be abandoned if they don't improve quickly.

Love also shows you what you feel, something trauma often does. People who have been through trauma think they are broken, unworthy, or impossible to love. But love tells them how powerful, gorgeous, and tough they are. When someone speaks life into you, they remind you of your worth, bravery, and progress. This fights the negative thoughts that trauma left in your heart. This emotional mirroring is a vital element of getting healthy. You begin to view yourself as more than just your hurt. You begin to perceive your wounds as distinct from your identity. This separation is a significant aspect of your journey toward healing.

Love also helps people get over tragedy in an incredible way by giving their pain purpose. Love doesn't make what happened right, but it can help you grow from it. When people feel supported and understood, they often become more empathetic, emotionally intelligent, and stronger. They use their healing to help others, halt patterns that have persisted for generations, and strengthen their relationships. Love will define their future, even though trauma may have affected their past. Love gives the healing process a purpose. It makes the suffering feel less like a prison and more like a means to grow and become a better person.

Chapter: 13

Ultimately, love provides those who have been through trauma something worth more than anything else: hope. Trauma often leads individuals to believe that life will be perpetually challenging, that relationships will consistently pose risks, and that trust is unattainable. But love doesn't fit with such notions. It brings up new possibilities, such as caring partnerships, safe connections, and enjoyable times. Having hope is one of the finest ways to recover from trauma. Love is what makes the heart feel hopeful. When love enters someone's life, it provides them with a chance at a future different from their past.

Love also helps people rediscover their voice. Those who have experienced hurt often hesitate to express their emotions, establish boundaries, or reveal the truth. But love helps people be honest. A person who cares for you profoundly allows you to express yourself freely without concern for potential repercussions. They care about how you feel, listen to what you have to say, and provide you space. You start to understand that what you say matters. You find out that what you need is fine. You learn that you can speak up. Getting your voice back is a significant step in healing from trauma, and love frequently gives you the strength to do it.

Love as a healing power reminds us that no heart is too shattered to heal, no history too terrible to forget, and no trauma too deep to recover from. Love gives back what trauma took away: a sense of safety, connection, self-worth, peace, patience, and hope. To heal doesn't mean forgetting what happened; it means learning to cope with it. And love is the calm, steady light that guides the heart out of the dark. When people receive sincere, gentle, and loving affection, they start to believe that recovery is possible. Love doesn't make trauma go away, but it does help the heart navigate through it.

Chapter: 13

Love has a powerful ability to reveal aspects of ourselves that we often find challenging to uncover on our own. Our perceptions of the environment and ourselves are altered by emotional scars, which can be minor or severe. This chapter demonstrated that although love cannot heal wounds, it can lessen their anguish, restore trust, and give individuals a sense of security. Healing begins when a person feels valued, supported, and emotionally seen. Emotional wounds can eventually heal rather than stay buried when love is present at all times, with patience, gentleness, and understanding.

Reflection Questions — How Love Heals Emotional Wounds:

1. In what ways has love, whether from a partner, friend, or family member, helped soothe wounds you once thought would last forever?
2. What does emotional safety mean to you, and who in your life has offered that feeling?
3. How has someone's patience or understanding helped you open up or become more vulnerable?
4. Which emotional wound still affects you today, and how might love help you begin healing it?
5. How has receiving love changed your view of yourself and your own worth?

The chapter also included numerous recovery experiences that demonstrated the value of love. These tales demonstrate that self-healing is not possible. A family member who took on the role of caregiver, a supportive friend, or a partner who showed compassion after years of trauma are all examples of this. Recovery occurs when someone is near enough to provide hope without being too close to overwhelm the person undergoing healing. Being present, dependable, and supportive are the ways that love operates.

Reflection Question — Stories of Recovery and Healing Through Love:

1. Which recovery story in this chapter resonated with you the most, and why?

Chapter: 13

Another important thing to know about this chapter is how love helps people deal with trauma. Trauma impacts how a person thinks, acts, and connects with others. Love provides the heart with something stable to grasp onto while it learns how to be healthier. Fear used to dwell in love, but now it teaches trust. It teaches being there instead of avoiding things. It teaches how to be soft when you use emotional numbness as a shield. It takes time, support, and kindness to get over trauma. It's not a short process. This page asks you to think deeply about how love has changed the way you deal with sorrow, grow, and be strong.

Reflection Questions — Love and Overcoming Trauma:

1. What is something trauma made you believe about yourself that love later challenged or changed?
2. How has love—romantic or otherwise—helped you regain a sense of safety or belonging?
3. What does emotional stability look like in your relationships today, and how did love contribute to that stability?
4. Which areas of your life still need healing, and what kind of love would support that process?

As you think about these questions, keep in mind that healing isn't about forgetting what happened; it's about getting back the pieces of yourself that grief previously silenced. Love is a strong healer. It inspires honesty, helps people become stronger, and makes hope seem feasible again.

Reflection Questions:

1. What does "healed love" look like in your life today?
2. How can you allow more healing, supportive love into your relationships moving forward?
3. In what ways can you become a source of healing for someone else—through presence, empathy, or compassion?

Chapter: 14

Love and Patience
The necessity of patience in nurturing love

Patience is one of the most crucial aspects of love, yet people often overlook it. These days, everything happens quickly: talking, making choices, and setting goals. But love often makes us take our time. Real love doesn't grow very fast. It needs room, time, and someone who understands. It takes time for love to grow. It enables relationships to evolve naturally, without imposing unreasonable time limits. You know that people develop, heal, and express themselves in different ways and at varying speeds when you are patient. You choose to be kind and curious instead of furious. Patience is the calm power that keeps love stable, especially when feelings are strong or misunderstandings arise.

Patience is vital in love since it shows that both people are human. Everyone has problems. People have weaknesses, worries, phobias, and behaviors that they had before they got into a relationship. If you don't have patience, small things that upset you might quickly become enormous difficulties. But if you allow them time, those shortcomings might help you understand someone better. Being patient doesn't imply putting up with rudeness or disregarding difficulties. It involves allowing them to help the relationship grow. It means knowing that troubles will come up, but they don't have to end the relationship. Instead, practicing patience allows you to reflect on difficulties rather than react impulsively, thereby strengthening the relationship rather than weakening it.

Being patient also helps you grow emotionally. Loving someone means sometimes being disappointed, confused, or failing to meet their expectations. You can respond with grace instead of rage if you have patience. It prevents you from saying unkind words when you are upset and helps you listen without passing judgment. It shows you that you can wait to confront situations and feelings. This emotional maturity makes the connection stronger, more stable, and better able to address issues. Patience is what keeps love strong through good and difficult times.

Chapter: 14

One benefit of being patient with love is that you know people will show who they are over time. You don't learn everything about someone in the first week, month, or even year. People reveal things about themselves in layers, and each layer provides you with more knowledge about who they are. If you are patient, this procedure can happen on its own. It stops you from making assumptions and makes you want to be open-minded and interested in your relationship. People are more willing to talk to you when they know you are pleased with their sentiments, their speed, and their personality. This kind of emotional safety makes the connection more intimate because it lets you be yourself without feeling pressured or condemned.

Another element of being patient is knowing that love is hard work and that effort takes time. You don't just suddenly enter into healthy relationships; you have to put in the effort by spending time together, talking honestly, and sharing experiences. Being patient helps you understand that some days will be imperfect and some moments will seem unromantic. There will be days when you are too busy, too stressed, or just don't feel like yourself. During these circumstances, patience keeps you steady. It reminds you that being separated for a short time doesn't mean you'll lose someone forever and that love may grow stronger when you talk to each other.

Being patient also helps you prepare for the challenging aspects of love, such as moving past hurts. In partnerships, many people carry emotional baggage like unresolved trauma, childhood phobias, or previous heartbreaks. The mere fact that you love someone does not ensure that they will change right away. It takes time for wounds to heal, and hurrying can make them worse. But if you are patient, you can get better. "Don't rush," I'm there when it says that. When people are not compelled to hide their pain or rush their growth, they are more open. This degree of emotional transparency is the only thing that can make love stronger. Patience can be used to turn past suffering into optimism for the future.

Chapter: 14

Being patient in love also entails learning to talk to each other deliberately instead of just saying what comes to mind. Patience encourages you to take a break before you respond when you're upset or frustrated. This lets you reflect on what you want to say before saying it. This break may seem minor, yet it makes a tremendous difference. It allows you time to think about what you want to say, what you need, and how you feel. It helps prevent unnecessary conflicts and facilitates smoother communication between individuals. When both parties are patient when they chat, they can figure things out quickly, and misunderstandings go away. This kind of communication fosters trust because everyone feels like their voice is heard, their opinion is appreciated, and they are respected.

Another benefit of being patient is that you can let the connection evolve. People evolve as time goes on. Their dreams alter, their personalities grow, and the things that happen in their lives affect what they value most. These factors can change, so instead of resisting them, practice patience. Being patient means recognizing that both you and your lover will become better. You have faith that the relationship will be strong even if you both change. Love moves from one stage to the next with patience. The outcome could be the excitement of new love, the steadiness of committed love, or the deep companionship of long-term love. Practicing patience strengthens the relationship, increases its flexibility, and contributes to its longevity.

Being patient can also help you be thankful. When you slow down and enjoy your partner rather than rushing through the relationship, you see how they enrich your life. You stop focusing on what's not there and start seeing what's already there. When you learn to be patient, you stop expecting things that aren't possible, and the result makes you more grateful. Instead, you should appreciate the simple things, the modest gestures, and the quiet ways your partner shows you love. Being thankful changes how you think about the relationship and strengthens your emotional connection.

Chapter: 14

One of the best things about patience is that it helps you handle challenges with grace. There is no such thing as a perfect relationship. Every marriage has times when it is stressed, upset, or emotionally distant. If you're patient, you won't give up too quickly. It reminds you that issues are merely steps along the way, not the end of the road. When you exhibit patience, you don't assign blame; instead, you strive to discover a solution. You don't keep quiet; you talk instead. You don't judge; you receive it instead. You and your partner can learn from the struggle instead of letting it ruin your relationship. Even when things are challenging, they might help you grow closer to each other over time.

Patience also teaches you how to love someone no matter what. When you're patient, you love someone for who they are, not for meeting your demands. You continue to love them when they're having a hard time, and you forgive them for being imperfect. Being patient helps you see beyond faults and flaws, which keeps love strong. This unconditional love sees things as they are and chooses kindness over anger. When both individuals demonstrate a willingness to love each other patiently, the relationship transforms into a safe space that nurtures growth without haste.

Patience is more than simply a modest virtue; it's the key to lasting love. It maintains robust, compassionate connections that can get back on track. It helps love grow strong roots that can last through storms. It shows you how to enjoy the trip as much as the destination. Patience teaches you that love isn't about how quickly things get better; it's about how much you want to walk the route together. Love becomes more than just a sensation when patience is a part of the relationship's basis; it becomes a powerful, steady force that lasts.

Chapter: 14

Love and Patience
How patience strengthens relationships

Being patient allows both parties to grow without fear of judgment or haste. There are times when any relationship is easy, challenging, or difficult to predict. If you are patient, you may get through each step with understanding instead of wrath. Being patient means letting your partner mess up, learning from it, and learning how to show love better. This doesn't mean putting up with terrible behavior; it just means knowing that it takes time to create a solid connection. Patience removes unnecessary stress and helps both hearts become adjusted to the rhythm of loving and being loved.

What patience actually does for a relationship is make it more stable on an emotional level. When you disagree or have a hard day, patience encourages you to stop and consider before you act, rather than act on impulse. Your partner will trust you more if they know you won't become mad or punish them for every little mistake. When things get too emotional, both couples might use emotional stability as a safety net. Patient couples realize that not every problem needs to be resolved right away. Some people need time, calmness, and the willingness to talk about them again when things have settled down. It is easier to have healthy conversations when you are patient. This decreases conflict and makes both people feel valued.

Patience also helps relationships thrive by enabling people to get to know each other better. Taking the time to really get to know your partner, their past, anxieties, triggers, and dreams, will help you better meet their needs. You stop taking things personally and start to see the big picture. If someone sounds frustrated, it could not be because of you. It could be because they had a difficult day, a troubling memory, or internal stress. If you wait, you can stand back and ask yourself, "What's really going on?" This mindset encourages a desire to assist rather than confront and fosters feelings of compassion rather than anger towards others. Being patient is the key to understanding your spouse, which is what makes partnerships work.

Chapter: 14

Another important way patience helps relationships is by fostering emotional connection between people. You have to be open to being vulnerable to be truly intimate, but it doesn't happen immediately. People often take time to open up, particularly those who have experienced past hurt. Your spouse will share their worries, fears, dreams, and hidden scars when you are patient. If people know you are patient with how they feel, they are more willing to talk to you. This makes your relationship stronger in ways that surface-level partnerships can't. Patience communicates a commitment to a long-term relationship and fosters closeness over time.

Patience also helps couples work through their disagreements without harming their relationship. People have distinct personalities, methods of talking, and ways of showing how they feel. If you don't have patience, these differences can make you angry. They can assist you in learning if you are patient. Being patient means you can see things from your partner's perspective instead of trying to make them your way. This regard for each other keeps people from becoming furious and makes them feel like they are working together. When you and another individual hold differing opinions, it is not a problem; rather, it presents an opportunity to foster greater closeness. Their love is much stronger when they embrace each other's differences rather than trying to change each other.

Being patient is also beneficial since it protects the connection during times of change. Life is full of changes, including getting a new job, taking care of family, and coping with personal, financial, or emotional problems. For a period, these shifts can make partners feel tense, apprehensive, or distant from each other. If you're patient, these seasons will keep you stable. It reminds you that love isn't about how easy life is but about how diligently you work when things go rough. Couples who are patient with change are stronger because they learn to rely on each other instead of giving up or criticizing.

Chapter: 14

Patience helps relationships thrive by letting love blossom naturally. When you first fall in love, everything appears new and exciting, and your sensations are intense. But over time, love becomes something more profound, built on partnership, understanding, and commitment. Impatient couples often get scared when the "spark" feels different because they fear something is amiss. But couples who are patient know that their love is not going away; it is getting stronger. When you're patient, you can accept the deeper connection that arises when the initial excitement fades. It helps the relationship grow into a secure, adult form of love, where both people feel safe rather than unsure.

Being patient also helps you avoid hurting yourself when you don't understand something. In every relationship, there are instances when one person becomes offended or doesn't understand something. Being impatient makes things worse rapidly, turning a simple mistake into a significant battle. But if you wait, things become clearer. Instead of making hasty assumptions, you ask insightful questions. You don't become frustrated; you strive to comprehend instead. You don't talk poorly; instead, you listen. This calm way of handling things protects the relationship from getting overly emotional and helps both couples learn how to talk to each other better. Over time, these patient responses build trust and emotional safety.

One of the best things about being patient is that it helps people get over problems. People will make mistakes, such as saying harsh things, forgetting to do things, or pulling away emotionally, no matter how much they love each other. If you don't have patience, these blunders will stay with you forever. But if you wait, you can forgive. If you give your spouse time, you can see their intentions rather than just their mistakes. It helps you say you were wrong without letting it change the relationship. Patient love realizes that neither person is flawless and that it needs time to evolve. This ability to forgive and move on is important for long-term love.

Chapter: 14

Being patient also makes it easier to talk to others, which is the most important part of having positive connections. If you talk to someone with patience, you give both of you a chance to be heard. You let the discourse run on without making assumptions or cutting off your partner's point of view. This kind of communication builds trust because neither participant feels they have to communicate or that they are being ignored. When you learn how to talk to patients, you learn to respond with understanding rather than anger. Over time, it strengthens your bond by ensuring your interactions are respectful and insightful, not full of rage and assumptions.

To retain the peace in the relationship, you also need to be patient. When both couples are patient, the house is a peaceful environment. You learn to cope with stress, comfort each other, and choose peace over pointless fighting. Being patient might help you prevent emotional outbursts that can damage someone or break trust for a long period. Instead of attacking each other, you work together to solve problems. This shared approach makes it clearer that both couples are on the same side and working toward the same goal: lasting love.

In the end, being patient strengthens connections because it demonstrates how much you care. When things are going well, it's easy to love. However, patience emerges when your heart is challenged, when you must choose between understanding and anger, compassion and judgment, and commitment and ease. When things are difficult, patience says, "I believe in us." It makes you stronger, makes you feel more connected to other people, and changes love from an emotion to a choice. Love grows stronger, steadier, and lasts longer when patience is part of the relationship's foundation. It becomes a love that lasts, not because it never had issues, but because it always found a way to endure through them.

Chapter: 14

Love and Patience
Practical ways to practice patience in love

The first step to being patient in love is learning how to slow down. This is particularly crucial in a world where everything demands immediate attention. One of the easiest ways to learn to be patient is to let your partner talk without cutting them off or making guesses. Not because one person doesn't care, but because both individuals rush to reply, defend, or react, many partnerships have problems. You make room for understanding to enter the discourse when you stop, breathe, and let the moment happen on purpose. Taking a moment before you react is a simple practice that can affect the way you talk to each other. It helps you pay closer attention when you listen, think through your responses more carefully, and avoid misunderstandings that can occur when you act on your feelings.

Another fantastic technique to exercise patience is to learn how to manage your expectations. Unrealistic expectations or not talking about them might slowly end a relationship. Don't expect your partner to read your mind; instead, talk to them clearly and compassionately. Please allow them the time they need to grow at their own pace. When you change your expectations, you don't have to compromise your standards. You just have to remember that love is a process, not a spectacle. Your relationship can progress if you stop trying to be perfect. People are less inclined to anticipate perfection and more likely to recognize minor developmental steps as a result of this change.

You can also learn patience by intentionally creating calm moments in your relationship. Couples sometimes don't know that stress, daily activities, or responsibilities can add up and make things tense. When things become uncomfortable, both partners might feel better by taking time to relax, such as going for a quiet stroll, conversing without interruptions, or doing simple breathing exercises. These relaxing activities teach your heart to slow down rather than react immediately. They serve as a reminder that not every problem requires immediate resolution. You need to be quiet for a minute to achieve peace and understanding.

Chapter: 14

Another beneficial technique to exercise patience in love is to learn more about your partner's feelings. Everyone has personal triggers that make them angry, stress them out, and lead to internal conflicts that others may not understand. You become more patient when you pay attention to these emotional patterns instead of making quick judgments. For example, if your partner pulls away during a fight, it could be because they handle their feelings differently, not because they don't care. Your partner may require time to trust you because of past wounds, but that doesn't mean they don't love you. When you slow down, pay attention to, and understand these emotional patterns, you stop taking things personally and start to feel what other people feel. This change is one of the best reasons for patients to appreciate their partners.

To be patient, you also need to believe that growth is more important than being flawless. Two people who aren't perfect are doing their best to make their relationship work. Instead of dwelling on problems, it can be helpful to appreciate modest wins. Recognizing progress provides you with a reason to keep going and strengthens your bond. When you choose to encourage instead of condemn, you become more patient.

Also, being patient implies being kind to yourself. You can't be patient with your lover if you aren't patient with yourself. You may behave in a hurry, misinterpret the situation, or become irrationally angry. You're not a lousy partner; you're just human. When you're feeling overwhelmed, you can practice self-patience by taking emotional breaks, writing down your feelings, or talking about your difficulties with someone you trust. You can think more clearly and feel more at ease when you pause and give yourself some space. The patience you show to others comes from being kind to yourself.

Chapter: 14

Working on how you talk to each other is a helpful, sometimes overlooked technique for practicing patience in love. Rather than hastily drawing conclusions or making assumptions about your partner's desires, engage in questioning to uncover their intentions. If you go into a conversation with the thought "Help me understand" instead of "I already know," it will be easier to talk to each other straight away. It helps people understand each other better and reduces defensiveness. Using soft tones instead of sharp ones can make a tremendous difference when things become heated. When you talk to someone thoughtfully, you can avoid misunderstandings and ensure that both individuals feel heard instead of chastised.

It's also good to know when to walk away when your emotions are too strong. Many think stepping away is avoiding something, but if done on purpose, it's a strong act of patience. When you're furious, and the conversation isn't going well, it's best to say, "I need a minute to calm down so we can talk clearly." Taking a break gives both parties time to think things over and return with a better understanding. When you realize that stopping is not giving up but choosing calm over emotional impulsiveness, you become more patient.

Being patient also entails seeing your spouse as a person. You and your partner will always do things differently, such as how you handle your feelings, fix things, and get things done. Patience doesn't want you to change each other; it wants you to accept your differences. This acceptance strengthens the connection by reducing stress and facilitating mutual understanding. Practical patience means letting your spouse finish things their way, letting them explain their perspective without rushing them, or encouraging their personal growth even when it doesn't mesh with your plans. Acceptance lets love blossom without any stress.

Chapter: 14

One of the best ways to learn to be patient in love is to show thanks. Focusing on your partner's positive traits makes you more patient. Being thankful transforms how you see things, from not having enough to having enough. You can see how diligently they work on their relationship, how kind they are, and how real their love is. This method of thinking makes the minor things that irritate you seem less important and makes you feel more connected to each other. A thankful heart is patient, and being appreciative can help you relax quickly.

Creating routines that enhance emotional connection is another effective approach. You may avoid misunderstandings and make things more stable by adding rituals to your relationship, such as weekly check-ins, shared meals, or even ten minutes of uninterrupted talk. This consistency helps you be more patient since it makes you feel less emotionally unstable. When both partners know they can talk, worries don't seem as important, and it's simpler to talk. Routines help us manage our emotions and let love blossom gently and on purpose.

Keep that in mind, being patient in love means choosing to understand rather than get angry, to be kind rather than get annoyed, and to grow over time rather than get angry right away. Being patient doesn't mean ignoring issues or suppressing your feelings. It entails being emotionally mature at all times during the partnership. It's a loving act that creates trust, brings the two people closer together, and offers them both a strong platform from which to grow. Love is calmer, kinder, and stronger when patience becomes a daily habit rather than just a notion. Rather than rushing in with optimism, you approach it with care, and it transforms into a love that endures.

Chapter: 14

Patience is a very important part of any relationship's health, yet it is frequently not given enough credit. This chapter showed how being patient makes you feel more emotionally comfortable, reduces unnecessary fights, and lets love grow at a normal, healthy pace. Patience teaches you to calm down and enjoy the process, rather than rushing your partner or trying to get them closer.

Reflection Questions — The Necessity of Patience in Nurturing Love

1. When you think about patience in love, what examples from your own relationships come to mind?
2. Why do you think patience is so challenging in relationships, even when you love someone deeply?
3. How has impatience affected any past or current relationship you've experienced?
4. What does nurturing love slowly and intentionally look like for you?
5. What would change in your relationship if you allowed more time, space, and grace for growth?

This chapter also made the point that patience not only stops fights but also strengthens the emotional bond between two individuals. Being patient makes things stable. When you choose to be patient rather than angry, your partner feels safe being open, vulnerable, and making mistakes without worrying about what others would think. This makes the link stronger and deeper.

Reflection Questions — How Patience Strengthens Relationships

1. How does your partner (or loved ones) respond when you show patience during difficult moments?
2. What relationship challenges could be softened or resolved through patience?
3. In what ways does patience help you communicate more clearly and calmly?

Chapter: 14

Patience is a skill you develop daily, not something you wish for. Being patient is a skill. It grows stronger when you are careful with your words, feelings, and reactions. Taking a moment to think before you act is one way to practice patience. Occasionally, it involves letting go of false hopes or giving your spouse time to reflect on how they feel.

Reflection Questions — Practical Ways to Practice Patience in Love

1. What is one specific situation in your relationship where you tend to become impatient?
2. What would it look like to pause, breathe, or step away in that moment instead of reacting?
3. Which expectations in your relationship might need adjusting to create more patience and less pressure?
4. How can you show yourself grace on days when your patience runs low?
5. What daily habits, such as gratitude, open communication, or calm conversations, can help you become more patient with your partner?

As you contemplate these questions, keep in mind that patience doesn't mean being quiet or passive; it means being purposeful. Being patient doesn't mean disregarding your needs or hiding your sentiments; it means showing them with kindness, timeliness, and intelligence.

Final Reflection

1. How has your definition of patience in love changed after reading this chapter?
2. What kind of partner do you want to become as you practice more patience in your relationships?
3. What is one immediate change you can make today to nurture a more patient, loving connection?

Chapter: 15

Love and Forgiving Yourself
The importance of self-love and self-forgiveness

Forgiving yourself is hard but vital. Forgiving others is simpler for many individuals than forgiving themselves. They keep going over their faults in their heads, criticizing themselves more harshly than anybody else ever could. But forgiving yourself doesn't imply pretending the past didn't happen or making excuses for the actions that damaged you. It's about knowing that you did the best you could with what you knew, how old you were, and how you felt at the time. It's about being aware that you are a person. When you forgive yourself, your heart can breathe again. You make it possible for others to heal, find peace, and evolve as people. You can't really love someone else until you forgive yourself. To have true love, you need a sensitive spot inside you where compassion can grow.

Self-love and self-forgiveness are inextricably linked; one cannot exist without the other. When you love yourself, you are gentle, patient, and understanding with your heart. It suggests you shouldn't let your darkest times define you. It requires deciding to perceive your value even when you don't feel like it. This doesn't mean you're full of yourself; it means you're emotionally mature. Loving yourself helps you appreciate your strengths, respect your needs, and set limits. Self-love doesn't make you feel awful about making a mistake; it helps you learn. It helps you improve instead of punishing yourself. If you don't love yourself, life is a never-ending cycle of doubt and regret. But self-love helps you see your worth, even when you feel weak.

Many people find it challenging to forgive themselves because they believe they have to "earn" it by going through hardship. They believe they must feel remorse indefinitely to demonstrate that they have learned their lesson. But feeling guilty for too long might be detrimental. Healthy guilt educates you, but excessive guilt keeps you from doing things. Letting go of the emotional ties that keep you locked in shame is possible when you forgive yourself. It serves as a reminder that making mistakes does not define your identity; rather, it enhances your growth. Forgiving yourself is the first step in getting your future back.

Chapter: 15

To forgive yourself, you also need to know where your negative self-talk comes from. It's not only your voice that tells you you're not good enough. It may be the voice of someone who injured you, judged you, or made you feel negative about yourself. You start to think of that voice as your critic. When you hear this voice, you feel like you don't deserve love, happiness, or grace. But as you become older, you start to understand that this voice is from the past, not the present. Forgiving yourself involves getting back to being who you are after being injured. It involves telling a better tale that acknowledges how far you've come, how much you've grown, and how much more you can do.

Letting go of your mistakes also helps you get along better with other people. When you don't forgive yourself, you typically make the people you care about confront your difficulties. You may be overly defensive because you fear others' opinions or think they'll judge you as harshly as you do. But if you learn to be kind to your heart, you will be more open to others. You talk to others better now that you don't feel negative about yourself. It's easier to trust other people when you trust yourself. You love more sincerely now that you use love to express emotional wholeness. You don't hang on to love out of fear; you give it. Forgiving yourself strengthens your love, making it more complete and healthier.

You realize that forgiving yourself isn't something you do once; it's a process when you think about your journey. You should treat yourself with the same care you would an injured part of your heart. Some days you will feel powerful and loving, while other days you can be hard on yourself again. But every time you choose grace, even in modest ways, you move closer to getting well. The goal isn't to be flawless; it's to improve. With each act of self-forgiveness, you let go of more emotional baggage. Forgiving yourself again and again is not a sign of weakness; it is the bravest way to show love for yourself.

Chapter: 15

When you forgive yourself, you also become stronger emotionally. You won't fear repeating past mistakes if you stop punishing yourself for them. You cease being careful with how you feel. You don't have to worry about letting other people down anymore. Instead, you begin taking healthy risks, trying new things, and allowing yourself time to learn. You get the guts to go after dreams that once seemed out of reach. This strength also shows up when things get hard on an emotional level. When things are rough, you don't let guilt or shame get to you. You tell yourself that you've gotten through challenging times before and that you'll endure through this one too. Forgiving yourself makes your heart stronger and steadier, which is wonderful for your inner strength.

Learning how to be polite to yourself is one of the most fundamental parts of forgiving yourself. What you say to yourself has a lot of power. They can help you or hurt you. When you express sentiments such as "I made a mistake, but I am learning" or "I am deserving of love even in my imperfection," you influence and alter your emotional state. Talking to yourself like this can make you feel better. It helps you treat yourself with kindness, just like you do with the people you care about. When your inner voice stops punishing you and starts helping you, it's easier to forgive yourself. Over time, this transformation will change your self-perception and influence how you handle life's challenges.

Taking responsibility for your actions without letting remorse take over is another component of forgiving yourself. To forgive yourself in a healthy way, you need to be honest and own up to the choices that wounded you or someone else. But you have to decide to move on after you admit them. If you keep harming yourself, you won't become better. We can learn from the past, but it shouldn't stop us from going forward. When you forgive yourself, you let go of the humiliation and keep the lesson. You become more emotionally mature when you find a balance between being responsible and caring. This helps you build a future that isn't focused on your mistakes.

Chapter: 15

When you forgive yourself, you also acquire the strength to set stronger boundaries. When you love yourself and care for your heart, you become choosier about what you let in. You cease letting others abuse you, lie to you, or be in relationships that make you exhausted. You begin to choose love over fear, respect over shame, and serenity over chaos. These restrictions aren't walls; they're shields that help you evolve as a person. They help you keep track of the recovery you've fought so hard for. Forgiving yourself makes you feel better about yourself, and when you do, you naturally set healthier boundaries.

Forgiving yourself also helps you remember to be proud of how far you've come. People don't often realize how far they've come because they're too focused on how far they still have to go. But you should appreciate every healed wound, every brave moment, and every step you take toward loving yourself. When you celebrate your healing, you foster greater emotional development. You begin to view yourself not as a flawed individual, but as someone who is evolving positively. When you celebrate your progress, you want to continue working on your mental health. Healing is no longer merely a task; it has become a journey that you take pride in.

The most important part about loving and forgiving yourself is that you can't extend love to someone else if your heart is empty. If you don't think you deserve love, you can't have a healthy relationship. You can't move closer to your goal if you're feeling guilty. Letting go of your mistakes frees your spirit. Loving yourself makes you more confident. They are the parts that make up a fulfilled, stable, and purposeful life. You may be truly present in your relationships and in your life when you learn to forgive yourself. You can do this with compassion, courage, and a heart that is finally at peace.

Chapter: 15

Love and Forgiving Yourself
How self-compassion leads to better relationships

Being kind to yourself is one of the best ways to strengthen your relationships, but it's often overlooked. Many people live their lives with old mistakes, fears, and scars that they haven't let themselves heal from. They are ready to forgive others, but they are often harsh on themselves, being demanding or judgmental. The reality is simple but powerful: how you treat yourself affects how you treat other people. When you practice self-kindness, you become patient with your problems rather than ashamed. This emotional tenderness automatically extends to the people you love. Self-compassion teaches you that your shortcomings don't make you unlovable; in fact, they make you more human. When you acknowledge your humanity, your relationships become safer, healthier, and more satisfying.

Being kind to yourself may strengthen your relationships by relieving others of the burden of making you feel complete. When you don't treat yourself well, you may expect your partner or loved ones to fill that emotional hole without even realizing it. You may need them to constantly reassure, validate, or confirm you, but these things have to come from inside. But when you are kind to yourself, you start to take care of your own emotional needs. You cease relying on others to resolve situations that only being kind to yourself can solve. Your love is no longer dependent on fear or insecurity, which makes your relationships healthier and more balanced. Instead, it becomes a choice based on your emotional stability.

Being kind to yourself also makes perfectionism less potent, which is a quiet enemy of many relationships. When you're relentless on yourself, you often treat other people badly. You want them to "get everything right" because you desire the same thing from yourself. People will criticize you, impose unattainable standards, and keep their distance emotionally because you need to be perfect. But if you learn to be kind to yourself, you can let go of your mistakes.

Chapter: 15

Another advantage of self-compassion is that it helps you manage your emotions. Because their inner world is unstable, people who aren't kind to themselves often get quite agitated when things go wrong or when they disagree with someone else. Because their inner critic is already harsh and loud, a small object can have a big impact—not because the situation is spectacular. This internal turmoil can be calmed by self-compassion. Your emotions become more balanced when you learn to calm yourself with kindness rather than criticize yourself. Speaking to them comes from a place of safety rather than fear. Emotional control improves relationships by reducing miscommunication, preventing unnecessary confrontations, and encouraging calm communication rather than defensive behavior.

Treating oneself with kindness can also improve one's ability to focus. Regular self-criticism keeps your attention on your issues, errors, and concerns. Being genuinely present for other people is difficult when your mind is filled with this clamor. But as you learn to be kind and patient with yourself, your mind calms down. You don't have to fight with yourself anymore, so you can listen to what your loved ones have to say. You listen without jumping right in and taking over the conversation. You can empathize with them without imposing your worries on them. This attentive, deep presence builds trust and strengthens emotional connection.

Being kind to yourself and forgiving yourself also helps you quit hiding your feelings. Many individuals approach dating cautiously, fearing potential hurt or rejection. They put up emotional walls that keep love away, not because they would rather not connect, but because they are still punishing themselves for earlier hurts. Being kind to yourself can help you break down these obstacles. When you start being kind to yourself, you don't worry about being weak anymore. You let people see you, know you, and love you. This flaw makes it easier to connect on a deeper level. Relationships do well when both individuals feel comfortable enough to be themselves, and self-compassion is one of the keys to unlocking that safety.

Chapter: 15

Being kind to yourself strengthens your relationships because it helps you take responsibility without feeling negative about it. Many individuals assume that being harsh with themselves makes them more responsible, but it often has the opposite effect. When people feel too guilty, they shut down, become defensive, or avoid challenging conversations. But if you're kind to yourself, being responsible will be easier on your emotions. You don't have to feel awful about saying you're incorrect. You may say you're sorry without being ashamed of how much you've grown. You don't have to freak out when you have a problem. This kind of responsibility makes relationships stronger by indicating that you are emotionally mature and by building trust.

Self-compassion also benefits relationships by helping people set healthy boundaries. When you are kind and respectful to yourself, you automatically safeguard your mental health. You reject relationships that cause you to feel terrible about yourself, fail to appreciate you, or deplete your energy. You start saying "no" when you need to. You stop prioritizing your own needs to maintain harmony. These limits come from a place of worth, not fear, so your love is healthier. Being kind to yourself lets you be yourself without risking your emotional well-being. The relationship becomes stronger, more balanced, and more respectful when both parties honor each other's boundaries.

Being kind to yourself might also help you figure out what makes you feel miserable. When you realize why you act the way you do, because of past breakups, wounds from childhood, insecurities, or memories that haven't healed, you confront relationship problems in a different way. You don't get mad or shut down; instead, you take a moment to think it through. You question yourself, "Is this episode genuinely about my partner, or does it pertain to an aspect I still need to address within myself?" Being conscious of your feelings is a great thing for any relationship. It stops unnecessary fights and helps both spouses grow together. When you practice self-compassion, you can take responsibility for your feelings without condemning yourself.

Chapter: 15

One of the best things about being kind to yourself is that it makes love feel lighter, easier, and more enjoyable. When you refrain from consistently belittling yourself, it becomes easier to smile, laugh, and engage in conversation with others. You stop being preoccupied with every minor detail during your conversations and instead begin to enjoy the experience. Being kind to yourself takes the pressure off of love. It allows you to be yourself—unfiltered, honest, and emotionally available. This kind of honesty makes relationships stronger in ways that attempting to be perfect never will. Love is a source of comfort, not a constant challenge to conquer.

Being kind to yourself also makes room for thankfulness. When you are kind to yourself, you are more thankful for the compassion others show you. You can see what they do, how they act, and how they are. You stop believing that you don't deserve love and start being grateful for the affection you do receive. Gratitude can improve relationships by shifting focus from what you lack to what you have. Instead of focusing on their imperfections and yours, it makes you appreciate the person in front of you.

In the end, self-compassion improves relationships because it transforms the most essential relationship you'll ever have: the one with yourself. When your inner environment is a place of kindness instead of judgment, you act differently in love. You converse with each other in a more polite way. You are more forgiving. You trust more. You connect in a way that feels more authentic. You don't need anyone else to make you full anymore; you are already whole and healed when you enter the relationship. Taking care of oneself is not selfish. It's incredibly crucial. This calm and steady love makes all other kinds of love possible. When you learn to love yourself, every relationship you have gets better, stronger, and more important.

Chapter: 15

Love and Forgiving Yourself
Steps to cultivating self-love

To love yourself, you need to learn how to be honest and kind to yourself first. The first thing you need to do is be honest about how you feel. Many individuals live their lives without ever taking the time to contemplate how they truly feel. They don't pay attention to what's going on inside them and instead spend their time working, being with others, or fulfilling their duties. But you have to know yourself to love yourself. You need to take a break and contemplate how you feel. What do I have on me? What do I need? Being emotionally honest may feel awkward at first if you're accustomed to hiding your concerns, but it becomes easier over time. The first step to loving yourself is to know yourself.

The second step to loving yourself is to treat yourself the same way you would treat someone else. People are quick to console friends who mess up, but they are hard on themselves. This emotional double standard goes against self-love. It advises you to treat yourself with kindness, even when you are angry or lacking confidence. Instead of stating, "I shouldn't feel this way," say, "It's acceptable to feel this." I'm trying my best. Don't say you're a failure; instead, tell yourself that you're learning. You may not think much of this change in your inner conversation, yet it impacts how you see yourself. Being compassionate makes you feel protected, which helps you recover and grow.

Taking time to rest is another way to show yourself love. In our culture, people value being busy, so taking a break can seem like a sign of weakness. But it's also a sign of emotional strength. You can't pour from an empty cup. Taking a break, whether it's sleeping, having quiet time, pursuing hobbies, or taking meaningful breaks, can help you replenish your mind, body, and spirit. Resting isn't selfish; it's something you need to do. Self-love tells you when you're mentally fatigued and urges you to rest rather than push yourself too hard. It reminds you that you deserve more than simply tension in your life. One of the most loving things you can do for yourself is to take time to rest.

Chapter: 15

Setting healthy limits is a crucial aspect of learning to appreciate yourself. Setting limits can be challenging for many people because they would rather not hurt others or be considered selfish. But limits aren't walls that keep people out; they're guidelines that protect you from getting hurt emotionally. If you don't set limits, you may overextend yourself, accept tasks that drain you, and let others take more than you can provide. Self-love helps you understand your limits and respect them. This could involve saying no when you're too busy, breaking off connections that don't match with your ideals, or getting away from problematic ones. Setting boundaries is a way to be kind to yourself, to improve your health, and to show respect in your relationships with others.

Another crucial step is to accept your imperfections. Many people don't love themselves until they repair what they think is wrong with themselves. Self-love doesn't come from perfection; it grows as you make mistakes. You need to learn how to cope with the aspects of yourself that are dirty, broken, and challenging to manage. Loving yourself while you grow doesn't imply neglecting your need to grow; it just means loving yourself. Expecting yourself to have flaws will help you feel more accepting, less critical, and less afraid of failing. You let yourself feel things so you can learn, try new things, and grow. Having flaws does not mean you are weak; it simply indicates that you are human.

The next stage in learning to love yourself is to spend time with people who love you. Your environment has a big impact on how you see yourself. You learn to love yourself more when you spend time with people who support and uplift you. On the other hand, relationships where you are criticized, controlled, or emotionally ignored make it harder to love yourself. When you choose helpful connections, it's not about being picky; it's about knowing your worth. Positive relationships can help you remember your strengths, feel better about yourself, and want to take care of your mental and emotional health. You may increase your self-love in settings where you feel comfortable and seen.

Chapter: 15

Another key step in learning to love yourself is to forgive yourself for both enormous and tiny mistakes you make every day. Many people feel negative about things they can't change. They blame themselves for decisions they made when they were less experienced, less healed, or just didn't know better. Forgiving someone lets you move on from past emotional baggage. It helps you move on without feeling bad about what happened. Self-love teaches you to acknowledge, "I made a mistake, but I'm learning," instead of holding on to shame. You don't just forgive someone once; you do it all the time. Every day, you can choose to be kind instead of mean.

You also need to appreciate your progress to love yourself. Many individuals don't give themselves enough credit for what they've done because they're too busy thinking about what they still have to do. But self-love stops showing growth, no matter how tiny. Did you set a limit today? Be glad with that. Did you stop? You should be thrilled about that. Have you ever said something pleasant to yourself? That's a step in the right direction. When you celebrate your triumphs, you feel better about yourself and become more emotionally powerful. It keeps you going, even when the trip seems to be taking a long time. It's crucial to see how far you've come, and loving yourself encourages you to do so rather than downplaying it.

Another key stage is to create habits that help you stay healthy. Routines provide you with structure, which helps you grow emotionally. This could include keeping a journal, meditating, exercising, saying nice things to yourself, going to therapy, or just spending a few quiet minutes every morning. You don't need a sophisticated plan; you just need modest, advantageous habits that remind you to put yourself first. These behaviors help you stay calm when things are rough and make you more dedicated to your emotional wellness. Doing things that are good for your mind and heart shows you care about your health.

Chapter: 15

A significant part of loving yourself is learning to trust yourself. Many people have trouble trusting themselves because they doubt their instincts or feel bad about past mistakes. But you have to rebuild that trust in order to love yourself. You learn to listen to your instincts, honor your feelings, and make decisions that are in line with your beliefs. When you trust yourself, you can learn, grow, and make healthy choices. When you trust yourself, you don't need others to tell you how to feel or act. You are the one who writes your story.

You can also practice being grateful for yourself. Be grateful for your surroundings, but also for who you are and what you bring to life. You could thank yourself for being strong, kind, growing, or willing to keep going. Being thankful helps you feel more confident and less unsure. It helps you remember the good things about yourself that you overlook because you're too busy thinking about what you lack. Complimenting yourself for your positive traits and progress strengthens your belief that you deserve affection, particularly from yourself.

Ultimately, self-love is a journey, not a destination. Some days you'll feel confident and strong, and other days you won't. But self-love is always with you, providing you with strength when things are hard and happiness when they are good. Self-love involves making a promise to be kind, honest, and caring to yourself. When you practice these things consistently, self-love becomes your normal state. Self-love transforms your life, fortifies your emotional resilience, and transforms your interactions with others. The more you love yourself, the more love you can extend to other people.

Chapter: 15

This chapter tells you to look inside yourself and reflect on how you feel about yourself. This is the relationship that most people disregard, but it's the most crucial one for their mental health. You learnt that how you treat yourself affects everything, including your serenity, your confidence, and how you love others, when you looked into the value of self-love and self-forgiveness. This chapter advised you to pay attention to how your inner voice sounds, how much weight your past mistakes have, and how being nice to yourself can help you progress. Think about how this chapter made you feel for a bit. This questionnaire is meant to help you go to the bottom of your heart and find out what needs to be healed, what needs to be cared for, and what needs to be let go of.

Reflection Questions

1. When you think about self-love, what parts of your life or identity do you realize you have neglected or undervalued the most?
2. What past mistakes or emotional burdens have been hardest for you to forgive yourself for, and why do you think they still affect you today?
3. How has your inner voice spoken to you over the years—was it harsh, gentle, demanding, or dismissive? How would you want it to sound moving forward?
4. What did this chapter reveal to you about the difference between holding yourself accountable and punishing yourself emotionally?
5. In what areas of your life are you still seeking external validation instead of affirming yourself internally?
6. How do you think your life would change if you practiced consistent self-forgiveness? Write down the emotional shifts you imagine.
7. What fears come up when you think about loving yourself more fully or releasing shame from your past?
8. If you could speak to your younger self right now, what words of compassion or understanding would you offer them?

Chapter: 15

This chapter also discussed how being kind to yourself can help those around you and offered some good advice on how to love yourself more. That's when real growth starts: when you resolve to do little things for your heart every day. This page asks you to think about how these steps affect your daily life, how you react, your limits, your emotional patterns, and the space you allow yourself to live in. Be honest with yourself and don't judge your responses as you go through these questions. It's not about being perfect; it's about being attentive and having noble intentions.

Reflection Questions

1. Think about your closest relationships—how has a lack of self-compassion in the past affected the way you communicated, reacted, or connected?

2. What emotional needs are you expecting others to meet because you're not meeting them yourself?

3. Which step of cultivating self-love (awareness, boundaries, changing your inner dialogue, rest, vulnerability, or gratitude) resonated the most with you, and why?

4. What is one practical change you can make this week to nurture yourself more intentionally?

5. Were there any emotional habits you realized you need to let go of—perfectionism, negative self-talk, self-neglect, or over-apologizing?

6. What makes it difficult for you to set boundaries, and how do you think honoring your limits could strengthen your relationships?

7. How would practicing self-compassion daily shift your confidence, your reactions, and your sense of peace?

8. Describe the healthiest, most self-loving version of yourself. What steps can you start taking today to move toward that version of you?

Chapter: 16

Love Without Expectations
Learning to love without expecting anything in return

One of the toughest but most freeing sorts of love is learning to love without expecting anything in return. People often love with hidden expectations, such as wanting to be praised, to be faithful, or to be emotionally supported in return. It's normal to want these things, but they can become emotional traps if you feel like you have to do them to gain love. Loving without expectations doesn't mean letting people treat you unfairly or failing to care about what you need. It indicates that your love should come from a genuine place, not from wanting to control someone or to receive anything in return. This chapter makes you consider how much of your love is given freely and how much is based on what you want from others. You become a more serene, balanced, and generous person when you stop expecting things from people you love.

Many of us were taught to show love in a planned way, believing that kindness should always be repaid, effort should always be matched, and compassion should always be rewarded. When this doesn't happen, people get more upset and frustrated. But love without conditions dissolves those emotional links. It tells you to love because that's who you are, not because you want something in return. When you love someone without expecting anything in return, you enjoy giving more than just the ultimate result. It helps you realize that love is pure because of the intention behind it, not the response. When you cease inquiring, "What will I gain from this?" and begin considering, "How can I demonstrate love in a genuine manner?" you no longer require others to affirm your worth. There is no longer a deal for love.

Loving someone without expecting anything in return is something you do inside yourself. You need to learn to be emotionally independent rather than relying on others. You learn to be happy with yourself instead of depending on how someone else acts, how much work they put in, or whether they fulfill your emotional standards. It doesn't mean you put up with unacceptable behavior or one-sided relationships; it just means you don't let unmet expectations change how you feel anymore. Loving freely provides you with the power to stay strong.

221

Chapter: 16

Loving someone without expecting anything in return also lets you see them for who they truly are, not who you think they should be. People can feel pressure from expectations that they don't even know they're under. You might imagine that someone will react in a specific manner, appreciate your work in a certain way, or understand how you feel without you having to say anything. When they don't, you grow more and more angry because you're not following your script. But loving freely rips that script away. It allows individuals to enter at their own pace, showcasing their unique strengths and weaknesses. This doesn't mean reducing your expectations; it means not letting your love for someone else dictate how they act. When you care more about being authentic than doing beneficial things, your interactions are more honest and less tense.

Loving without feeling you deserve it provides you with a lot of emotional freedom. You can connect with someone more deeply when you stop believing that they owe you love, attention, or emotional recompense merely because you offered them those things first. Love becomes less of a business deal and more of a cheerful, joyful thing. You can give without fear, communicate without getting mad, and be pleasant without keeping track. You would rather not feel like you have to be generous. This shift can help a lot with relationship disputes because many of them develop when one person feels unappreciated or that they're the only one. You get rid of the emotional scorecard that converts tiny disappointments into big wounds when your love is no longer related to what other people do.

Being able to love without expecting anything in return also makes you stronger emotionally. When events don't unfold as expected, you no longer crumble. People don't answer messages, acknowledge your attempts, or return your gestures. Instead, you respond clearly and fairly. You recognize that not every action you do needs to be returned in kind and that people love in different ways and to varying degrees. False hopes or assumptions can't injure you, since you are emotionally strong. It helps you handle relationships in a mature, patient, and understanding way.

Chapter: 16

Learning to love without expectations doesn't mean dismissing your sentiments; it means finding ways to meet those needs from within. One reason why expectations build up in relationships is that people often need reassurance, approval, or security from others. When those requirements aren't met, it feels like the disappointment is intended at you, even though it usually isn't meant to hurt you. When you really love yourself, you stop expecting other people to fill emotional wounds that they didn't make. You enter into partnerships with a whole heart, not an empty one. This change makes things a lot less stressful for everyone else and enables your love to flow more freely and honestly.

Another key component of loving someone without expecting anything in return is setting and keeping healthy limits. Many people confuse unconditional love with unconditional acceptance. Loving freely doesn't imply putting up with terrible behavior, taking on someone else's emotional burdens, or staying in a location that hurts you. Boundaries protect your love by making sure no one can use it against you. When you limit your feelings, thoughts, or relationships, you can be sure that the love you give comes from a place of strength, not need. Boundaries help you stay balanced. You can love someone and still have self-respect. What keeps unconditional love going is not giving up on yourself.

The more you accept love without conditions, the better you will be at enjoying the good times and not letting the bad ones get to you. You begin to understand effort for what it is, not what you believed it should be. A little thing becomes a big deal. Just being there for a short time is enough. It doesn't feel like a list of things to accomplish; it feels more like something we both did together. Being appreciative is something you learn when you love without conditions. When you contribute without expecting anything in return, anything you receive feels like a gift rather than something you have to do. Being thankful for someone strengthens the bond between them, brings them closer together, and makes love feel truer for both.

Chapter: 16

Learning to love without expecting anything in return can lead to a sense of ease. You don't spend your days worrying about things, comparing your work, or going over moments when you were let down. You cease monitoring who apologized first, who initiated the last message, or who demonstrated greater concern. Your heart settles down because it doesn't have to keep checking constantly. This calm lets you enjoy your relationships as they are. You may be close to someone without being too clingy, serve others without sacrificing yourself, and embrace love in any way it comes. When you love freely, you feel soft inside, as if your heart is guided by honesty rather than fear or insecurity.

Loving someone without expecting anything in return makes your connections more real. When you contribute without expecting anything in return, people feel more at ease around you. They don't fear that your love is conditional or that your kindness is only for them. Loving someone without expecting anything in return lets them be honest, flawed, and authentic in their interactions. People typically express more when you express love freely, not because they have to, but because they want to. Love that isn't forced spreads. Love that isn't coerced is dependable. And love that isn't counted lasts.

Ultimately, learning to love without expecting anything in return is a transformation of your inner self. It teaches you not to let how people treat you affect how you feel about yourself, to value giving over controlling, and to value being real above emotional exchanges. It isn't easy to love this way; it requires emotional maturity, self-awareness, and a willingness to change old behaviors. But once you learn how, love will be deeper, calmer, and more satisfying than ever. The best part of loving freely is who you become, not what you receive. Someone who loves without expecting anything in return loves completely, honestly, and with courage. That type of love will always be there.

Chapter: 16

Love Without Expectations
The freedom found in unconditional love

You feel really free when you love someone without fear, pressure, or hidden demands. When you love someone unconditionally, you don't ignore your needs or give up who you are. Instead, you let your heart give without asking anything in return. We desire love to make us feel valued, acknowledged, or seen because we need comfort. However, when we cling too tightly to these hopes, we unknowingly impose emotional restraints on ourselves and those we care about. Unconditional love dismantles those walls. It enables you to love without being afraid. You learn to ask, "What will I receive in return?" instead of "Who can I become through this love?" That shift alone makes it possible to love more freely and peacefully.

You don't have to keep track of your sentiments when you love someone unconditionally. When love becomes a bargain, like "I did this for you, so you should do that for me," it loses its purity. You begin to care more about what you get than what you give. But as you learn to let go of the invisible ledger you keep in your relationships, your emotional world grows lighter. You don't feel bad about every attempt that doesn't go your way or every gesture that isn't returned. You no longer consider small things to be failures. When you love someone unconditionally, you don't have to worry about calculating, comparing, or overthinking. It lets you love without having to work at it or take an exam. This helps your heart give freely without concern about running out or being rejected.

This kind of love also helps you get over your doubts. Often, it is fear that leads us to hope. For instance, you might harbor fears of falling behind, not achieving enough success, or losing someone. Love based on fear is weak and seeks to control you. But unconditional love shows you that your value doesn't depend on how others treat you. You don't need to gain approval or cling to affection. You can allow closeness without worrying. You may love with confidence because your love emanates from a solid, stable place inside you. The feeling of safety within you is what provides you with freedom. The less reliance you have on others to feel complete, the greater your capacity to love them.

Chapter: 16

One of the best things about love without conditions is that it relieves you and the people you love of emotional burdens. When you love someone, you let them be their authentic selves without imposing your expectations on them or drawing closer attention to their true connection or desires. People are at ease being themselves when they're with you. They don't have to do anything, please anyone, or achieve impossible emotional demands. They think they can come as they are, with all their shortcomings. Additionally, your heart is free because you are no longer striving to make things happen. You stop stressing about whether love is "balanced" and start paying closer attention to the true connection happening right now. When you can love this way, relationships become partnerships instead of negotiations.

Unconditional love also prevents you from feeling let down by your thoughts. The quickest way to ruin a relationship is to believe that someone should know what you need without you having to express it. Expectations grow without anyone saying anything, and when they aren't met, frustration grows, even if the other person didn't know about the hopes. When you love someone without restrictions, you learn to talk to them instead of expecting them to always do the right thing. You communicate what you need clearly, honestly, and without resentment. You stop the emotional guessing game that often causes problems. Such behavior gives you freedom because communication becomes a bridge rather than a conflict zone. Love becomes easier, safer, and more stable.

Unconditional love is also beneficial because it strengthens your emotional well-being. If you express love freely, you won't break apart every time someone lets you down. You learn to see people for who they are, not who you wish them to be. This doesn't mean you have to tolerate rude people or stay in undesirable places. It means you don't let your love stand in the way of your urge to be in charge. You begin to see others as unique individuals and cease expecting them to satisfy your needs. You may prevent needless suffering and manage relationships more effectively if you have this emotional fortitude. You give, and you love without losing who you are.

Chapter: 16

Additionally, unconditional love breaks the habit of emotionally needing someone else. When you require someone else to like you to feel positive about yourself, your heart becomes unstable. Your emotions fluctuate in response to their actions. But loving someone unconditionally can help you learn how to value yourself. Your love is no longer a means to improve your well-being; it has become a way to express your true self. You cease relying on other people to make you content. This independence inside oneself allows for emotional breathing space. You may love a lot and still be content. You can donate everything you have and still feel full. And you can help other people without putting your own emotional needs on hold.

Loving unconditionally also relieves you of the burden of constantly predicting or controlling the future. Expectations often arise from wanting to know how a relationship will turn out, how someone will react, or how they will love you back. But unconditional love shows you how to be there. Enjoy the present moment without worrying about its outcome. You learn to appreciate the connection without needing certainty. This allows you space to feel things. You learn to let go of your fear and trust the flow of love. You become more conscious, more grounded, and more grateful. Being able to live in the present makes you more secure emotionally and helps you love more profoundly.

Another liberation that comes with unconditional love is letting go of anger. If others don't meet your expectations, it can make you frustrated and bitter, even in previously calm relationships. When you love someone unconditionally, without expecting anything in return, there is no need to monitor or track every action they "should" be taking. You cease being upset and punishing yourself. You cease penalizing individuals for not being perfect. And you begin to pick kindness over criticism. Not letting rage wreck your heart doesn't imply disregarding your sentiments. Love becomes healthier, lighter, and easier to maintain because it no longer has to confront unspoken demands.

Chapter: 16

Unconditional love lets you go when you need to without feeling frustrated, guilty, or emotionally unstable. Many people believe that unconditional love entails unconditional acceptance, but the two are completely unique. If you love someone unconditionally, your love stays pure, even when you choose to stay away from relationships that aren't beneficial to you anymore. You don't keep someone around because you think they will meet your requirements. You don't stay in situations where your emotional safety is at stake. You may say, "I still love you, but I have to choose peace." That's not a cold way to leave; it's brave. It teaches that to love someone unconditionally, you have to love and respect yourself.

Another wonderful thing about unconditional love is that it makes you appreciate even the slightest acts of compassion, love, or connection. When you don't constantly measure your effort or compare what you provide to what you receive, the simple things seem enormous. A simple "thank you," a modest act of kindness, a moment of understanding, or a delicate touch means something since it wasn't asked for; it was offered freely. Being thankful is easier. Being thankful becomes a habit. And partnerships feel more compassionate when there aren't any expectations or emotional conditions that make them feel awful.

Unconditional love lets you be who you truly are. When you stop expecting things, your heart can love freely, boldly, and honestly. You stop loving because you're scared or unsure, and then you resume loving from a place of emotional fullness. You become more stable, patient, and understanding. You learn that love is strongest when it comes and most beautiful when it is given without expecting anything in return. It's not dumb or weak to love someone unconditionally; it's daring and grown-up. This kind of love frees your heart, lifts your spirit, and helps you sense relationships in their purest form.

Chapter: 16

Love Without Expectations
How to let go of unrealistic expectations

To stop having unreasonable expectations, we first need to realize how much they shape how we love, behave, and understand how other people act. Many people have secret ideas about how their friends, family, or partners should treat, love, talk to, or prioritize them. These expectations often stem from anxieties about yourself, past disappointments, or ideals shaped by culture and the media. However, when real-life events don't align with your expectations, it exacerbates your upset and agitation. The first step to eliminating unrealistic expectations is to realize they are just made-up rules that don't reveal the full person. When you realize the unspoken rules, you've been following, you make space for new, healthier ways to interact.

It's also vital to note that unmet demands that you don't know how to speak or address in yourself can make you anticipate too much. For example, expecting someone to constantly know how you feel without you ever saying it is a sure way to get let down. Another example is expecting someone to love you or to behave the same way you do. When you expect other people to think, feel, or act exactly like you do, you unwittingly establish a love dynamic built on pressure instead of freedom. The first step to learning how to let go is to be responsible for stating your demands and giving people the freedom to be themselves. Instead of having inflated expectations, this adjustment makes talks more authentic.

Letting go also means detaching your identity from desired outcomes. If you believe that how someone else responds to you decides your worth or value, you may be expecting too much. When someone doesn't do what you want, you could feel that they disregard or overlook you. But if you let go of expectations, you may accept that your worth doesn't depend on how someone else acts; it rests on who you are, not how they act. Once you learn to value yourself, you won't need other people to constantly comfort you, match you, or act precisely. This inner change allows for emotional freedom and a more genuine, healthy love.

Chapter: 16

Another key step in letting go of unreasonable expectations is learning to recognize people as individuals with their own past, emotional language, and limitations. You expect others to see things as you do, but they don't. People express love, address issues, communicate their wants, and convey gratitude in many ways. When you accept these variances, you stop trying to make others fit into emotional molds they were never meant to fit into. When you let people be themselves instead of trying to make them the best version of themselves, relationships are more natural, calm, and honest. You realize that effort is more important than getting things right.

Letting go also implies not needing things to be the same all the time. When you have unreasonable expectations, you believe that things should always happen a certain way. For instance, you might think that someone should always stay calm, put their needs first, or know what to say. But life is full of surprises, and people aren't perfect. When you have very high standards, you become emotionally weak; every change feels like being let down or betrayed. You allow relationships to evolve when you realize that other people will have terrible days, misunderstandings, and periods of weakness. Being able to change makes you emotionally powerful. You remain calm when your expectations aren't met. Instead, you respond with understanding and inquiry, which pull people together rather than drive them apart.

Letting go and shifting from assumptions to open communication is a powerful way to achieve this. You have false hopes because you want things but don't ask for them. But people can't know what you're thinking. When you learn to communicate what you need directly, without accusing, hinting, or expecting perfection, it becomes easier for people to understand you. Talking to each other turns unrealistic hopes into a shared understanding of how you feel. Instead of condemning the other person for not knowing what you need, it lets them see within you. This adjustment eliminates misunderstandings, eases stress, and increases mutual trust. Unrealistic expectations are transformed into real, potential connections through effective communication.

Chapter: 16

You also need to think about yourself to get rid of unrealistic hopes. You seek the same things from other people that you want from yourself most of the time. You may expect to always have someone there for you emotionally, since you struggle to do it yourself. You could expect other people to be stable because you are scared of instability. Alternatively, you may seek continual praise due to feelings of inadequacy. Thinking about the emotional causes behind your expectations helps you identify the underlying scars that require attention. This enables you to modify your expectations in a manner that fosters love and well-being for yourself. Self-reflection is not about blaming yourself; it's about learning more about who you are.

Another strong technique is to be aware of the present moment. Unrealistic expectations are usually regarding the future, including what someone "should" say or do next and how things "should" go. You analyze relationships based on reality, not on how you think they should be. You learn to like actual gestures instead of hoping for flawless ones. It's easier to let go of expectations when you focus on others' actions rather than what you want them to do. When you're present, you can see real effort and love that you might miss if you're distracted.

You need to avoid issuing emotional ultimatums if you want to let go even more. People often have unreasonable expectations when they don't say anything, like "If they love me, they'll do this" or "If they care, they'll respond exactly how I want." These emotional tests are detrimental because they terrify people, push them away, and make love into a show. Taking away these internal conditions helps love blossom on its own. Stop testing others or connecting love to certain actions, and you'll make room for honesty. Instead of rejecting love because it doesn't fit your mental script, you learn to accept it as it is. This makes things a lot easier for you and the people you care about.

Chapter: 16

Learning how to be emotionally independent is one of the best ways to quit expecting too much from others. When you rely on others to meet all your emotional needs, validation, comfort, and security, your expectations rise too high, and your relationships suffer. But when you learn to meet many of those demands alone, you ease your relationships. Being emotionally independent means you can love others instead of needing their affection. You become more balanced, less needy, and less reactive. It's about being strong inside so you can share in relationships rather than rely on each other.

Letting go means accepting people as they are, even if they're different from you. Acceptance doesn't imply lowering your standards or putting up with unacceptable behavior; it means facing the facts instead of holding on to dreams. It means appreciating someone for who they are, not who you believe they could be if they changed. Acceptance means letting go of wrath and resentment. It tells you to make friends based on what you know is true, not what you assume will happen. Your love is calmer, your feelings are steadier, and your communication is more sincere when you accept people.

Letting go of unreasonable expectations is an indication that you are growing emotionally. It takes effort, focus, and courage, but the payoff is worth it. When you stop attempting to control what happens, you start to feel love in its truest form. You feel better now that you don't have to endure disappointment. You feel freer now that you don't expect everything to be flawless. You let relationships bloom on their own, without any worries or stress. And you learn that love becomes better, deeper, and more fulfilling when you stop expecting too much from it. This is the heart of unconditional love, which comes from freedom, understanding, and truth, not from demands.

Chapter: 16

Chapter 16 urges you to reflect on how your expectations affect your relationships, often in ways you don't even notice. You need to stop loving someone conditionally and start loving them for who they are. This chapter made you contemplate the "scripts" in your heart that teach you what love should seem like, how people should act, and how relationships should go. As you read about the freedom that unconditional love brings, you should let go of unrealistic expectations and find the calm that comes with it. Think about the thoughts that made you feel something for a while. These questions can help you see how you love and move toward a healthier, more stable manner of loving.

Reflection Questions

1. What expectations from your past relationships—romantic, family, or friendships—did you recognize as unrealistic after reading this chapter?

2. In what ways have your unspoken expectations created stress or disappointment in your relationships?

3. How do you typically react when someone doesn't meet an expectation you never communicated? Does this chapter help you see that reaction differently?

4. What does "loving without expecting anything in return" mean to you personally, and how does it differ from how you usually show love?

5. When have you loved someone freely, without keeping score or waiting for a specific reaction? How did it feel compared to conditional love?

6. Which fears arise when you think about loving without expectations—fear of being taken for granted, fear of being hurt, fear of giving too much?

7. After reading this chapter, what do you now understand about the difference between unconditional love and emotional self-neglect?

8. What is one expectation you know you need to release in order to experience more emotional freedom?

Chapter: 16

This chapter also discusses how to let go of unreasonable expectations and how unconditional love may emotionally release you. Letting go doesn't mean reducing your standards or putting up with bad behavior. It means liberating your heart from expectations, subtle demands, and the need to control what happens. You were told to think about how fear, insecurity, or unvoiced wants can make you expect things. This page urges you to reflect on the specific places where you can grow, be more open with others, and receive love in a balanced, emotion-independent way. Be honest and open when you answer these questions. They are meant to help you understand what love without expectations looks like in your life.

Reflection Questions

1. Which part of the chapter resonated most with you: loving freely, the freedom that unconditional love creates, or letting go of unrealistic expectations? Why?

2. What expectations do you notice yourself placing on others that may come from your own insecurities or unexpressed emotional needs?

3. How would your relationships feel different if you stopped keeping emotional score or comparing effort?

4. What does emotional freedom mean to you, and how does unconditional love help you move toward that freedom?

5. Which unrealistic expectation feels the hardest for you to release, and what belief is keeping it in place?

6. How could better communication help you avoid building invisible expectations that others don't know about?

7. What steps can you take this week to practice loving openly without trying to control how others love you back?

8. Imagine a relationship where you truly let go of expectations—how would you show up differently, and how might that change the dynamic?

Chapter: 17

Love in Parenthood
The transformative power of parental love

Parental love is one of the strongest factors that can transform a person's life. Because the world is no longer just about you, it's about someone who needs you for everything. This phenomenon changes how you think, feel, and make decisions. Before you have kids, love is frequently built on giving and getting, being emotionally compatible, and having the same aspirations. But when a child comes into your life, love shifts from something you feel to something you provide, defend, and care for without even thinking about it. You learn about emotional levels you didn't know were there. You can't fully prepare for this transition; it happens when you realize your heart is no longer in your body but in the small hands of someone who needs you totally.

One of the best things about being a parent is how it changes the way you see your life. You keep going even when things are challenging, including when you're weary, anxious, or out of patience. That's because your love is bigger than any obstacle. Being a parent can be challenging but also rewarding, as it helps you forget your troubles and focus on caring for someone else. You start to think more about the decisions you make, the habits you develop, and the role model you are. Love is your compass. It tells you how to act, how to talk, and how to show up. This transformation will change your life because it teaches you a greater kind of responsibility that comes from love instead of duty.

Every moment, regardless of your activity level, is invaluable because you are witnessing someone's growth firsthand. Days that seem lengthy evolve into years that go by quickly. You start to understand how every milestone, hardship, and tiny victory is a part of the story you're helping your child write. This information impacts how you approach being patient, being there, and building connections. As a parent, you learn that love grows in the simple things, like late-night feedings, tiny hands reaching for yours, odd talks, and blunders that teach you lessons. These little things that happen every day affect both you and your child. You become more conscious of your sentiments, more thoughtful, and more purposeful when you know that your love is making a difference in someone's life right now.

Chapter: 17

The love that grows between you and your child is one of the most significant changes of parenthood. You love your child for who they are, not what they do. This love that doesn't ask for anything in return makes your heart broader and more open to understanding and compassion than you ever believed it could be. It teaches you to forgive fast, to softly push, and to kindly correct. You teach your youngster that errors are chances, not failures, so they won't be frightened to make them. This form of love transforms you by instructing you to be kind rather than resentful and to exercise patience rather than anger. When you give love without expecting anything in return, you start to comprehend how powerful it can be.

Parental love also makes you stronger emotionally. Being a parent tests your patience, strength, and emotional strength. But even on your darkest days, something inside you rises. This thing is stronger than your exhaustion, shields you, and is determined. You keep going because love makes you keep going. You can use this strength in other sectors of your life as well. You become more patient with yourself, more understanding of others, and more stable when things become challenging. As a parent, you learn how to be flexible without losing your mind. It shows you how to manage fear, keep calm, and retain hope even when circumstances seem too difficult. You don't teach your child to be strong by making things easy for them. You teach them to be strong by showing them deep and unwavering love.

When you become a parent, your ideas about sacrifice alter. You learn that giving up sleep, comfort, personal space, or convenience is no longer a hardship; it's an act of love. You learn to put someone else's needs before your own without feeling angry since your motives for doing so have changed. You stop worrying about what you receive and start worrying about what you offer. You don't keep count of or hate the things you give up; they just become a natural method to demonstrate you care. You become more compassionate, generous, and unselfish when you consider sacrifice in this new perspective. It makes you stronger emotionally and shows you that real love is often conveyed through modest, ordinary gestures of care that no one else may ever witness.

Chapter: 17

Love from your parents can also help you repair portions of yourself that you didn't know were wounded. When you look at your child, you often think of things from your childhood, including how curious, innocent, and needy they are. Some of those recollections make me cheerful, while others make me sad. But having a parent helps you shift how you perceive things. You can show your child love, patience, or understanding that you might not have received from your parents, and by doing this, you become better. Having a child provides you with a second chance to feel love in a deeper, more meaningful way that affects both your heart and your child's. This healing is deep, peaceful, and will change your life.

As a parent, your empathy increases. Having a child changes how you see the world. You are conscious of people's intrinsic frailty, their intense need for affection, their susceptibility to injury, and their desire for approval. You start to see that every child and adult was once a baby in need of love, care, and safety. Knowing the past makes you more compassionate toward everyone. You don't pass judgment as much, and you pay closer attention. You know that everyone has invisible issues. Being a parent reminds you that everyone wants to feel loved, accepted, and as if they belong, and it also makes you feel special.

Being a parent also alters your perspective on fear. Before you became a parent, fear may have disrupted your plans or made you anxious. However, fear becomes more severe when you love a child because you realize you have something important to protect. The greatest thing about love, however, is that it teaches you to face fear with courage instead of fear. When necessary, you become more cautious, but when it's important, you become bolder. You gain self-defense skills while maintaining your trust and respect for others. This change brings about a new sort of courage, one that stems from love rather than pride. The ultimate result is a fearlessness that empowers you to raise a child with confidence and stability.

Chapter: 17

Your level of happiness may be greatly impacted by parental love. Before having children, you might have found fulfillment in relationships, achievements, or other aspects of your life. But having a child makes happiness easy, pure, and essential. It is joyful to hear them laugh, see their grins, watch their first steps, or listen to their stories. Being a parent teaches you to discover joy in the mundane, to enjoy quiet times, and to value the small things. Now that the incident has occurred, your perspective on life has changed. You begin to appreciate the moments rather than rushing through them. Instead of constantly focusing on the future, you learn to live in the present. Being a mother teaches you that happiness comes from being present, not from being flawless.

Furthermore, having kids impacts what you leave behind. You start to realize that the love you offer your child now will affect their future, including how they love others and how they see themselves. They hear what you say in their brains. They feel better about themselves when you help them. Your patience helps them keep their emotions in check. You want to live deliberately, be kind, and be strong while yet being modest, since you know this. You start to nurture seeds of love, strength, curiosity, and bravery in your child's heart. These seeds will live on in the individual you helped grow. They are a gift that will last forever.

The most essential thing about parental love is that it alters who you are. You become more patient, more kind, more observant, and stronger emotionally than you ever believed you could be. It expands your heart in ways you never thought imaginable, teaches you things you couldn't learn anywhere else, and provides your life a depth of purpose that can't be measured. It takes more than just raising a child to be a parent. It also implies growing into a stronger, more intelligent, kind, and better person. Parenting transforms the giver and the recipient, and the effects last a lifetime.

Chapter: 17

Love in Parenthood
How parents demonstrate love that never fails

Parental love is a timeless expression of love. Parents demonstrate this kind of love not through large gestures, but by the little things they do every day to make their child's life better. A parent gets up early for school, stays up late with a sick child, and worries about topics they never talk about. They keep giving even when they feel like they don't have any energy. These things illustrate that love is more than simply feelings; it is dedication, strength, and selfless devotion all the time. Parents love their kids by being there for them, keeping them safe, giving them advice, and sacrificing everything to protect and support them. They act without thinking, expecting that their child will grow, thrive, and know that they are truly loved, not that they will be flawless in return.

Being constant is one of the best ways parents can express their love. Children may not always understand rules, limitations, or discipline, but your unwavering love for them is demonstrated by your consistency. A parent demonstrates to their child that love is not just for the good moments; it shows up every day, no matter how worn out or anxious they are. Rather, children learn from constant love that trust is the most important element of healthy partnerships. Children feel comfortable and secure when they know that their parents will always be there for them. Such behavior includes bad choices, mistakes, and emotional outbursts. A subtle message of consistency is "I'm here for you, even if you don't accomplish it right." The foundation for a child's lifetime emotional stability, trust, and sense of self is that message.

Parents' patience is another way they show their unwavering love. Parenting isn't always simple, and children frequently test boundaries, push boundaries, or engage in behaviors that make life more difficult. Love enables a parent to see past the frustration and the bigger picture, which is why they remain patient—not because everything is simple. "I know you're still learning," together with patience, demonstrates your concern. When a child is patiently cherished, they feel valued rather than condemned. Children learn to be patient with others as adults through their parents' love.

239

Chapter: 17

Parents show their love by keeping their kids safe in every way, including physically and mentally. A parent creates a safe space for their child to express their concerns, questions, and dreams without fear of ridicule. They listen to their child when they are upset, comfort them when they are terrified, and cheer them on when life seems too big or too challenging. This kind of love tells youngsters that they are worth fighting for and caring for. It also makes kids stronger, since knowing that someone is on their side provides them the strength to confront life's adversities. One of the most basic ways parents show love is by keeping their kids safe. They do these acts because they want to protect children from physical and emotional injury that could influence how they see themselves.

Another way parents often express their love is by giving up something. Parents give up sleep, spare time, money, comfort, and even their dreams to make things better for their kids. People don't always talk about these sacrifices, yet they are tremendous evidence of love. A parent may work multiple jobs, forgo meals to feed their children, or postpone personal objectives to be present during significant moments in their child's life. Parents who put their kids' needs first show their love by sacrificing. Being a live example of selflessness reminds kids what it really means to act from the heart.

Parents also display their love by teaching and helping their kids. Being pleasant isn't the only thing that love is. Love is also about correcting, directing, and giving advice. A parent teaches a child how to apologize, make beneficial decisions, stand up for themselves, and be kind to others. These lessons can be challenging, especially when they involve discipline, but they stem from a desire to help the child grow into a strong, capable, and grounded adult. When a parent tenderly guides their child, they are crafting a future built on character instead of ease. This counsel sticks with the youngster for the rest of their life and changes how they love, work, cope with issues, and make friends.

Chapter: 17

Forgiveness is another constant feature of parental love. Kids make mistakes. Children who are emotionally immature do not listen to, dispute with, defy, or purposefully harm their parents. But a parent's heart is quick to forgive, since love overlooks the mistake and focuses on improvement. This kind of forgiveness is a powerful way to show kids that they can make mistakes and still be loved. It shows children that love perseveres in the face of adversity. When a child receives forgiveness, they develop the ability to forgive others and themselves. A parent's ability to forgive their children shows that their love is resilient despite hardship. Instead, it is strengthened by compassion and understanding.

Another meaningful way that parents show love is by being there. Kids may not remember every toy, gift, or amazing time, but they will never forget being there. Being there for school activities, having deep conversations, spending time at the dinner table, or just sharing little moments throughout the day might help you feel emotionally safe. Being there for a youngster conveys, "You matter to me." Your life is crucial. Even parents who are incredibly busy make time for their kids. These small but crucial acts show that you care about a child and make them feel like they matter. Being present and available for your kids is one of the best ways to show you love them.

This behavior gives them a sense of belonging and lets them show their love for their children by believing in them, even when the kids can't see their greatness. A parent guides their child through their insecurities, finds strengths in them that the youngster hasn't yet noticed, and celebrates every little step forward. This idea makes a child feel positive about themself. When kids see that someone else has done well, they start to think they can too. Having faith in your parents is a strong incentive. It makes you feel positive about yourself, builds your confidence, and helps you overcome challenges. Even when the world doesn't believe in them, a child draws strength from their parents' unshakable faith. Such trust is one of the best things a parent can do for their kid.

Chapter: 17

Parents who persevere through difficult times also demonstrate unwavering love. You have to endure stress, anxiety, disappointment, and unavoidable uncertainty as a parent. However, a parent loves their child no matter what, even if they don't sleep, act like a teenager, get sick, struggle financially, or face family problems. Unfailing love endures; it is not perfect. By continuing to love their children during difficult times, parents demonstrate their tenacity. They continue to make an effort, show up, and express concern. A child who possesses this emotional power learns what true love is and how to maintain faithfulness in relationships as they grow older.

Another significant sign that a parent loves you is their willingness to let you leave when the time is right. Parents spend years protecting, guiding, and caring for their kids, but part of loving them unconditionally is knowing when to let them go. Letting a youngster make their own decisions, cope with the repercussions, and design their own destiny demands trust and bravery. This kind of love doesn't imply telling someone what to do; it means giving them authority. It indicates that a parent doesn't want to keep their child close forever; they want to help them learn to be independent. Letting go is often the hardest way to show love, but it is also one of the most lasting since it indicates that you value the child's freedom, growth, and individuality.

Ultimately, parents provide their children with unwavering love by being kind, resilient, and consistently present. This love shows kids how to love themselves, be brave and compassionate, and make friends. Parental love is a lifelong anchor that shapes a child's identity and worldview. This love doesn't fade away; it grows stronger as you grow older. Being there for your child, making sacrifices, being patient, protecting them, forgiving them, or offering them guidance are all ways that parental love leaves a mark that lasts forever. This is the kind of love that lasts forever and illustrates that real Love Never Fails.

Chapter: 17

Love in Parenthood
Lessons on love learned from raising children

You can only learn these things about love by being a parent. You might not expect it, but being a parent can help you grow in ways you didn't expect, like being more patient, caring, and emotionally strong. You learn that love is a daily activity that you depend on, not just a feeling. Children remind us that love is not about grand gestures; it is expressed through small acts that demonstrate care, such as being present for them and choosing to spend time with them even during difficult moments. They convey that love is not always orderly, predictable, or perfect, yet it remains profoundly beautiful. Kids demonstrate a kind of love that is real, basic, and pure because they are innocent and weak. They bring you back to the essence of human connection and serve as a constant reminder of what truly matters.

Kids teach you how to love with patience right away. Their constant learning, asking questions, making mistakes, and mood swings reveal your limits, prompting you to pause and breathe. Kids move at their own speed, which can be too quick or too slow. You learn soon that you can't rush love. When you're patient, kids can feel loved, and they trust you back. You also learn to allow yourself more time. As a parent, you learn about your weaknesses, what makes you angry, and what makes you sad. It does not induce negative feelings about oneself; rather, it encourages greater humanity and compassion toward oneself. You also realize that you are still growing and that love requires giving yourself time to figure things out. These lessons also change how you show love to others, because patience is a natural part of growing up.

Children also teach you how vital it is to be there. Before having kids, it's easy to become engrossed in work, responsibilities, and personal aspirations. However, having children brings you back to the present moment. They expect you to observe them, share in their laughter, and offer them your focused attention. They don't care when you're free; they simply want you to be there. Kids remind you that just being there is often enough and that the memories you form in these little moments are priceless.

Chapter: 17

Children also teach us a lot about love by showing us how vital it is to love people no matter what. They don't know who you should be when they are born. They don't care about your past mistakes or successes. All they want is to be secure, loved, and understood. Kids teach you that love isn't about what you do but about where you belong. You start to understand what it means to love someone without expecting anything in return. As time goes on, you learn to love yourself. When you have a child, you come to understand the profound warmth of being loved simply for who you are. This lesson alters how you perceive love in all of your relationships. It teaches you that being kind is better than judging. Kids also show you how crucial it is to let go of things. They forgive quickly after a disagreement, a misunderstanding, or a moment of fury. They don't become angry or keep grudges as grown-ups do. You can see that letting go of anger makes your relationships stronger when someone can forgive you.

Forgiving someone shows strength, trust, and closeness. Being a parent also teaches you how to say sorry when you mess up. You learn to express your heartfelt apologies, understanding that acknowledging your mistakes does not diminish your strength but rather strengthens your relationship. You realize that love needs forgiveness to last, which makes you a better friend, partner, and person. One of the most surprising things kids can teach you is how to be joyful again.

As adults, we sometimes cease being impressed by things because life grows monotonous or challenging. But kids bring you back to a world of pleasure, wonder, and make-believe. They tell you to enjoy the little things, have fun, and try new things. You can see how love grows when you're pleased. Kids show you that happiness isn't only for kids; it's vital for everyone. They commemorate small victories, build forts, dance in the living room, and make amusing faces. This happiness you've found again makes you stronger emotionally because it gives you something real and lovely to grasp on to when times are hard.

Chapter: 17

Being a parent also teaches you humility. As a parent, you must accept that you often do not know everything. Kids ask many questions, test your limitations in ways you never thought of, and provide you with experiences you never could have imagined. They cause you to question your perceived knowledge and reveal your vulnerabilities. This kind of humility doesn't make you weaker; it makes your love stronger. You recognize that love does not need to be flawless or constantly in control. Love, on the other hand, wants people to be honest, open, and willing to grow. When you are humble, you are more open-minded, flexible, and eager to adjust. You can use this lesson in other relationships, too. It teaches you to be more compassionate, listen more thoroughly, and speak softly.

Additionally, children teach you how to be tough. They have a natural desire to embrace life, take risks without fear, and bounce back swiftly from obstacles. This strength in love serves as a reminder that love is resilient and can endure adversity while becoming stronger. Being a parent teaches you to control your emotions, even when you're feeling exhausted, nervous, or perplexed. Because others rely on you, you gain the fortitude to persevere, remain present, and stay dedicated. As you move through life, this strength provides you with greater self-assurance and emotional depth. It also emphasizes that overcoming setbacks is a key component of becoming strong in love.

Children teach us that when it comes to expressing affection, actions carry more weight than words. Children see how you behave, manage stress, talk, and take care of yourself. You soon discover that making promises is not as effective as keeping your word when it comes to showing affection. To show love, you must be understanding, tolerant, truthful, and consistent in your behavior. You will become a better person, friend, partner, and parent as a result of this knowledge. Kids teach you that choosing to love is a daily decision.

Chapter: 17

You learn that love entails making sacrifices when you have kids, but these sacrifices don't always feel like much work. Instead, they make things feel more connected and important. You find out that real love frequently means putting someone else's needs ahead of your own, even if it means giving up sleep, changing your lifestyle, or changing your priorities. These sacrifices make your relationship stronger and show you what it really means to be selfless. You begin to realize that love, which sacrifices something for another person, does not diminish you; it enhances your character. This lesson shows you that love isn't always simple, but it's always worth it. This will help you manage adult relationships more maturely.

Children also teach you how crucial it is to have boundaries in love. It's natural to assume you should give someone everything when you love them. But being a mom teaches you that part of love is setting limitations for your kids. Kids feel comfortable when you set limits for them. It also teaches children how to be responsible, respectful, and emotionally stable. Boundaries also show you how to look after your own mental health. You discover that love is stronger when both people can be themselves, grow, and rest. These teachings make you think differently about the limits in all of your interactions. They teach you that love needs rules, respect, and clear communication to be healthy.

In the end, being a parent teaches you that love is something you have to work diligently for. The things you teach your kids today will shape who they become as adults. Your love shows them their worth, your trust, and their identity. Parenting is like a mirror that reflects your growth and your kids'. You discover that love isn't a place to go; it's a lifelong journey of growth, healing, and change. The things you learn from being a parent impact your heart in ways that affect all of your relationships. And that is the remarkable quality of parental love: it transforms both the parent and the child.

Chapter: 17

Parental love, one of the most powerful and transforming types of love, was introduced in this chapter. This chapter challenges you to consider how having a child may affect your feelings, morals, and even your conception of love. It makes no difference if you are keen to learn more about love, are a parent, or hope to become one. You examined how parental love enhances your sense of purpose, helps you manage your emotions, increases your patience, and increases your awareness of what matters most. We aim to inspire you to pause and contemplate how this chapter has transformed or enhanced your understanding. Take your time, take a deep breath, and provide an honest response as you consider how parental love changes both the giver and the recipient.

Reflection Questions

1. Which part of the chapter about the transformative power of parental love resonated most deeply with you, and why?

2. How do you think parental love can change a person's priorities, habits, or emotional patterns?

3. What examples from your own life, whether from parents, guardians, or people who raised you, remind you of the sacrifices and commitment shown by parental love?

4. What does "love that never fails" look like in the context of parenthood, and how did this chapter reshape your understanding of that phrase?

5. How do consistency and emotional presence influence a child's sense of safety and trust?

6. In what ways do you think parental love teaches resilience? Write about a moment from your life when a parent or caregiver's support helped you through something difficult.

7. This chapter highlighted that parental love often appears in small, quiet actions. What small acts of love do you believe shape a child's life the most?

8. How does understanding parental love help you see other forms of love, romantic, family, and friendships, in a different or deeper way?

Chapter: 17

This chapter also discussed real-life instances of love that show how being a parent can teach you so much: patience, making sacrifices, offering guidance, forgiveness, and being there. It taught you that becoming a parent can reveal things about yourself you didn't realize you had. It teaches you to be modest, to keep your emotions in balance, and to convey love through your actions. This last page is meant to help you remember what you've learned about loving others without expecting anything in return, about always being there for them, and about evolving as a parent through the good and the terrible times. These questions will help you recall the wisdom, healing, and clarity this chapter instilled in you.

Reflection Questions

1. What lessons about love did you find most meaningful when reflecting on how parents demonstrate love that never fails?

2. How did this chapter challenge any assumptions or expectations you previously held about parenting or parental love?

3. What did you learn about forgiveness from the way parents forgive children quickly and wholeheartedly?

4. How do you believe raising children teaches humility and emotional maturity?

5. What sacrifices mentioned in the chapter stood out to you, and how do they demonstrate the depth of parental love?

6. Think about the lesson on presence: How can being emotionally available—not just physically present—transform a parent-child relationship?

7. How do you think children teach adults to rediscover joy, wonder, and appreciation for small moments?

8. Looking at all three parts of this chapter, what is one principle you want to carry into your own relationships or future parenting journey?

Chapter: 18

Love in Aging Relationships
How love evolves over time in long-term relationships

When people first fall in love, they rarely consider how love will change over time. In the beginning, love is enjoyable, unexpected, and full of things to learn. But love grows bigger, deeper, and more complicated as time goes on. Long-lasting relationships show that love is more than simply a sensation; it's a bond that grows and changes over time as you share experiences, hardships, and achievements. People who stay together for a long period discover that love is never the same. It grows bigger and smaller, changing with each season of existence. This versatility is what makes love linger so long. It's not about having ideal moments; it's about being willing to pick each other over and over again through all the changes, challenges, and chapters.

Love is less about always being excited and more about being solid, having a buddy, and feeling comfortable emotionally as couples grow older. The thrill of a fresh relationship fades into something calmer but more profound, a love that seems like home. Couples begin to value stability more than passion and connection over flawlessness. They make a language of love out of the experiences they share, the inside jokes they have, the routines they know well, and the things they don't say. This emotional intimacy grows stronger over time, making you feel protected in a way only a long-term relationship can. You realize that you can't rush this kind of relationship; it takes years of choosing to be patient, forgiving, honest, and committed. The quiet certainty that your partner still loves you and sees you is where the beauty of love, cultivated over time, truly shines.

As relationships grow older, one of the most significant adjustments is how love deals with the ups and downs of life. Long-term spouses go through sickness, money challenges, job changes, family issues, personal growth, and surprises together. These things make love stronger. You learn to rely on each other more and discover strength in your connection. You discover that love doesn't fade when things turn worse; rather, it grows stronger. Love that lasts teaches you that being truly committed doesn't mean avoiding storms; it means going through them together.

Chapter: 18

Love also changes into a deeper type of acceptance over time. When people first start dating, they often strive to present their best selves. But as time goes on, people stop pretending and start being honest, which is what brings them together. Long-term couples know each other's strengths and weaknesses, as well as their flaws. They learn to love each other completely, even the challenging parts. Both couples feel emotionally safe because they know they don't have to be flawless. Love that grows older reveals that acceptance isn't automatic; you have to choose to embrace your spouse as a person. It is appreciating the individual they are in the present moment and supporting their growth toward becoming the person they aspire to be.

Love changes over time in other ways, too. In long-term partnerships, both people evolve, sometimes in subtle ways and sometimes in enormous ways. People and goals evolve, and the way we see things grows deeper. For love to last, both people need to be willing to evolve and grow together instead of apart. People who care about their relationship recognize that progress isn't a threat; it's a chance to grow closer. They support each other in attaining their goals and allow each other room to flourish. Such behavior keeps the partnership from becoming stale. It can be challenging to grow, but it can also provide you with a fresh start. Couples who are willing to change keep their love alive by getting to know each other better over and over again. In this sense, love that grows old becomes a lifelong voyage of learning, curiosity, and change.

As time goes on, love likewise becomes softer and more caring. People learn that life is fragile as they grow older. They start to notice the tiny things that they might not have noticed previously, such as calm mornings, breakfasts together, short talks, or light touches. Love is less about grandiose gestures and more about little acts that demonstrate you care in long-term relationships. You begin to realize that the small things in life are what really bond people. This transformation makes you more grateful and brings you closer together emotionally. Many couples who have been together for a long time say they feel more connected during these quiet times than when they started dating. It is a love that originates from presence, gratitude, and genuine affection for someone.

Chapter: 18

Love also becomes quite stable over time. In long-term partnerships, couples provide each other with an anchor, a consistent presence in a world that is continually changing. It's not only the regularity that makes things stable; it's the profound trust that comes from living together for a long time. It's challenging to locate someone who has always been there for you when things are unclear. As we become older and our goals alter, this steadiness becomes even more crucial. Love turns into friendship, a partnership, and helping each other out. You come to realize that real love isn't about avoiding troubles; it's about having someone you can trust to help you cope with them.

Long-term relationships reveal how love evolves over time and across distance. The excitement of a new romance may wane, but love grows more meaningful and intentional. Touch makes you feel better. Words of support become increasingly important. Being open becomes easier. You learn to love each other through the good and difficult times that come with getting older, being sick, and having feelings. Couples who stay together grow closer not just because they are physically attracted to each other, but also because they feel close to, respected by, and connected to one another. This stage of love shows that closeness evolves with age. It also becomes easier to communicate with one another after having been together for an extended period.

When partners have been together for a long time, they get into a rhythm that helps them understand each other without having to explain everything. Couples learn how to talk to each other about their needs, feelings, and what makes them mad. They learn to settle arguments more quickly and to talk to each other with understanding rather than pride. Even when problems still come up, love that has grown over time offers you the wisdom to manage them with patience instead of acting on instinct. This emotional maturity keeps the partnership safe and makes love feel more stable and tranquil. It's not so much about being right as about staying in contact when you talk to someone.

Chapter: 18

One of the beautiful things about love is how couples come to appreciate each other's company over time. As time goes on, you start to realize how crucial it is to have friends. You value having someone who understands you well more and more as you spend time together. You love the person who remembers your past, knows who you are, and loves you no matter what. This admiration deepens as you grow older, making even the little things extraordinary. What counts is not so much what you do as it is who you do it with. A relationship that gets stronger over time is one of the most important emotional ties a person may have.

Long-lasting relationships demonstrate the importance of leaving a legacy. Long-term couples often contemplate how their relationship has affected their kids, families, and communities. They witness how their love sets an example for others, changes family customs, and teaches them to forgive and be loyal. This knowledge makes you even more thankful and strengthens your friendship. Couples know that their love has produced something bigger than just the two of them. It becomes a story that people will remember, a foundation for future generations, and evidence that love can endure.

Long-term relationships teach you that love is a choice and a journey. It requires significant effort, patience, giving up things, and starting over again and again. But for those who are open to its transformations, love is one of the nicest things in life. It goes from excitement to devotion, from desire to cooperation, and from romance to a friendship that lasts a lifetime. Love that lasts reveals that love doesn't fade; it grows stronger, deeper, and more real. It reminds me that the best love stories aren't in the first chapter; they're in the ones that come decades later, when love has been tested, grown, and matured magnificently.

Chapter: 18

Love in Aging Relationships
Nurturing love in the later stages of life

To cultivate love in later life, one must develop a unique form of intentionality, grounded in wisdom, shared experiences, and a profound understanding of what is truly meaningful. In the early years, love typically centers on passion, excitement, and novelty. Later in life, love focuses on friendship, gratitude, and emotional closeness. As couples grow older, they typically discover a more meaningful and peaceful way to be together. It doesn't feel rushed or dramatic; it feels like two hearts coming together gently after choosing each other over and over again. During this time of year, nourishing love means being grateful for what you've built together, recognizing the journey you've been on, and finding joy in the slower, more meaningful moments that come with age.

One of the best ways to keep love alive as you get older is to put emotional presence first. When couples don't have to worry about raising kids, developing careers, or keeping the house clean, they can spend more time together. But being there takes effort. It means choosing to talk rather than get distracted, listening patiently, and being open and honest after years together. Being emotionally present makes a relationship stronger and allows each partner to realize that their feelings are important, their voice is heard, and they still matter. When couples develop love through presence, it serves as a powerful anchor, ensuring they feel safe, supported, and fully understood.

Being grateful is another key part of keeping love alive as you become older. As you become older, you realize how essential the people in your life are and how precious time is. Being grateful makes your heart softer and your bond stronger. Couples who make an effort to show each other how much they care, whether it's for help, friendship, shared experiences, or tiny acts of kindness, keep their love alive and full of feeling. You don't have to do large things to demonstrate how much you appreciate someone. Small things like saying "thank you," acknowledging their hard work, or appreciating little things they do every day are just as beneficial. Grateful partners focus on what they have, how lucky they are to have each other, and what has changed.

Chapter: 18

As couples grow older, showing love also includes being compassionate and understanding when things change. We go through experiences and changes as we become older, such as retiring, getting sick, changing our roles in the family, losing friends or family members, or even feeling melancholy. These changes can either help or hurt a relationship. Couples who stay emotionally attached learn to confront change together rather than resist it. They help each other resolve new problems, celebrate new successes, and alter their expectations in a polite way. They don't contemplate what they can't do anymore; instead, they enjoy what they can still accomplish.

This ability to change is a kind of love in and of itself, indicating that commitment isn't about having everything perfect but about being willing to develop together. If you want to keep love alive later in life, you also need to make closeness a priority. Such proximity encompasses physical proximity as well as emotional and spiritual closeness. Couples' closeness varies as they get older, yet it never ceases to be crucial. Holding hands, spending quiet time together, reminiscing about the past, or just sitting next to one another are all wonderful ways to show how close you are. Emotional connection improves when partners are more honest with each other about their worries, dreams, and flaws. People have more time to discuss topics they put off when they were younger.

Honest couples strengthen their relationship and relish the joy of deepening their understanding of each other once more. Making new memories together is another key way to keep love alive in long-term relationships. It's still possible, and very beneficial, to try new things as a pair, even after being together for a long time. A relationship may gain vitality and passion from doing something new, visiting a location that holds memories, or simply pursuing a shared interest. They remind one another that their bond is still growing rather than waning. These fresh recollections energize the partnership and create hope for the future. They show how love may grow with time.

Chapter: 18

As people grow older, talking to each other becomes one of the best ways to show affection. Couples who have been together for a long time sometimes think they know everything about each other. But as they grow older, their feelings change, and they need to keep talking. Couples can maintain their emotional bond by discussing their anxieties, aspirations, health issues, and future objectives. By helping people understand others' thoughts, this communication fosters trust and helps them avoid mistakes. Each partner can express their needs without feeling ashamed or afraid when communication is effective.

When life slows down, conversations tend to become more serious and profound. This reminds couples that love stays alive through emotional connection. You also need to learn to forgive even more easily as you get older. You will hurt, misinterpret, and make mistakes with each other over the years. Being mad at someone simply makes things worse between you two. Older couples often recognize how important time is and are more likely to move on from past troubles. Forgiving someone is an act of love that implies letting go of the past and moving on. This form of forgiveness helps you recover emotionally and feel closer to someone. It also helps partners trust each other, making them feel safe being honest about their imperfections because they know love will accept them without criticizing them.

Couples can keep their love alive as they age by reminiscing about their shared wonderful times. When you recall the things you've done in the past, including raising kids, navigating challenging times, helping each other through losses, and achieving goals, you feel proud and connected. The stories you both share illustrate how powerful and long-lasting your love is. Celebrating the trip also helps couples recall how far they've come and how much they've grown as individuals and as a pair. This thought helps couples be thankful, feel closer to each other, and genuinely appreciate the love they've developed over time.

Chapter: 18

Choosing kindness daily is one of the best ways to keep love alive as you age. As time goes on, it becomes clearer that being kind is more important than being right, being perfect, or winning arguments. Small things like being kind, helping, being patient, and expressing concern can help maintain a strong relationship. Being nice makes fights less serious, relieves stress, and creates a tranquil environment in the house. Being kind to each other every day strengthens the relationship and makes love seem warm, safe, and comfortable as partners grow older.

Caring for each other in practical ways is another way to show affection. Helping with medicine, performing chores, making meals, or just being there for someone while they are sick are all small acts that show how much you care. These acts of kindness show that love isn't only a sensation; it's also a responsibility and a privilege. Couples who are kind to one another build trust and safety that grows stronger over the years. Taking care of each other becomes a sacred element of the partnership, strengthening the commitment that has kept them together through all of life's ups and downs. In the end, nurturing love in the later phases of life requires choosing to be with each other on purpose.

You need to know that love fluctuates, yet it never stops developing. Couples who have maintained a long-standing relationship understand that love does not simply happen; it requires effort, consistent presence, gratitude, and kindness to sustain. When partners are open to the later years, they discover a sort of love that is mature, quiet, and highly rewarding. It is a love that has endured hardships, reaped rewards, and endured the passage of time. When it matures and softens, it becomes one of life's most beautiful ways to show love.

Chapter: 18

Love in Aging Relationships
Stories of lifelong love

L ifelong love is one of the best ways to show how powerful and deep the human heart can be. People who believe in love that lasts a lifetime think of couples who have been through many changes over the years, including romance, struggle, joy, sorrow, and growth. They still choose each other with a quiet faithfulness. These stories demonstrate that lasting love does not develop instantly or solely because life is always perfect. It comes when you promise to be together through the seasons, forgive each other, and feel at home. We can see how precious it is when two people never give up on each other in stories of love that endure a lifetime. The best love tales aren't the ones with ideal moments; they're the ones that are kept together by strength, sacrifice, and never-ending love.

A powerful love tale that will last a lifetime is about couples who went through tough times together and yet loved each other. Consider a couple who married young and had nothing but ambition and determination. They had money troubles, worked long hours, raised kids, and faced pressures they didn't expect. They could have given up at times, but they didn't. They learned to talk, make deals, and help each other when things got tough. They struggled for their love, which is why it lasted. These couples show us that love that lasts a lifetime isn't perfect; it lasts. Every time two individuals refuse to allow anything to stand in the way of their connection, it grows stronger. Another typical narrative about lifelong love is of couples who support one another through challenging times, such as illness or grief.

Deep and painful tests put love to the test when health deteriorates, or life takes a turn for the worse. Long-term couples often talk about when one had to care for the other. This period entailed giving them medicine, going to their appointments, and being there for them when they couldn't sleep. These circumstances reveal how profound the promise was: "in sickness and in health." Love is a daring and beneficial act during these times. It goes from being romantic to being an act of service. These stories show us how strong devotion can be and remind us that love is strongest when it stays strong through challenging times.

Chapter: 18

Friendship is the start of many love tales that endure a lifetime. People who have been together for a long time often state that being each other's best friend helps them endure through the years. When things were difficult, they made them laugh; when things were uncertain, they made them feel better; and when things were calm, they made them feel better. They liked the same things, cheered each other on when things went wrong, and talked for hours about their hopes, fears, and everything else. Friendship kept them close as romance faded and life got busy. It provided them with a home to go back to, a safe environment where they could be with friends and feel important and appreciated.

Friendship in a lifetime of love shows us that desire can start a relationship, but it's friendship that keeps it going. Another story that couples who have been together for a long time tell is how they learn and evolve as people. People who have been together for a long period often talk about how they've evolved throughout the years. They changed into other people, becoming more stable, more patient, more mature, or more confident. But the most remarkable aspect of enduring love is that they did not merely improve as individuals; they also grew stronger as a couple. They didn't always have an effortless time growing up. At times, it could be a nuisance or lead to confusion. But couples who stayed together learned to discover each other again and again. They stayed interested, open, and willing to adjust. They let each other grow, and their love grew too. The narrative of little traditions is one of the most beautiful love stories that will last a lifetime.

People who have been together for a long time often discuss the little things they do together, like having coffee on the porch in the morning, going for walks in the evening, having dinner on Sundays, writing notes to each other, sharing inside jokes, or listening to a song that always makes them think of each other. These traditions may not mean much to other people, but they are what keep the connection strong. They helped the couple feel at ease and at home, reminding them of the life they established together. Over time, these small moments become precious memories. There is quite proof that the little things we do every day to demonstrate we care make love blossom.

Chapter: 18

Forgiveness is another recurring theme in stories about love that lasts a lifetime. Couples that have been together for a long time talk about the times they wounded each other, their blunders, and their growing pains. They also talk about choosing to forgive, and they do so more than once. For love to last, both people need to be able to say they're sorry and let go of their grudges. This forgiveness helps people heal, rebuilds trust, and keeps anger from hardening the heart. People who have been together for a long time know that forgiving someone is not a sign of weakness; it is a sign of strength. This perspective emphasizes that maintaining the relationship is more important than being right. This lesson is highly important for long-term relationships since time is more important than anger. These stories show that forgiveness is a small act of love that keeps individuals close to each other through good and bad times.

Loyalty is also a big part of many love stories that last a lifetime. Being loyal means more than just being together in person. It also means being emotionally committed, even when you want to be upset, busy, or sad. People who want to be together for life discuss how to keep their relationship safe. They chose to be honest rather than keep secrets, to work together rather than alone, and to be together rather than apart. Because they were faithful to each other, they felt safe in each other's love and sure about the future. Over time, loyalty becomes a strong form of devotion. It builds trust and respect between two people, making them a true team. This loyalty that can't be broken is one reason why love lasts forever. For both lovers, it gives them the comfort of mind that they will never have to face life alone.

One of the most poignant stories is about couples who had loved each other for a long time and then found each other again. These two have been together for a long time, but they still find new things to love about each other. Perhaps they discover a new interest, a new strength, a new weakness, or a new goal. Long-lasting relationships are constantly evolving; they never remain the same. Couples who are constantly observing one another maintain their curiosity, interest, and emotional connection. The connection feels fresh and significant because of this rediscovery. It teaches children that love endures and grows stronger over time.

Chapter: 18

Love tales that last a lifetime also highlight the importance of having friends. As people grow older, their perspectives change. They value being there more than being passionate, being calm more than being perfect, and being real more than looking appealing. In the later years of love, it's important to have someone by your side who knows your background, your peculiarities, your problems, and your accomplishments. As partnerships grow older, being with someone becomes one of the best things you can do. Couples enjoy simply sitting together, sharing stories, observing the sunset, or holding hands during peaceful moments. This friendship doesn't have to be loud or theatrical; it's steady, calm, and very vital.

Long-term partnerships typically develop into love when two individuals are delighted to be together, doing nothing. Couples who have been together for a long time tell the narrative of thankfulness over and over again. As spouses grow older, they start to think more highly of one another. They are thankful for the sacrifices, the fights they had together, and the memories they made over the years. They show their thanks every day by thanking each other for small acts of kindness, acknowledging each other's hard work, and recalling the past that brought them together. This thankfulness makes the bond stronger and keeps the love fresh, even after a long time. It makes regular days feel more special and helps partners pay closer attention to what the other person wants.

In the end, stories of love that last a lifetime show us that love isn't about how long it lasts, but how deep the devotion is during that time. Lifelong love is all about choosing each other again and again, even when things are tough. It is based on loyalty, friendship, forgiveness, sacrifice, and small acts of kindness every day. These stories teach us all something: love grows better, stronger, and more rewarding over time. They remind us that love can start a relationship, but dedication is what keeps it going. As time goes on, everlasting love becomes a precious treasure, a silent promise that two hearts will always be together, no matter how long it takes.

Chapter: 18

Chapter 18 provides a close look at love and how it changes and grows over time. In the beginning, love may be full of passion and excitement. But as time goes on, love becomes a bond based on trust, patience, friendship, and emotional depth. Couples realize that love isn't always the same; it changes, grows, and grows stronger with each new season of life. This chapter made you go beyond the idea of love as a single moment and see it as a lifelong journey full of choices, sacrifices, rediscovery, and strength. The questions below will help you contemplate how love changes over time and what it means to love someone for a long time.

eflection Questions

1. What part of the chapter changed or deepened your understanding of how love evolves over time?
2. How do you think long-term relationships move from passion to partnership, and why is this shift valuable?
3. What emotions or thoughts came up when you considered the idea that love matures rather than fades?
4. How have you seen commitment and consistency build emotional connection in the relationships around you?
5. Which challenges mentioned in the chapter, such as illness, change, or emotional growth, do you think have the most significant impact on long-term love?
6. In what ways do you believe love becomes more powerful as partners age together?
7. How does the idea of "rediscovering each other" throughout life resonate with you?
8. What qualities do you think are essential for allowing love to evolve in a healthy, meaningful way?

Chapter: 18

This chapter also discussed the importance of being kind and intentional in keeping love alive as you age. It talked about how friendship can be strong even when things are challenging, how being thankful can help you heal, and how stories of couples who stayed together through many changes can teach you. These stories of love that lasts a lifetime aren't made up; they're proof that two people keep choosing each other, even when things grow challenging or confusing. The questions below will help you reflect on how these tales and lessons can shape your perceptions of long-term relationships, aging together, and the kind of relationship you want to develop or maintain.

Reflection Questions

1. What aspects of nurturing love later in life felt most meaningful or inspiring to you?

2. How do you think emotional presence becomes even more important as couples age?

3. Which examples of lifelong love in the chapter reminded you of relationships you have witnessed in real life?

4. What did you learn about the role of gratitude in strengthening aging relationships?

5. How did the chapter shift your perspective on intimacy and connection in later life?

6. What elements of lifelong love, such as forgiveness, loyalty, shared traditions, or companionship, stood out to you the most?

7. In what ways do you think aging love reflects a deeper, more settled form of commitment than early romance?

8. Based on everything you learned, what kind of long-term love do you hope to create or nurture in your own life?

Chapter: 19

Love and Boundaries
Establishing healthy boundaries in relationships

Setting and keeping healthy boundaries is one of the most crucial things you can do to develop and keep love relationships, but many people don't understand or follow them. People sometimes think that love involves giving all the time, making sacrifices all the time, or saying "yes" to everything. But real love, love that keeps people safe, fosters connections, and inspires respect, needs to have some rules. Boundaries are not walls; they are paths. They help you articulate what you need, what you care about, and what you can provide without losing yourself. Setting healthy boundaries is a kind thing to do since it lets both people be their best selves. It teaches you to respect both your own and others' needs. Love becomes muddy, complicated, and tiresome when there are no rules. When there are restrictions, love becomes obvious, purposeful, and very rewarding. One of the first things you need to do to set healthy boundaries is to get to know yourself.

Understanding yourself enables you to respond with honesty rather than anger, preventing you from saying things you do not genuinely mean. This self-awareness also helps you figure out when your restrictions are too tight or too loose. Healthy limits aren't always the same; they change depending on how old you are, what kind of relationship you have, and how emotionally strong you are. Knowing where those lines are is the key to polite communication and emotional equilibrium.

Saying "no" can mean you're being honest, even if you love someone. It protects your vitality, mental health, and emotional stability. Refusing things that don't suit you keeps the relationship from becoming frustrated, burned out, or unstable. When you say "no," you show respect for yourself and the relationship, keeping things authentic and lasting. People become closer when they are honest with one another because they both know they can trust each other.

Chapter: 19

When you set healthy limits, you also need to be unambiguous. Many people believe that their lovers, friends, or family members can read their minds and know what they want and need. But relationships work best when people talk to each other on purpose. This involves saying what you do and don't want. It implies stating things like, "I need time to recharge," "I don't like it when this happens," or "I like it when you do this." These things don't tell you what to do; they help you get to know each other better. When individuals communicate and express themselves, they become less frustrated over time. When both people are honest about their needs, the connection grows stronger because they don't have to guess. Respect for one another is another crucial part of having ethical limits.

If only one person complies with the rules, they are useless. Both partners must respect each other's time, needs, emotional space, and personalities for love to develop. You can demonstrate respect in small ways, including giving each other space, not getting defensive while you listen, and respecting each other's boundaries even if you don't fully understand them. Respecting each other also entails knowing that your partner doesn't have to be there for you all the time. There is space for friends, hobbies, rest, alone time, and personal interests in a beneficial partnership. When you respect each other's space, it means that neither spouse has to be "everything" for the other. Love flourishes when both individuals feel accepted, supported, and free to be who they are. Setting your limits also requires understanding when someone has crossed them and knowing how to respond.

Everyone is human, and our limits will be tested. The most crucial element is how you handle violations. To set a healthy boundary, you need to be honest about how you feel hurt, say what you need again, and work together to ensure it doesn't happen again. When partners learn to confront boundary-related mistakes in a mature and understanding way, their relationship grows stronger. When they show that mistakes aren't the end but rather chances to learn more, they trust one another more.

Chapter: 19

People can also maintain relationships by setting healthy limits. Being in love doesn't imply losing who you are. Instead, it means staying connected with people while being true to yourself. Setting boundaries helps you grow as a person, pursue your interests, make friends, and be yourself. This independence makes the partnership stronger because each person adds something unique. When two whole individuals choose to share their lives, their relationship becomes a place of abundance instead of neediness. Keeping your individuality doesn't push partners away; it makes the bond stronger by letting each person grow. Setting healthy limits helps both partners learn more about themselves, keeping the relationship fresh and intriguing.

Managing your feelings is another key component of boundaries. Setting limits helps you manage your feelings and keeps you from having to cope with someone else's. This implies caring about how you feel; it means knowing where your obligation ends and the other person begins. You can support your partner without taking on their stress, worries, or frustrations by setting clear limits. This emotional transparency maintains the partnership in balance and eliminates fatigue. Furthermore, it creates a healthier emotional space because both partners can speak their minds without being judged or condemned. The partnership becomes a safe, stable environment when you learn to manage your feelings and set limits. Setting healthy boundaries also helps keep passion and connection alive over time. Many people think that boundaries make people less close, but the truth is that they make people closer.

When partners feel safe being themselves, they are more honest about how they feel. When they feel valued, they become kinder and trusting. People are more willing to communicate about their concerns, dreams, and wants when they think someone is listening. Boundaries protect intimacy by ensuring that both parties feel comfortable emotionally. This sense of security helps the partnership stay strong through all of life's ups and downs. When partners feel comfortable and understood, their enthusiasm for each other grows. Boundaries are not barriers; they are ways to keep love alive without losing its spark.

Chapter: 19

Healthy boundaries can help relationships stay healthy by stopping things like codependency, resentment, emotional manipulation, or burnout. One partner can provide too much, and the other can mistakenly take too much if there are no limitations. This imbalance will lead to anger, distance, and arguments over time. Setting boundaries helps keep things in balance by making sure that both partners contribute to the relationship in healthy, long-lasting ways. They help people take responsibility for their actions, encourage emotional independence, and prevent anyone from having to carry the whole relationship. This balance is vital for long-term love, as it keeps the bond healthy through mutual effort rather than obligation. Setting limits is also critical, as it helps you feel emotionally safe in the long term.

When you know that your spouse respects your boundaries, listens to your needs, and provides you space to be yourself, you feel safe opening your heart. It's easier to be honest, discuss your anxieties, and have tough conversations when you feel safe emotionally. It also reduces conflicts because both spouses know how to state clearly and quietly what they want. Setting boundaries is one of the best ways to create emotional safety, which is key to sustaining love. Putting emotional safety first brings couples closer over time, as they trust the relationship to protect their hearts. Setting healthy limits is one of the best things you can do for yourself and your relationship. Boundaries safeguard individuality and strengthen connections. This aspect keeps love real and lasting. They teach you how to love without losing yourself, how to give without feeling guilty, and how to acquire without feeling guilty.

People's relationships develop better when they respect each other's space. They change from locations of tension or confusion to places of joy, support, and emotional growth. When there are appropriate boundaries, love stays balanced and respectful and lasts a long time. These connections help you build stronger relationships over time, founded on honesty, clarity, and mutual respect. Ultimately, boundaries are not constraints; they are liberties that facilitate the development of love into its most robust and salubrious manifestation.

Chapter: 19

Love and Boundaries
How boundaries protect and preserve love

Many people don't accept them at first, yet boundaries are one of the best ways to protect love. Some individuals believe that boundaries push people away or make them feel remote. However, the truth is that appropriate boundaries are what keep love strong, balanced, and emotionally safe. They provide a place where each person can grow as a person and as a pair. Love might become fuzzy, challenging to understand, or too much. People lose touch with themselves, anger builds up without them knowing it, and emotional problems slowly start to arise. Boundaries safeguard love by giving it structure, such as clear expectations, mutual respect, and emotional clarity. They let love flow freely without hurting anyone. In this manner, limits aren't walls; they're soft guardrails that keep both hearts on a safe road.

Boundaries safeguard love in part by protecting individuals from getting too emotionally depleted. Individuals who excessively contribute without taking breaks or seeking assistance will eventually exhaust themselves. Love becomes a burden rather than a source of delight. When you're emotionally drained, you become frustrated, distant, and annoyed, making it difficult to connect. Setting limits breaks this pattern by informing each partner of their rights and obligations. This protection keeps everyone from getting too worn out, which makes them more present. It also helps people contribute and receive more effectively, which makes the partnership feel more stable. Partners can prevent their relationship from progressively coming apart because of underlying resentment by respecting each other's need for relaxation, space, time alone, or emotional clarity. Boundaries ensure that love is something you want to do, not something you have to do.

Boundaries can protect love by stopping people from becoming too dependent on each other. If you don't set limits, you may feel like you have to take care of everything your partner does. You can lose your freedom, sense of self, or personal space if you strive to make them content. This protection helps each spouse stay true to themselves and preserve a strong sense of who they are.

Chapter: 19

Boundaries also safeguard love by making individuals feel emotionally safe. When partners know they can discuss their wants, anxieties, or restrictions without feeling ignored or attacked, they build trust. This emotional comfort lets you be honest. It helps individuals connect on a deeper level, be honest, and feel something. This is the fundamental understanding: "I will respect your feelings." Because it prevents emotional wounds from worsening, emotional safety is one of the best ways to keep a relationship secure.

When partners feel free to be themselves without faking, hiding, or treading carefully, love grows stronger and lasts longer. Limits also contribute to the longevity of love by minimizing disagreements. People don't always aim to injure each other when they quarrel; sometimes, they just have unstated expectations. When limits are explicit, there are a lot fewer misunderstandings. Partners know each other's interests, what makes them feel bad, and how to become closer. This transparency makes it easier to talk to each other. Partners don't become mad or confused; they reply with understanding. Boundaries also discourage people from doing things that aren't good for them, including blaming someone, making them feel unwell, or using their feelings to control them. They encourage responsibility by making each partner responsible for their choices and feelings. This prevents the partnership from forming habits that can undermine trust and connection. Boundaries help people dispute in a way that is more beneficial and less hurtful.

People can be themselves when there are boundaries, which helps love stay strong. Every relationship needs to be tight, but it also needs room to breathe. If partners don't have time to do things on their own, like pursue hobbies, develop friends, or grow as people, they may start to feel stuck or excessively dependent on one another. Setting limits helps both people preserve their sense of self and emotional balance, which strengthens the connection over time. When both partners are free to grow as individuals, they bring new energy, new ways of seeing, and new emotional depth to the partnership. Freedom becomes food instead of space. Love keeps alive because it doesn't stifle people; it respects their independence while bringing them closer together.

Chapter: 19

Boundaries also keep love safe by helping you preserve your self-respect. When you explicitly clarify what is and isn't acceptable, you show that you care about yourself. This self-respect shows your partner how to treat you, and it also makes them want to respect themselves. When both partners respect each other, their relationship is stronger and more fulfilling since neither feels like they are being stepped on, disregarded, or undervalued. Setting boundaries helps you stay true to your values, beliefs, and emotional needs, which is vital to long-term happiness.

When partners consistently show consideration for one another's personal space, they say, "I see you." You are important to me. I will not jeopardize the bond we are developing. This type of respect sustains love even in the face of adversity. Boundaries also shield you by offering long-term emotional stability. Without limitations, overwork, repressed rage, or unmet expectations could cause emotions to shift drastically. Setting limits will help you better control your emotions. They support each partner in discussing their desires, facing their emotions, and surviving stressful situations without going insane. Emotional stability is one of the most crucial aspects for keeping love alive, especially in long-term relationships. Couples can resolve their issues without being irritated because of it.

Boundaries help keep your emotions in balance by limiting things that make you feel too much or make it challenging to understand your feelings. Boundaries also safeguard love by keeping closeness safe, both emotionally and physically. People often think that becoming close to someone is simple, but it truly takes trust, safety, and emotional clarity. Boundaries protect intimacy by preventing resentment, emotional neglect, or imbalance. When partners communicate about their boundaries on time, affection, vulnerability, or physical intimacy, both people feel more at ease and safe. This comfort strengthens the link and helps closeness flourish rather than dissipate. Setting limits ensures both parties feel at ease and that intimacy is grounded in genuine connection rather than coercion or duty. Love remains vibrant, robust, and warm when closeness is safeguarded.

Chapter: 19

Boundaries also safeguard love by keeping the relationship solid when things go wrong. It's okay to differ, but without boundaries, fights can grow harsh, hurtful, or even dangerous. Healthy limits inform you how to fight fair: no yelling, name-calling, shutting down, or punishing. These restrictions help people disagree without harming the emotional core of the partnership. They also help partners take breaks when needed, communicate calmly with each other, and return to the conversation with love rather than anger. Boundaries keep love safe by making arguments safer, more productive, and more polite. Boundaries can help keep love alive by keeping anger and resentment at bay.

People who ignore their limits to keep their partners happy build up animosity in subtle, silent ways. Over time, this rage translates into emotional estrangement. Boundaries stop such behavior by ensuring that donating is always an option, not something that has to be done. When partners say "yes" because they actually want to, not because they feel they have to, the relationship improves. Setting limitations keeps the partnership fair and stops one spouse from bringing emotional baggage that the other partner can't see. When there is no resentment in the heart, love stays open, compassionate, and connected.

In the end, limits safeguard love by making it honest, fair, and safe for feelings. They prevent relationships from being detrimental, draining, or one-sided. They remind both people to treat themselves and each other with respect. Boundaries help love last by making it a relationship that can develop and adapt without falling apart when things become challenging. They keep the love alive, strengthen the relationship, and protect the emotional bond that keeps two people together. Boundaries that are imposed with kindness, consistency, and respect let love not just survive but also thrive. Therefore, boundaries do not hinder you; they protect your heart, maintain your connection, and sustain love.

Chapter: 19

Love and Boundaries
Respecting the limits of others in love

Being in love means respecting other people's boundaries, which is one of the most grown-up things you can do. It means understanding that love isn't about having someone; it's about being partners. Many individuals believe that being close to someone means being able to control them and that loving someone involves being able to affect every area of their life. But true love gives people freedom. It doesn't need to be watched, agreed on, or proven all the time. When you respect someone's limits, you are saying, "I trust you to be yourself, and I feel safe enough to let you be alone." Love that doesn't respect boundaries can soon become suffocating, yet love that does respect boundaries becomes stronger with time.

Learning to love in this manner will strengthen your relationships. The first step to respecting boundaries is to be empathetic. It's important to know that everyone has their limits, routines, and emotional strengths. What one person thinks is safe might not be safe for someone else. When you love with empathy, you learn to pay attention, listen, and understand before you act. You learn that saying "no" doesn't imply you would rather not do anything; it means you want to keep yourself safe. It's a way for someone to stay mentally healthy and be totally present in the relationship. When you perceive limits as love instead of distance, you stop taking them personally and start to see them as a sign of emotional awareness.

Boundaries also teach you how to be modest. They remind you that love is not about what you desire or when you wish it to occur. Occasionally, you need to step back, put some space between yourself and others, and let things happen on their own. To respect someone's limits, you have to think that love remains even when you're not in charge. When both parties feel protected, the relationship develops stronger. You create trust when you allow someone else space. Your love is strong, selfless, and based on mutual respect, patience, and understanding.

Chapter: 19

Respecting other people's space also helps you keep your feelings in balance. When both people can say what they want without feeling awful about it, relationships work best. When you let individuals set their limits, you make it safe for them to be honest. People are more likely to talk openly when they know they won't get into trouble for being honest. This kind of freedom makes love stronger, not weaker. It makes the relationship one of mutual care instead of anger. True love cares about how both individuals feel emotionally.

Many people struggle to respect boundaries because they see them as space. In reality, boundaries are bridges. They bring together two healthy people who can love one another without being afraid. You eliminate disputes and uncertainty when you know where you end, and the other person begins. You can love simply and honestly if you respect other people's boundaries and don't try to dominate them or become emotionally involved. It allows love to blossom naturally. A relationship without room is like a plant without air: it may look full for a time, but it will die under too much pressure. You have to keep your limits in control if you want to respect someone else's. You might not recognize love when you see it.

Occasionally, the person you care about needs time or space instead of solutions. Respecting someone means honoring how they do things, even if it's not the same way you do. It's about putting understanding above pride. One of love's hardest lessons is that how someone heals, matures, or shows their feelings may not be what you want. But you can connect more deeply and attain peace if you quit wanting to be in command.

Chapter: 19

Boundaries are rules for lasting love, not walls. They show the boundary between being kind and assuming responsibility. Both partners in a good relationship are aware that they can say, "This is what I need," without fear of the other person's reaction. Respectful love promotes individuality rather than stifles it. You value the real person, not the one you've created to keep yourself feeling good about yourself. Love remains genuine when boundaries are respected. It allows intimacy to coexist with development, creativity, and self-fulfillment.

When two people can be themselves, their friendship grows stronger. Being respectful in love also entails being mindful of how your feelings affect others. Everyone becomes worn out, distracted, or overwhelmed at some point. A devoted partner does not require constant supervision; they provide you with personal space. They know that love doesn't need to be told it's right all the time; it needs faith. If you respect their bounds, you can love someone without holding on to them. Instead of saying, "You have to give me what I want now," it's saying, "I'll be here when you're ready." That little modification turns love into a sanctuary instead of a combat zone. Each heart has room to breathe in a healthy love.

People will respect your boundaries if you respect theirs. It becomes a dance of trust and respect between us. You don't worry that love will fade with time because you know that it increases over time. You learned that understanding each other is more important than being close all the time. When there is a balance between freedom and connection, love can last a long time. There are limitations to every relationship, even the most passionate ones. Love stays strong, lasts, and grows with it.

Chapter: 19

Being conscious of yourself at all times is important if you want to respect other people's restrictions. You need to pay attention to how you react when someone says "no" or needs time alone. Does it make you feel terrified, jealous, or insecure? It's normal to feel this way, but it shows you where you need to recover. You have to learn how to regulate your feelings before you can learn how to respect other people. When you stop taking someone else's boundaries personally, you start loving from a place of maturity rather than emotional dependence. You realize that someone can love you passionately and still require space.

Both of these things can be true at the same time. Another crucial way to respect boundaries is to talk to each other. Love can't last if you make assumptions. Talk about what you both need, what makes you feel safe, and what goes too far. Setting good limits means not expecting things to happen without talking about them. It's simpler to respect each other's space when you are open. Talking to each other clears things up and keeps anger from getting worse. It turns boundaries into obvious, agreed-upon norms that protect the partnership, rather than walls that are difficult to notice.

Respecting other people's boundaries in love demonstrates how much you've evolved as a person. It demonstrates that you recognize that love is not about controlling someone but about caring for them and working together. When you let others be themselves, you build honest, calm, and enduring connections. Respecting boundaries may not always feel wonderful, but it always fosters trust. "I see you; I accept you, and I will respect your space because your peace is important to me," love says. At that time, love becomes unbreakable, strong enough to last, kind enough to heal, and wise enough to last.

274

Chapter: 19

Boundaries aren't walls that keep people out; they're doorways that let people in. This chapter makes you consider what it actually means to love someone while still having appropriate boundaries. Many people believe that love implies giving everything, saying "yes" to everything, and putting our needs aside to show how much we care. But love doesn't grow when you're angry or exhausted; it grows when you care about each other. Boundaries are the quiet protectors of love; they help people get along, feel protected, and understand each other.

Reflection Questions — Establishing Healthy Boundaries in Relationships:

1. What does a healthy boundary look like to you? Can you describe one that has helped you feel emotionally safe?

2. When was the last time you felt your boundaries were crossed, and how did you respond?

3. Why do you think many people feel guilty about setting boundaries in love?

4. How can you communicate your needs without fear of losing someone's affection or approval?

5. What boundaries do you still need to strengthen in your relationships today?

Boundaries are also love's anchor; they keep relationships grounded during emotional storms.

Reflection Questions — How Boundaries Protect and Preserve Love:

1. In what ways can boundaries actually make a relationship feel safer and more secure?

2. How does knowing your partner's emotional limits make you a more understanding partner or friend?

3. Have you ever noticed that setting clear boundaries improved the quality of your connection with someone?

4. What happens to love when there are no clear boundaries?

Chapter: 19

One of the most important markers of emotional maturity is knowing when to respect other people's limits. It implies loving someone without trying to change them into the person you want them to be.

Reflection Questions — Respecting the Limits of Others in Love:

1. How comfortable are you with giving the people you love personal space when they need it?
2. What emotions come up for you when someone sets a boundary with you: hurt, confusion, understanding, or peace?
3. Can you think of a time when respecting someone's boundary actually strengthened your relationship?
4. What's one small way you can show someone you care while still honoring their limits?
5. How do you remind yourself that love and control cannot exist in the same space?

Setting limits doesn't mean you don't love someone; it means you love them in a healthy way. When you care about your own needs and those of others, relationships are built on balance rather than fear. This chapter reminds us that the best relationships are not the ones without limits, but those that embrace them. Loving someone doesn't mean taking away their uniqueness or making your own voice quiet. It involves making a rhythm of giving and getting that helps both hearts grow.

Final Reflection Questions:

1. What boundaries in your life reflect love, peace, and mutual respect?
2. How can you practice better listening when someone expresses their limits to you?
3. What do you need to forgive yourself for, crossing your own boundaries or ignoring someone else's?
4. How can you remind yourself that saying "no" is sometimes the most loving thing you can do?

Chapter: 20

Love in Times of Loss
How love helps us cope with loss and grief

L ove and loss are integral aspects of life. You can't fully know one until you've met the other. When we love deeply, we let happiness, connection, and significance into our lives. When loss breaks that love, we also allow pain to enter. When experiencing the loss of a loved one, the conclusion of a relationship, or witnessing the fading of something beautiful, it is natural to feel sadness. But love doesn't end when life or connection does. In many ways, love helps us cope with loss. It keeps us together when everything else goes wrong. It reminds us that what we had was real, meaningful, and worth remembering.

At first, grief feels like a storm: loud, confusing, and never-ending. You may think you'll never see the sun again. But love is the silent anchor that protects you from becoming lost in your emotions. When someone dies or goes away, your love for each other doesn't go away; it lingers in your heart, your routines, your prayers, and your memories. You can hear it in the tunes that once made you feel fulfilled. You may sense it in the traditions you still follow. Love is what connects the past to the present and provides sorrow a purpose. Love helps you heal, not by taking away your pain, but by helping you carry it with grace.

When you lose someone, realizing that love endures forever can be the most comforting. It changes its shape. It passes from the body to the spirit and from what is said to what is remembered. You stop holding hands and start clinging to the past. You no longer hear their laughter, but their presence remains palpable in the serenity. Love is what keeps you connected to the past as you learn to live in the now. It's not about "getting over" someone; it is about progressing forward with the love they have left behind.

Chapter: 20

Strangely, grief illustrates how profound love can be. You realize how much you cared when you cry. It can be challenging to cope with grief, but it also demonstrates how much you can love. Knowing that can affect how you feel; it turns melancholy into gratitude. You cease questioning, "Why did I lose them?" and begin acknowledging, "I'm grateful for the opportunity to have loved them." Love turns suffering into memories. It teaches you that every pain has a story, every cry has a purpose, and every time you say goodbye, you change yourself.

Love also provides us the strength to keep going when we feel like we can't. Even when we want to hide, it makes us want to keep coming back. Think about how a parent keeps going after their spouse dies, or how friends join together to help someone sad to show them they are not alone. That is love in action; it enables you to do what you are otherwise unable to resist. It communicates with you through others when you feel completely drained. Love is a bridge that moves you from feeling hopeless to feeling hopeful.

Love can help us cope with things by letting us remember without being scared. The pain of losing someone never goes away completely, but love makes it hurt less over time. You begin to grin at the recollections that used to make you cry. You take comfort in the idea that love doesn't die with people; it lives on in you, shaping how you care for, understand, and are patient with others. When you lose someone, a portion of them lives with you. You express that part of them through the way you love other people in the future. Grief teaches us, and love is the lesson that stays with us forever.

Chapter: 20

We also acquire the strength to forgive when we lose someone we love. When you're grieving, you could feel frustrated, depressed, or guilty, which might make it challenging to become better. Love teaches you that forgiving someone doesn't imply forgetting; it means letting go of your heart so it can heal. It's about letting go of your anger and moving on. Forgiving someone who injured you or even yourself makes it possible to find peace. Love teaches you that being frustrated just makes you feel worse. Letting go of it lets you maintain the memory of the person or event, but without the burden that once weighed you down.

Love also enables you to ask others for help when you can't handle the loss on your own. You could feel that no one else can comprehend how you feel when you're upset. But you can recover by letting other people love you through it. They can do this by sitting with you, listening, or just holding your hand. Love from other people might be the best treatment for your heart. You start to realize that talking about your pain makes it easier to manage. Every embrace, every conversation, and every kind thing you do will help you get over your loss. And when you start to feel better, love makes you want to exchange again. It may not happen immediately, but it will happen eventually.

You become more conscious of how other people are hurting when you lose someone you love. You start to experience pain in places you used to ignore. You become more patient, compassionate, and open. A loss is love's modest win; it turns pain into understanding. You used to feel empty because of the agony, but now you want to help others. Loss is like dirt that helps love bloom into a more profound understanding of life.

Chapter: 20

Love is what makes mourning meaningful, but it's also what makes healing possible. Love heals wounds, not time alone. When you recall the wonderful times, forgive the difficult times, and start to open your heart again, that's love. Love teaches that healing is not forgetting; it's learning to cope with the past. Love doesn't heal loss, but it reminds you of how deeply you lived.

Love can also help you discover meaning after a loss. People often find new ways to discover purpose in their lives after losing someone or something. They start charities, publish books, raise their kids with a new sense of purpose, or live with more thankfulness. The result is love's eternal power; it converts grief into purpose. It says, "You're still here for a reason." It tells you that the story isn't over simply because a chapter has concluded. When love leads, grieving focuses on what you have and what you used to have, not what you lost.

In the end, love doesn't just help us cope with loss; it changes what loss means. Loss can take away things that are real, but it can't affect things that are forever. The love you have given and received will continue to shape your soul long after you bid farewell. Love connects you to the dead, gives you strength in hard times, and gives you hope. Love stays while all else goes away. It becomes the invisible thread that connects you to the people and events that shaped you. And even amid the silent pain of loss, love whispers one simple truth: you haven't lost everything; you've just learned to carry love in a new way.

Chapter: 20

Love in Times of Loss
Stories of love that persist even after death

Love doesn't mean the end of life. It transforms, taking on new shapes, meanings, and ways of being felt. Stories of love that continue long after death show us that the human heart can connect with other people in ways we can't perceive. The relationship doesn't stop when someone we love dies; it changes. The laughter fades into memory, the voice becomes an echo in the heart, and the presence becomes a feeling that never really goes away. When someone dies, it can feel like we've been divided, but love keeps the living and the dead apart. It sticks with us in little ways, like a song, a smell, or a remark that pops into our heads at the opportune time.

These reminders aren't accidents; they're love's way of saying, "I'm still here." Many people believe that love feels stronger than ever shortly after a loss. A mother may feel her child's warmth in a light wind. A husband thinks his dead wife is helping him make difficult decisions. A daughter dreams about her father's grin and wakes up feeling calm for no reason. These aren't just coincidences; they're connections that stretch beyond death and time. If you genuinely loved someone, that love will remain with you throughout your entire life. You can't bury that kind of link; it grows stronger the more you learn to perceive it freshly.

Love after death isn't just a memory; it's a presence, an energy, and a gentle friend who stays with you through all the changes in your life. Little things that happen every day provide the best stories of lasting love. It's the widow who chats to her husband every day, the child who writes to a parent who has passed, or the friend who keeps their loved one's rituals alive every year. These actions of remembering are love's method of keeping love alive. Even after death, love changes how we live, act, and see the world. Love doesn't go away; it merely shows itself in new ways.

Chapter: 20

Love that lasts after death is beautiful because it makes us stronger. When we grieve, we change, but love that lasts provides us the strength to keep going. A woman still wears her late husband's old flannel shirt because it makes her feel safe. Every spring, a father plants a tree for his daughter. He does this because it makes him feel like she's still growing up with him. A man visits the grave of his closest friend to converse with him about his day, as he used to, not to mourn.

These are not sad things; they are acts of love. They prove that love can still give life significance even when death has taken it away. Love is holy because it never ends. It shows us that death can separate bodies but not spirits. You can lose someone's voice yet still hear what they say. You can lose their touch, yet you can still feel their warmth. That's because love becomes a part of you. It transforms who you are, makes you more open-hearted, and affects the decisions you make long after they're gone.

When people claim that their loved one lives "in their heart," they genuinely mean it. Their spirit is still with you, helping you discover your way when times are tough. Love that lasts after death influences how we see life, too. It reminds us that the connections we create will stay forever. People we love leave marks on our souls that time can't erase. That love shows you lived fully and felt real emotions, even when sad. You heal by letting love replace the pain, not by forgetting it. Love is what makes you unhappy and what helps you endure through it.

Chapter: 20

Some people feel like they should love beyond death. Many people extend their affection to other people instead of the person they used to adore. A mom who lost her son works as a volunteer at a children's hospital to make sick kids feel better. Somebody whose wife had died established a charity in her name to offer others hope. A daughter who misses her mother becomes a mentor to other girls, teaching them what her mother taught her. These stories of change illustrate that love may still provide life even when it hurts. These things make love last longer than the body and turn it into something eternal.

People who can love after losing someone have a quiet strength. They don't deny death; they remember it. They have items like pictures, souvenirs, or even recipes that make them think of the person they lost. When they discuss the person they've lost, their eyes light up, not with agony but with gratitude. Love makes it easier to endure sadness when we know that the relationship hasn't ended but has transformed from being present to being a spirit. These times remind us that love is more than just the physical world. It's an energy so enormous and pure that it can't be broken.

You may see this fact in how love has lasted over the years. A granddaughter who never met her grandfather feels very connected to him since her mother told her stories about him. Love is taught through stories, rituals, and the kindness we show others. If you love someone profoundly, you do not merely recall them; you continue their legacy through your actions. Following the passing of an individual, love extends beyond mere attachment; it involves embodying and exemplifying the principles and convictions they held dear. That's how love lasts longer than death.

Chapter: 20

One thing that all stories of lifelong love have in common is that love is stronger than loss. It's the hand that still reaches across time, the whisper that calms the lonely night, and the bond that makes you feel better when you can't acquire the words. Death can change how things look, but it can't break ties. The heart that was loved will always be loved. This fact gives people who are still depressed hope. It reminds us that the people we love will always be in our hearts. We keep them alive by the way we talk, laugh, forgive, and dream.

Love doesn't go away when someone goes; it just grows quieter, more spiritual, and stronger. Love that lasts after death teaches us how to live better throughout time. It instructs us to exhibit kindness, engage with others, and offer support when needed. It tells us to appreciate every moment we have and to say "I love you" while we can. When we lose someone, their love becomes a mirror that informs us how to love others better by being more patient, thankful, and kind. Death can take someone away from you, but it can never take away what they gave to your soul. You keep them alive with love, which you show in your deeds as well as in your mind.

Love that lasts beyond death is the best proof that we will live on forever. Love doesn't die when the body does; it lives on as light, warmth, and an invisible thread that connects hearts over time and place. That's why there is always hope, even when you lose. Love doesn't die with the individual; it lives on in every heartbeat that remembers. When you love someone sincerely, that love becomes a part of the world. It is always there, indestructible, and never-ending.

Chapter: 20

Love in Times of Loss
The eternal nature of love

In its purest form, love is eternal. It lasts longer than space, time, and even death. One of the most comforting things about life is that love never ends. We often view love as something that begins and ends, depending on individuals and conditions. But real love, which is profound, selfless, and based on the soul, goes beyond those bounds. It exists beyond the body, beyond language, and beyond the distance that separates us. Love still flows like a stream beneath the surface of life, bringing hearts that once beat as one back together. Our love for someone who dies doesn't go away; it changes into something quieter, softer, and somehow stronger. It becomes a whisper in our hearts, a warmth in our memories, and a strength that helps us keep going when everything else seems lost.

We know this is true at odd times. When we hear a song that reminds us of someone who has died, it makes us cry, but it also comforts us. A fragrance in the air can evoke the sensation that they are still present and embracing you. These aren't just coincidences; they're love's way of showing us that it never ends. The love we share with others changes how we feel, what we do, and how we grow. Even if sadness transforms us, love still binds us to all that matters. The body will decay, but the soul will always have love.

Love lasts forever, and one way it achieves its end is by inspiring a legacy. You can maintain that love by performing acts of kindness for others, imparting knowledge, and dedicating quality time to their company. People offer it to their kids, friends lend it to their friends, and partners distribute it to everyone else. Even when one life ends, love's power continues to spread and change others' lives in ways that can't be seen. It is the legacy we leave behind that no one can see, the confirmation that something inside us lasts. We know that we are never really disconnected from the individuals we have lost since love lasts forever. They live on in our hearts and in our actions, not just in our memories.

Chapter: 20

It's easy to focus on what we don't have anymore when someone dies: the silence, the empty chair, and the words we didn't utter. But love helps us see more than we can. It reminds us that relationships don't actually end; they merely change. Love lasts forever; thus, we shouldn't think of loss as the end but as a shift. Love changes form, but it never loses its core. For example, water turns into vapor yet stays water. It moves from touch to memory and from words said to understanding inside. When you truly love someone, that connection is a part of who you are. It changes who you are and how you feel. Love endures eternally in every heartbeat that recalls it.

Many people progressively come to comprehend this fact when they are alone with their thoughts. They might obtain consolation in their dreams, feel a presence in their prayers, or experience a serenity that can't be put into words. Love isn't just a positive thought; it's something people feel deep down inside. It provides us the strength to continue living fully, even when we feel like we're missing something. Love is there for us, and we may experience it through our gut feelings, indications, and the peculiar feeling that someone is looking over us. And those whispers do benefit us in some manner.

Love that lasts becomes a memory and a guide, reminding us that ends aren't always what they seem. We perceive life differently when we love this way. It teaches that the most important things can't be taken away. Fame, money, and other possessions disappear over time. But there will always be love, absolute, unselfish, and unconditional. It spans generations, connects spirits over long distances, and endures even through pain. When you genuinely love someone, you stop seeing eternity as a place and start seeing it as a feeling. It's the quiet knowledge that everything lovely lasts. You keep doing the job of love every time you choose to be kind instead of angry, hopeful instead of hopeless, and compassionate instead of angry. Love never goes away; it just stays with you.

Chapter: 20

The way love heals reveals that it lasts forever. Love eventually converts suffering into wisdom, no matter how horrible it seems. The love that once brought tears to your eyes is now the love that restores your happiness. The heart is saying, "I'm still here, still beating, and still able to feel." Love lasts through healing because it doesn't hold on to negative feelings; it only wants to connect. When we let love guide our mourning, it helps us recall what we received instead of what we lost. Death can't take away the moments we were close, the lessons we learned, and the fun. Love converts sadness into gratitude, teaching us that even when it hurts, it can serve a beneficial purpose. Love also teaches us how to forgive and move on.

Occasionally, when we're sad, we wish we had said or done something different. But love teaches us that those relationships run deeper than time. Words can't describe what the heart knows. We remember people we've lost more honestly when we think of them with love instead of guilt. Love doesn't want you to be flawless; it just wants you to be there for them. Love doesn't go away when that person is gone; it grows. It becomes more spiritual, more thoughtful, and more cognizant of its eternal roots. We begin to see that death cannot extinguish the love we have cultivated, as love has never been solely a physical phenomenon.

You are still loving someone every time you think about them. These aren't sad rituals; they're ways to remember someone who has died, like lighting a candle, going to a spot you used to go with them, or speaking their name. Each one says, "We still have a link. Love lasts forever; thus, being away is only for a short time, and being together is forever. Everyone we've loved has changed us. It is through the way we love others, our perspective on the world, and our ability to discover strength even in moments of silence. Love, in its eternal form, connects us to the past and the future.

Chapter: 20

Knowing that love lasts forever doesn't make the sorrow of loss go away, but it does give it significance. It enables you to cry with trust, mourn with hope, and remember with calm. The agony of losing someone you love never goes away completely, but it becomes easier to endure. Love teaches you how to deal with loss rather than trying to escape it. And as time goes on, you start to realize that love didn't die with the person; it evolved into something you can't see but can feel strongly. In love, eternity does not seem like infinite sadness but rather endless presence.

Love also reminds us that every goodbye is merely a break in the grand story of being connected. The love you once shared remains, poised to resurface in various forms, such as dreams, memories, or even the spirit. You will be together again in another life. Love is eternal, which keeps religion alive. It tells us that death isn't the end; it's only a halt in the sentence of the soul. You know that everyone you meet will always be a part of your journey when you love deeply. Love feels boundless because it increases with every person you care about, every hour you give, and every act of kindness you do.

Ultimately, love's everlasting essence imbues existence and loss with significance. It tells us that love doesn't really say goodbye. It sticks with us in our memories, the decisions we make, and the individuals we become. It goes through time, turning grief into calm and endings into new beginnings. Even when hearts break, love carries on. It is stronger than grief, greater than distance, and more profound than death. That may be the most extraordinary truth of all: love is not confined to this world; it endures throughout eternity.

Chapter: 20

When we lose someone, we may feel different, but love reminds us that we are never really alone, even when we are sad. This chapter highlighted how love flows through sadness like a calm stream, keeping us solid when all else feels unstable. Consider how love has assisted you or an acquaintance in overcoming challenging circumstances. This reflection is meant to help you remember and understand those memories and realizations. It should help you see love as something that will always be there, living on in every heartbeat, thought, and act of compassion.

These ideas can help you remember how strong love is.

1. Think of a time you experienced loss, whether through death, distance, or change. How did love help you begin healing, even when the pain felt unbearable? Describe the emotions that surfaced and how love helped you manage them.

2. In what ways did your understanding of love evolve after experiencing grief? Did it deepen, soften, or challenge you to see love differently? Reflect on how loss reshaped your perception of connection and compassion.

3. This chapter emphasizes that love never truly ends; it changes form. Can you recall a moment when you felt the presence of someone you've lost, through a dream, a memory, or an unexplainable peace? How did that moment affirm that love continues beyond death?

4. Think about the ways you keep love alive for someone who's no longer here. Do you honor them through traditions, stories, or quiet remembrance? How do those acts make you feel connected to them today?

5. Grief can sometimes feel isolating, but love often finds ways to reach us through others. Who has shown you love during your times of loss, and what did their care teach you about the healing power of connection?

Chapter: 20

Love that endures through loss doesn't just comfort us; it changes us. It teaches resilience, compassion, and a deeper appreciation for life itself. As you complete this second page of reflections, think about how love's eternal nature has touched your own story. Every answer you write is part of your healing journey, an affirmation that love's power doesn't fade; it transforms.

6. When you think about "the eternal nature of love," what does that phrase mean to you personally? Does it give you hope, comfort, or a sense of peace about those you've lost?

7. Some people find that love after loss inspires them to help others or live differently. Have you ever been moved to honor someone's memory by giving, serving, or creating something meaningful? How has love guided your actions beyond grief?

8. Love leaves behind invisible gifts, patience, wisdom, and empathy. What qualities or strengths have you gained from loving and losing? How do these traits continue to influence how you love others today?

9. The chapter discusses how love connects souls across time and space. What does that truth mean for your life moving forward? How might it change the way you approach relationships, forgiveness, or gratitude?

10. Finally, how can you let love, rather than grief, guide the rest of your life? Think about one way you can embody the love you've experienced by being kinder, more patient, or more open to others.

As you finish this reflection, remember: love never stops at loss. It is the invisible bridge between what was and what still is. Through every tear, memory, and moment of peace, love continues its quiet work, reminding us that we are forever connected and that nothing truly beautiful is ever gone.

Chapter: 21

Love and Selflessness
The power of putting others first in love

L ove in its simplest form is not about taking, controlling, or possessing someone. It's about giving. Love grows as it learns to be selfless, which involves placing the needs of others ahead of your own. Selfless love tells us something different than what the world tells us: that taking care of someone else makes us truly happy. When you love someone selflessly, you don't keep count of what you receive in return. You're giving solely because love is naturally kind. It's about helping others, even if it means giving up something. It's about seeing your beloved as part of your soul and knowing they alone can make you happy.

Loving someone selflessly doesn't mean losing yourself; it means discovering a deeper part of yourself. Giving because you really care opens a part of your heart with no limitations. Think about the parents who stay up all night with a sick child, or the partner who gives up their comfort to help the other person achieve their goal. These situations don't make people weaker; they reveal how strong love can be. Being selfless in love doesn't mean being passive or allowing someone to mistreat you. It is choosing to value someone else as much as you value yourself. Love becomes real and transcends mere affection when it is balanced with mutual respect.

One of the most admirable qualities of selfless love is its capacity to develop and flourish. You gain more when you offer more. It may not always manifest in tangible ways, but it can do so through trust, peace, and a more profound sense of friendship. When you love without conditions, you make room for grace. When you are unselfish, it is easier for relationships to mend, as it makes pride, anger, and resentment weaker and understanding more possible. "I care about you more than I care about myself" is what love that puts others first says. This type of love endures through all challenges, regardless of how often they occur.

Chapter: 21

To love selflessly means to see past yourself. It involves being patient and listening, even when you're exhausted; forgiving, even when you're upset; and being kind without asking anything in return. Those moments were heavy on your heart. But love's power is also shown: it can affect both the giver and the receiver. You begin to see that putting someone else's needs before your own doesn't make you less valued; it makes you more human. Loving someone without expecting anything in return doesn't take away from your spirit; it adds to it. It teaches you that being happy means giving freely and not taking more.

You can also discover a lot of tranquility in this kind of love. When you stop worrying about what you receive out of each connection, you start to feel love in its simplest form. There is no need to worry, feel pressured, or fear losing your love; simply trust that it serves a meaningful purpose. It's not about being perfect; it's about being present. You can love passionately even if you make errors and aren't flawless. This is because you're no longer trying to protect yourself; you're seeking to connect with other people. You don't overlook your wants when you love selflessly. You contribute from a place of strength, not from a place of need. You fill yourself with love, faith, and patience, and then you transfer that energy to others.

There are many examples of love that are not selfish in history and in modern life. Think about soldiers who risk their lives to protect others, friends who are there for each other when things go disastrously, and couples who stay faithful despite years of change. Putting others first means doing little things, like listening instead of arguing, being quiet to soothe someone, or choosing to forgive instead of being proud. Every time you do something kind for someone else, you plant a seed of love that keeps blooming long after the moment has passed. This shows that kindness is never wasted, even if no one sees it.

Chapter: 21

Being unselfish doesn't mean giving up oneself; it means loving in an innovative way. It's crucial to establish a balance between being generous and preserving your sense of self. When both people respect each other's space, they can be unselfish in a healthy way. Love shouldn't make you stop following your aspirations; instead, it should make you want to help each other flourish. Putting people first doesn't imply you're always last. It signifies, you know, that love is when two people care for each other. Two selfless people can meet in the middle with elegance. One person's strength makes up for the other's weakness, and one person's patience makes up for the other's struggle. They build something lovely together: they stay true to themselves while being together.

Love that isn't selfish teaches you humility. It shows us that relationships aren't about who wins and who loses; they're about assisting each other. When you love someone profoundly, you start to feel their anguish as if it were your own. Rather than questioning, "What can I gain from this?" consider asking, "How can I assist them?" That shift makes everything different. It creates a link that can't be broken, built on understanding rather than on expectations. Empathy replaces the ego. When you make modest sacrifices that no one else sees, like getting up early to help, saying sorry first, and offering your time without complaining, your love grows stronger.

Being selfless also makes the simple things in life more important. You begin to perceive love as the little things you do every day, like providing dinner for someone who is exhausted, listening without judgment, and being there for them when no one else is. These small things have a lot of power because they communicate, "I see you, and I choose you." Love that comes from a place of selflessness makes everyday things appear heavenly. It makes relationships secure places where both parties may be honest and transparent. In this kind of love, giving is a pleasure, not a chore.

Chapter: 21

Prioritizing others is strong because it demonstrates the true nature of love, which is to give rather than to possess. Selflessness can lead to the blossoming of love. It serves as a reminder that being present and compassionate is what creates a meaningful connection, not being in charge or flawless. By prioritizing others over yourself, you are demonstrating your importance to them. They remember the message long after the words have faded. The development of authentic relationships is based on humility and compassion.

When you go back to the peaceful days in your life, you'll discover that the times you gave without expecting anything in return were the best. Love is powerful because of what it provides, not what it receives. When you love without expecting anything in return, you turn walls into bridges. You become a reflection of the type of love that heals, brings things back to life, and makes you feel better. Even if no one sees it, your compassion matters because it changes you. Giving freely makes your heart stronger, so it can love more deeply the following time.

So, when life tests your patience, when your relationships don't feel right, or when love feels too hard, remember that affection is a choice, not a deal. Putting people first doesn't make you weak; it makes you unique. You now know the most crucial secret of all: when you share love, it never runs out. You get more back when you give more, even if you can't see how. Selfless love is a miracle because it grows, heals, and lasts, turning ordinary lives into wonderful stories of kindness that never fade.

Chapter: 21

Love and Selflessness
How love grows when we act selflessly

Love grows strongest when we choose to do things for other people, not when they are simple. Every time we offer without expecting anything in return, we make love grow stronger. It's simple to adore when things are fair and balanced. But we really grow when we put someone else's needs ahead of our own, even when it's unpleasant or painful. That's when love grows, becomes stronger, and takes on a different meaning. To be selfless doesn't mean losing oneself; it means understanding that love grows when you offer. When two people care enough to offer assistance, listen, and help one another without keeping score, their relationship becomes more than just feelings. It turns into a bond of grace and understanding that lasts.

Love, by its nature, reacts to compassion. When you choose to be selfless, like by being patient, forgiving, or kind, love might blossom in ways you didn't expect. The heart tends to regard acts of kindness as food. Giving up even the most minor things makes your relationship stronger. Think about how a tiny thing, like staying up late to console a buddy or forgiving someone who injured you, might transform how you feel about each other. During that era, love was not about perfection; it was about showing up with an open heart. When we do things out of love, we demonstrate it more.

Love blooms when you stop contemplating what you can gain and start imagining what you can offer. It alters both the one who provides it and the one who takes it. When we are unselfish, our egos are weaker, which helps us perceive people with compassion instead of judgment. It takes away the fear of losing and offers you the happiness of giving. And when we provide more freely, something amazing happens: our hearts grow bigger. Love doesn't seem rare anymore; it flows, connects people, and heals them. That's how love grows: by doing things for others without expecting anything in return.

Chapter: 21

Being selfless is what all strong relationships, whether they be romantic, familial, or platonic, have in common. Trust grows when people pledge to take care of each other for no other reason than that. Unconditional love grows in a place where people actually care about each other. It does not seek repayment; it merely aims to uplift your spirit and bestow blessings upon you. And love becomes stronger as you extend it. Being selfless teaches us that being in charge isn't as vital as being connected. Love grows deeper and steadier over time when you stop trying to change it and let it flow naturally.

The most admirable aspect of selfless love is that it provides a sense of security and protection. Being compassionate to someone even when they mess up fosters trust that words can't. This is why selflessness and love are inseparable. You don't just say you love someone; you show them. It's the simple things that matter, like taking the time to listen, being patient when you don't comprehend something, or choosing peace above being right. These little things are what keep love going. When we consistently act for the benefit of others, we foster an environment where love feels secure, vibrant, and resilient.

Furthermore, remember that being selfless doesn't mean being weak or ignoring your needs. In reality, unselfish love grows stronger when both people do it for each other. You demonstrate the proper conduct by donating out of genuine concern, rather than out of exhaustion. Both individuals experience a sense of importance, recognition, and receiving assistance. Love grows best when both people are willing to provide as much as they gain. It becomes a never-ending cycle of offering and getting grace that keeps the partnership going strong.

Chapter: 21

Being unselfish also transforms the way we view love in our daily lives. It makes ordinary times feel spectacular. Doing tasks for your partner without being asked, supporting a friend during a stressful time, or just smiling at a stranger are all ways to show love that spreads. It doesn't take enormous acts of kindness to grow love; it takes modest, intentional actions of compassion that happen all the time. Love becomes a way of life when we live for other people, not just a feeling. From that vantage point, life itself begins to feel more whole and vital, and it alters our perception of other people.

Being selfless shows what love really is: how long it can stay. Putting someone else first provides a strong foundation that can manage tough times and disappointments. Love that grows when you put others first is strong, not weak. It realizes that partnerships aren't about taking turns winning; they're about being there for each other no matter what. When you can let go of your pride, forgive, and let others in, love grows. The more you do it, the more you see that being selfless enriches you. Your heart grows stronger as you act freely, making it easier for love to flow through you.

The happiest people are those who express love, not those who receive it. When you focus on giving, you stop attempting to obtain what you want. You start to think of love as a choice, not something you have to do. In such a place, where genuine care and no pressure exist, love blossoms spontaneously. As love grows, it becomes based on who you are and what you do, not just how you feel. Being selfless teaches us that love doesn't go away when things become rough; it grows stronger because it learns to adapt and last.

Chapter: 21

Most individuals are primarily concerned with their interests; therefore, performing a kind act for another person is one of the most effective ways to demonstrate genuine affection. It's a strategy to fight against your pride and ego. Putting others first teaches us that love isn't about being in charge; it's about working together. We make love flourish when we choose love over wrath, compassion over judgment, and understanding over blame. Selflessness is like water for relationships; it helps them develop even when they are dry. It transforms "me" into "we," thereby ensuring that love endures eternally rather than merely for the present moment.

Love that is not selfish also lasts. People will pass on the kindness you show them. Your kindness makes other people kind, your patience teaches others to be patient, and your compassion reminds the world that love is still there. Doing little things for others every day is how love grows. The more you offer, the more you spark that same fire in other people. It makes the world a little warmer, one heart at a time. It's a chain reaction that happens quietly but has a significant effect.

Be unselfish if you want your love to flourish. Even if no one is watching, choose to contribute. Don't interrupt when someone is talking, forgive without recording what they did wrong, and serve without expecting anything in return. It grows when we see love as something we can give rather than get. The hearts that are the happiest aren't the ones that were loved flawlessly; they're the ones that learned to love without expecting anything in return. And that kind of love keeps expanding once it has started.

Chapter: 21

Love and Selflessness
Balancing selflessness and self-care

I t is an admirable quality to love someone unconditionally, without anticipating anything in return; however, it is equally prudent to recognize the appropriate moment to cease. Real love isn't about giving up everything to make someone else content. It's about giving from the heart, not an empty one. Many people think that being unselfish means putting their needs last, which is wrong. But love that lasts isn't built on rage or tiredness; it's built on balance. When you learn how to care for yourself while still caring for others, your love grows stronger and healthier. It goes from harmful to healing, from taking to giving.

To establish a balance between caring for yourself and caring for others, you need to understand that you can't offer when your cup is empty. Giving your time, energy, and heart to the people you love is excellent, but not if it hurts you. You should never compromise your identity to love someone. Instead, it tells you to be the finest version of yourself, both mentally and spiritually. You may be more patient, understanding, and kind to others when you take care of your peace. It's not selfish to take care of oneself; it's getting ready to be selfless. It makes sure the love you provide is authentic, not forced or used up.

We sometimes think that saying "no" means we aren't concerned about someone. However, genuine love understands when it is necessary to pause. Setting limits doesn't mean shutting people out; it means retaining your ability to love well. It is recognizing that you need to take a break, think, and breathe some fresh air before you can act freely. Saying "I need time to breathe" means you are wise. That break allows you time to heal and prepare your heart to help again. Love shouldn't make you feel empty; it should fill you up. You can only do that if you learn to care for yourself and others.

Chapter: 21

The truth is that if you don't take care of yourself, being selfless will wear you out over time. You can start to feel irritated, unappreciated, or emotionally depleted. Previously appreciated gestures can become laborious. That's why you should check in with yourself often. "Am I giving because I want to or because I have to?" Love that isn't selfish grows best when it's based on happiness, not duty. It's about giving because you want to, not because you have to. When you feel good about yourself, it's easy to give, and it feels terrific. But when you're exhausted, even the tiniest thing might feel like a lot. Love stays real when you take time to relax, ponder, and rejuvenate.

Self-care doesn't always mean traveling to a spa or a quiet place. A lot of the time, it's about making modest, conscious choices. It involves selecting to pray or meditate when concerned, to rest when fatigued, or to walk when in need of reflection. It concerns allocating time for activities that bring you joy, as happiness nourishes your well-being. When your spirit is whole, you can love without worry. Your heart is like a flower bed. If you solely tend to the flowers of others and neglect your own, everything will perish. But if you take care of your soul, love can bloom for everyone else.

In a relationship, being selfless and caring for yourself means being honest about your needs. People who are honest with one another grow in love, not when they keep quiet about their problems. Occasionally, we mistakenly believe that loving someone means avoiding arguments or constantly yielding. However, silence can cause people to feel distant rather than connected. You can say something like "I need help" or "I need space." You don't have to feel terrible about it. True love understands that loyalty entails truthfulness and fairness. A relationship's rhythm of giving and receiving is maintained when both partners look after their own emotional well-being.

Chapter: 21

You don't have to give up who you are to be selfless. Love was never meant to change who you are; it was designed to make you better. If you love someone without expecting anything in return and respect your limits, you can still be yourself and be connected with them. That balance improves relations between people. You bring your complete self to the table, not a version of yourself that is worn out from giving too much. Choosing to be selfless is more meaningful than doing it out of habit or obligation. There is a distinction between giving out of desire and giving out of necessity. One comes from being brave, and the other comes from being afraid.

Relationships are often more peaceful and pleasurable for those who practice balanced love. When both individuals, whether partners, friends, or family, give each other room and energy, love blossoms stress-free. People are essential not only for what they do but also for who they are. That kind of love lasts because it's grown-up, thoughtful, and shared. It doesn't need to be sacrificed all the time; it celebrates shared understanding. When you respect your limits, you show others that they should do the same. Together, you develop a relationship that feels free, not forced.

Balancing selflessness with self-care is a more profound spiritual truth: both are ways to show appreciation. You can express respect for the life and love that God or the universe gave you by taking care of yourself. When you serve others, you are sharing that blessing. You can't have one without the other. Love at its best is a cycle of giving and receiving, resting and serving, and breathing in and out. Selflessness makes connections, and self-care makes you stronger. One needs the other to live. The balance between them keeps love alive for you and others.

Chapter: 21

Mastering the art of balancing Selflessness and self-care is not something you can do just once. It's critical to recognize when you're overexerting yourself and to have the fortitude to stop when necessary. Love can sometimes demand sacrifice, but it should never take away your peace of mind or your identity. The best connections allow both parties to contribute and develop. You can have a deep affection for someone and still be vibrant. That is something that will endure; it is not self-serving. Being more balanced allows you to support the people who are most important to you.

When you love from a place of fullness, everyone benefits. You give because you have enough, not because you feel guilty. You like helping other people and taking care of yourself. This kind of equilibrium keeps people from getting upset, makes them grateful, and brings serenity. Love that is built on caring for each other lasts because it grows. When you're weary, it doesn't work; when you're connected, it does. And that bond grows stronger when both people recognize that love isn't about who can give up more; it's about who can take care of the other person. Taking care of yourself and others is an integral part of one's relationship. One makes the other stronger.

You love people best when you love yourself well. And you love yourself most when your heart is open to others. The idea isn't to provide too much or to guard yourself too much; it's to discover that hallowed middle ground where love flows freely in both directions. When you find out that balance, love is like a mirror of peace: it stays constant, is gentle, and is powerful enough to last. The best approach to express what it means to provide without losing yourself is to love in a way that is both generous and grounded.

Chapter: 21

One of the most challenging things to do is to learn selflessness, which is one of the purest kinds of love. This chapter covered how love blossoms when we prioritize others, give genuine gifts, and take good care of ourselves. Sit down for a moment and think about what you know about non-selfish love. The purpose of this questionnaire is to assist you in comprehending the key ideas of these lessons.

1. Think of a time when you chose to put someone else's needs before your own. How did that experience make you feel: drained, fulfilled, or something in between? Reflect on what that moment taught you about your capacity to love selflessly.

2. In what ways do you believe putting others first strengthens relationships? Consider moments when your compassion, patience, or forgiveness made a difference in how someone else felt loved or valued.

3. The chapter discussed that love grows when we act selflessly. Can you think of a specific relationship that improved because you chose to give without expecting anything in return? What changed in that connection, and what changed in you?

4. Sometimes we mistake selflessness for self-denial. Have you ever found yourself giving too much, to the point where you felt depleted or taken for granted? What lessons did that teach you about the need for balance in love?

5. Love that endures requires awareness of one's own limits. How do you recognize when your love is coming from a healthy place, and when it's crossing into self-neglect? Reflect on how you can protect your energy while still showing up for others.

6. What does "the power of putting others first" mean to you personally? How does it shape your understanding of love in family, friendships, or romantic relationships? Write about one small, intentional way you can apply this principle in your daily life.

Chapter: 21

Being selfless means caring about others and yourself. If you want to love genuinely, you have to love wisely. These ideas prompt you to consider how self-care and giving can complement each other, how establishing boundaries can foster love, and how selflessness, when rooted in strength, enhances both the giver and the recipient.

7. The chapter made it apparent that love grows every day via modest acts of kindness. What are some small gestures you can perform for others that require minimal effort but help strengthen your relationships?

8. Think about what it means to give in a fair way. How does taking care of yourself help you love other people more? Write about how being kind, patient, and forgiving is easier when you take care of yourself.

9. Consider your limits. Do you find it challenging to say "no" when you need some time alone? How do you set loving limits that keep you calm and able to care for others?

10. How can you make altruism a daily habit? Think about how you can be kind, understanding, and graceful every day.

11. Think about how you would describe selfless love to a kid or a younger version of yourself. What does it mean to contribute without losing yourself? What do you think people can do to love themselves and others at the same time?

12. Finally, take a deep breath and ask yourself what a healthy, selfless love looks like in your life right now. What small thing can you do today to take care of it, both for yourself and for others? Remember, love and prioritizing others are inextricably linked. When you learn to balance giving and growing, serving and resting, you'll find that your passion develops and lasts. Love that originates from the heart and gives freely is the healthiest kind. It always takes care of itself.

Chapter: 22

Love in Service to Others
How serving others is a profound act of love

L ove is more than simply a sensation; it's something we do. Helping others is frequently the best way to show you care. It is being willing to devote your time, energy, and concern to others without expecting anything in return. Serving others is an excellent way to demonstrate love, as it is rooted in actions rather than emotions. Anyone can say "I love you," but showing love through actions, particularly when it is challenging, proves that love is genuine. When people help others, they can sense love. It makes love real. It's in the food we cook, the hands we touch, and the moments we choose to be there when it would be easier to remain away.

We offer a part of our heart when we aid others. When we help others, we learn to be humble because we have to set our wants aside and focus on theirs. It reminds us that love is about kindness, connection, and giving, not money, power, or gain. Authentic service does not seek recognition or acclaim; it simply acts out of genuine love for others. Each time you assist someone—whether by helping a friend move, volunteering in your community, or merely listening to someone in need of support—you send out a ripple of compassion that extends beyond what you may realize, touching the lives of many more individuals than you might imagine.

When we assist others, we undergo internal transformation. It helps us be more open-minded and kinder. We begin to perceive the world differently when we aid those in need. We begin to notice beauty in small things and feel thankful in areas we didn't anticipate. Being of service makes us humble because it reminds us that everyone is valuable and capable of kindness. Serving others shows us that love is more than words; it's also actions. And when we serve, we discover that love isn't something we give away; it's something that grows within us.

Chapter: 22

Helping others is a way to show love that transcends differences. It brings together people with different backgrounds, opinions, and problems. When you serve someone, you are saying, "I see you, and you matter." That simple "thank you" can make someone's day or perhaps alter their life. Loving in service doesn't mean fixing people or addressing every situation. It's about being open-hearted and there. Occasionally, the best way to help is to be there for someone. Sitting in silence next to someone, smiling at them, or helping them may seem like a tiny gesture, but it means a lot to them. Service illustrates that love doesn't necessarily need extravagant gestures; it blossoms in small things.

You should also know that helping others doesn't imply losing oneself in the process. Service is healthy when it comes from a place of compassion, not duty. When you support others, they can energize you rather than drain your energy. Being there for someone is more important than attempting to save them. There is a calm beauty in doing what you can with what you have and where you are. It doesn't matter how enormous the act is; what matters is how real it is. A gift given with love is holy, no matter how modest.

Helping others can also help people get to know one another better. Helping our family, friends, or even strangers fosters a more profound understanding and builds trust. Love grows stronger when individuals help each other. In a service-based relationship, you care for each other rather than fight or control. You start to perceive love as a group effort, where every thoughtful thing you do strengthens the bond. When you help other people, you are telling them, "You're not alone." And living that reality all the time makes connections that last.

Chapter: 22

Helping others out of love also teaches us to be grateful. When you allow other people, you realize how interwoven life really is. You learn you're lucky not because you have more, but because you can contribute. Assisting someone who is experiencing a difficult period reminds you of your humanity. It keeps you kind, grounded, and attentive. Understanding that giving is a reciprocal relationship deepens your thankfulness. Every time you provide, you receive something back. You learn to have fun, be modest, and see things from other people's perspectives. Love in service reminds us that we are all in the same class of life and learning how to care for each other.

It can also be a spiritual act of helping others. Serving others is a way to exhibit love that extends beyond yourself. Many individuals claim that doing charitable deeds brings them closer to God, the universe, or a greater sense of purpose. That's because love's purest objective is to offer freely, and service fits that goal. When you do something extraordinary for someone else, help them, or show them kindness, serving becomes a form of worship. When we love in deed, we touch something that will last forever. Doing things for others out of love is excellent for both the giver and the receiver. It turns into a living sign of grace.

Service also teaches us that love is beneficial. It's not far away or hard to understand; it's occurring. Love has the power to clean floors, accompany someone to the doctor, or alleviate depression. We show we care about others by the tiny things we do every day. Making small sacrifices, putting in consistent effort, and being willing to help even when you're weary are among the most significant ways to demonstrate love. When you serve out of love, you improve every day. And that light can change lives, one item at a time.

Chapter: 22

Doing enormous things isn't always what it means to help others. It means doing the right things out of love. The smallest things can sometimes have the most significant effect. A handwritten note, a dinner together, or a kind remark can mean more than a tremendous speech. People can sense when you do things with a charitable heart. Individuals may not recall your exact words, but they will invariably remember the way your love made them feel. That's what makes service so strong: it leaves an imprint of kindness that lasts forever. In a culture that often prioritizes acquisition, those who choose to serve exemplify love in action.

Serving others with love also challenges us to be better than we are. It fights arrogance, self-centeredness, and apathy. Because helping others requires paying attention to their needs, listening to their experiences, and understanding their viewpoints, it fosters humility. To have an impact, we only need to be willing; we don't need to be experts. When we serve, we are reminded that love is more than just an emotion; it is also an action. The more we share love with others, the more we learn about it.

Helping others is one of the best ways to show love in the end. It makes us think differently about ourselves and the world around us. When you make service a part of your life, love becomes more than simply a word; it becomes who you are. You start to feel positive about yourself, not because of what you receive, but because of what you offer. The best part is that helping others out of love never leaves you empty. Love has a way of coming back and making your heart feel joyful in a way that nothing else can. That is the essence of service: nurturing love, fostering its growth, and ensuring its enduring presence.

Chapter: 22

Love in Service to Others
Stories of love expressed through service

Not romantic novels or fairy tales, but acts of kindness convey some of the most powerful love stories. Love offered through service is apparent even when silent. It doesn't always look like enormous things or big sacrifices; sometimes it shows up in small, everyday ways. It's the neighbor who checks on an elderly acquaintance every morning, the nurse who treats a patient like family, or the parent who works long hours to provide their kids a better life. Each of these things offers a narrative of love that decides to help.

One example of this kind of love is a woman who worked at a local shelter every weekend for years. She didn't have much money, but she was always charming and warm. She knew their names and birthdays and would sit with them on cold nights. When asked why she kept coming back, she answered, "Love doesn't wait for the right time; it just comes." Her tale shows us that serving others doesn't require the correct instruments; it only requires a willingness. When we help others out of love, we track what we give, not what we have.

There is also a story about a young man who taught kids who didn't have much money how to read in the afternoons. At first, he thought he was helping them, but over time, he learned just as much from them as they did from him. Their humor, strength, and curiosity taught him more about love. He added, "I went there to devote my time, but every day I came home feeling like I got something valuable." This anecdote proves that service is never one-sided. Love grows stronger when you give it away. It transforms the person who offers it and the person who receives it.

Chapter: 22

Acts of service are frequently the most honest ways to show love in families. It's touching to see a father take care of his ill child. He would read stories to his son every night until he fell asleep, no matter how worn out he was. It wasn't simply a job; it was a calling. His service was a daily demonstration of love that didn't need words. Years later, the youngster remembered the love that stayed with them through every sleepless night, not the misery of being sick. You don't always have to say you love someone; sometimes you have to show them.

A tale of a couple who turned their hopelessness into something positive is also included. They started a nonprofit to help children in need of school supplies after their daughter died in an accident. Each year, they distributed hundreds of backpacks brimming with pencils, notes, and optimism. They also claimed that helping others made them feel better and that loving other kids brought them closer to their daughter's spirit. Their experience serves as an excellent reminder that you can help others get back on track. Pain is transformed into eternal love via compassion. It lasts longer than sorrow and provides a sense of purpose to the lost.

Being friends with someone is another fantastic method to help. One woman said that her best friend helped her when she was having a difficult time with depression. Her pal didn't tell her what to do; she just came. She sent her letters, brought her food, and told her she was loved, even when she couldn't see it. You don't have to do that kind of service; you do it because you know how strong love can be. Love's true power is shown when it helps others, like lifting them when they can't do it alone.

Chapter: 22

Communities are also made up of love stories shared via service. Think of the small-town folks who worked together to repair a neighbor's house after a severe storm. They didn't wait for someone else to take the lead. Instead, they brought tools, prepared food, and collaborated to repair the house. A simple act of kindness turned into a movement for peace. The best part about helping others is that it draws people together. When individuals collaborate, barriers dissolve. Serving others out of love transforms neighborhoods into places of hope and turns strangers into family.

Healthcare workers who risk their lives to aid during emergencies are another positive example. A number of them worked long hours away from their families, taking care of sick people and helping lonely people feel better. Not only were they professional, but they were also quite personal. They comforted and held the hands of patients who had no one else. These little bold things showed a lot about love. When people were scared and unsure, service was the light that led them through the dark.

There is also a story about a retired teacher who continued to serve kids in her neighborhood. When she left the classroom, she kept teaching. Every week, she opened her home for tutoring and help. When inquired about her persistent actions, she responded, "Because love endures forever." Her story proves that service doesn't end. As long as we are alive, we have something to offer. Love expressed through service doesn't depend on who you are, how old you are, or your position. It is constantly there, strong, and incredibly human.

Chapter: 22

Even little, secret acts of service can demonstrate a lot of affection. One anecdote is about a man who dropped groceries at his neighbor's door without telling anyone. Another is about a woman who went to the nursing home every week merely to hear the stories of folks who didn't have any visitors. They never begged for acclaim, yet what they did made a difference in people's lives. Their love was subtle, yet it carried a powerful message. That's what genuine service is: it doesn't need an audience. It works because the heart can't ignore the need to care.

One of the most moving anecdotes came from a volunteer who remarked, "The more I serve, the more I realize that love isn't what I feel; it's what I do." She learned that love is in every meal served, every kind deed, and every time she chose to keep assisting people experiencing homelessness after years of doing so. She realized that love does not need to resolve every issue; it merely needs to be present. Her story reminds us that love through service doesn't have to be perfect, just real.

These stories show that helping others is part of our identity. Every time we choose to help, we add to the story of love. We illustrate that love is strongest when it goes beyond words and that kindness and compassion remain crucial. Our actions of service, no matter how great or small, become part of something bigger, a legacy of love that will live on long after we're gone. In the end, every service tells a narrative, and every tale of service indicates that love is still alive.

Chapter: 22

Love in Service to Others
How to cultivate a life of loving service

Y ou live a life of loving service on purpose. Every day, you have to decide to act with love. It starts with a way of thinking that values everyone and sees every moment as a chance to make a difference. To live with purpose means to build a life of service. It's not about how much money you have, what title you have, or what platform you have. It's choosing to look outside of yourself and ask, "How can I help?" That one question can change your life and the lives of others. Start small with service. It begins with an open heart that is ready to see, care, and do.

Being aware is the first step toward a life of loving service. You can't serve what you can't see. Many people are so preoccupied with their issues that they overlook when others are in pain. You need to slow down and look outside of your group to become more conscious. It means being aware of the single mother who is trying to manage her job and family, the neighbor who lives alone, and the friend who is always "fine" but never talks about how they truly feel. We begin to serve when we look beyond individuals' appearances and acknowledge their true identities. When you show love by being attentive, it becomes compassion in action.

The next step in service is to show empathy. You love someone more when you let yourself experience what they feel. It doesn't mean you take on their troubles; it means you care enough to learn about their life. Empathy makes people feel like they are part of something bigger. When you consider how someone else feels, your heart automatically becomes kind. You start to understand that helping others is not a duty but a gift. Serving others out of love gives you a sense of purpose, reminding you that your life should impact others.

Chapter: 22

After understanding and feeling for someone, the following stage is to take action. You must take action regarding the service before it becomes significant. When you do something about it, love develops. You need to make little, steady improvements every day to live a life of service. You don't have to create a charity or travel the world to help people. Usually, your best opportunities are just where you are. It could include helping a coworker who is too busy, giving advice to a young person who needs it, or going to see someone who feels alone. Usually, the most helpful things people don't get reported. Every day, they happen without anyone noticing. You make every day exceptional when you behave out of love.

Consistency is what makes service go from something you do to something you are. Occasional kindness is pleasing, but constant love builds trust and hope. To create a service pattern, you must show up even when it's challenging or no one sees it. A parent who consistently supports their children, a friend who regularly checks in on them, and a volunteer who consistently returns week after week are examples of this. These gestures of kindness, again and again, illustrate that service is more than a profession; it's a way of life. When you always assist others, you become a light in a world that is often gloomy.

You need to be humble if you want to live a life of loving service. When pride is the primary motivator for service, it loses its effectiveness as it shifts from serving honestly to seeking attention. When you're modest, you may help people without wanting anything in return or demanding accolades. It's fine if you don't see the most important acts of service. People shouldn't look up to service; it should make a difference. When you serve others with true humility, you say, "It's not about me." This fundamental truth lets love flow through you freely. When you stop wanting to be recognized and start wanting to make a difference, your service becomes pure, and love flows effortlessly.

Chapter: 22

Being thankful is another crucial part of living a life of loving service. Being grateful transforms how you give. You serve out of gratitude, not guilt. When you recognize how lucky you are, your heart will want to share those beneficial things with others. Being grateful helps you stay focused on what you want and where you are. It serves as a reminder that everything you possess, including your time, energy, and money, is a blessing that you should share. Grateful people enjoy serving because they know giving adds to what they have.

Community also helps businesses grow. Love and service were never meant to be separate. When you come into contact with others who want to help, you set off a chain reaction. One good deed leads to another. People can do far more collaboratively than individually. You learn how to cooperate with other people, be patient, and have a common objective when you build a life of service in a community. It makes you remember that love is for everyone, not just one person. When you cooperate with others to help, you become part of something bigger than yourself. This is a movement of kindness that will never end.

Another key part of leading a life of service is taking care of yourself. Many people start with noble intentions, but quit when they don't manage their feelings. When you are whole, you can best help others. If you neglect your well-being, you will ultimately be compelled to either surrender or harbor resentment. When you take a break, pray, contemplate, or breathe, love can fill your spirit anew. You can't give away something you don't own. Balance isn't selfish; it's essential. The more you take care of your peace of mind, the more you can love others via your work.

Chapter: 22

You need to set aside time to reflect on your purpose: to live a life of loving service. Periodically, pause and reflect: "Am I continuing these actions driven by love?" It's easy to let routine take the place of meaning. Reflection helps you stay on track with your goals and keep your heart open. You can remain true to your purpose by journaling, praying, or reflecting on how your actions affect others. When you look back on things, you remember how beneficial it feels to help others and how even the tiniest act of service can have ramifications that reach far beyond what you can see.

Love is shown via service. Service often takes place in the background, yet it leaves a lasting impact. You have to learn to be patient if you want to live a life of service. You might not see the consequences of your work immediately. The person you help today might not say thank you, and the benefits you achieve might go unnoticed. But love doesn't measure success by how many people cheer; it measures it by how loyal you are. No matter what, keep serving. Even if you can't see it, every kind act you do leaves a mark. When love is patient in service, it communicates, "I trust that what I'm doing matters." You'll start to understand that even modest acts of kindness can, over time, change other people's lives for the better.

Living a life of loving service ultimately requires having a purpose every day. It's waking up to improve the world and sleeping knowing you did something good, even if no one saw. It's choosing to be friendly instead of easy, to provide instead of take, and to be present instead of being prideful. If you make service a part of your life, loving others will come to you. You realize that loving service is about who you become as you help others. Every time you do something beneficial for someone, your love for them deepens, strengthens, and lasts longer. That is the most crucial thing to contemplate when you want to live a meaningful life.

Chapter: 22

Doing things for others is one of the best ways to demonstrate love. When we help others, we move from words and sentiments to actions, where love is genuine and can be seen. This chapter discusses how helping others changes both the person who helps and the person who receives it, how love is demonstrated through simple acts of kindness, and how living a life of service affords a sense of purpose that lasts longer than praise.

1. Think of a time when you served someone out of love, without expecting anything in return. How did that experience make you feel? Did it bring a sense of peace, fulfillment, or perspective? Describe the emotions that came with that act of service.

2. Reflect on a moment when someone else served you out of genuine care. What did their kindness teach you about love and humility? How did their act of service impact your understanding of giving and receiving?

3. This chapter emphasized that serving others is a profound act of love. What do you think makes service so powerful? Why do you believe helping others can heal hearts—including your own?

4. Out of all the stories shared in this chapter, which one resonated with you the most? What lesson about love did you take away from that story, and how does it inspire you to serve in your own way?

5. Service often happens in simple, unseen ways. What small acts of kindness can you practice daily that would bring light to someone's life? List examples of how love can be quietly expressed through service at home, at work, or in your community.

6. Sometimes, people hesitate to serve because they think they have too little to give. Reflect on how you can serve even with limited time or resources. What does this teach you about the heart of service being more important than the size of the gift?

Chapter: 22

Service is motivated by love. It changes people's hearts, creates bonds, and gives life purpose. We must learn to combine humility with intention, awareness with empathy, and constancy with gratitude in order to live a life of loving service. Discover how to integrate service into your everyday life by thinking about these concepts.

7. What motivates you to serve others? Is it compassion, gratitude, faith, or personal experience? Take time to explore your "why" and how it shapes the way you love through service.

8. How can you cultivate a heart that notices the needs of others more easily?

9. Many people struggle with burnout when giving too much of themselves. How can you maintain a healthy balance between serving others and caring for your own emotional and physical well-being?

10. Reflect on a person in your life who models loving service. What do they do that makes their love so genuine? What qualities do you admire in their approach to helping others?

11. Think about the community around you, your family, workplace, neighborhood, or church. What are some meaningful ways you can bring love into action there? How can your service inspire others to do the same?

12. Finally, describe what a life of loving service looks like to you. If someone observed your daily actions, what would they see as evidence of love in motion?

Serving others doesn't require perfection; it just requires a willing heart. Every time you act with compassion, you're building a bridge of love that connects you to something greater than yourself.

Chapter: 23

The Joy of Loving Fully
The fulfillment that comes from loving wholeheartedly

No level of fame, wealth, or achievement can ultimately provide the same fulfillment as loving someone wholeheartedly. It's the deep happiness that comes from knowing you poured your heart into something worthwhile and essential. You can love someone even if you are imperfect and feel sorrow. Even if it costs you something, you have to be there for someone. When you express your love freely, without holding back or placing conditions on it, you start to sense a richness that words can't fully convey. When you express love honestly, it always comes back, even if you don't anticipate it. If you want to love completely, you have to choose openness over protection. It's the option where the prospect of connecting is worth the chance of being let down.

Loving with all your heart means enduring hurt, but you will also feel an indescribable beauty. People who love truly aren't concerned about what they receive in return; they care about how their love helps them grow. Every sincere act of love, no matter how small, makes your life slightly brighter. It reminds you that love isn't about having someone; it's about being with them. It's all about being there for someone else, heart to heart.

Many people don't demonstrate love because they're scared of losing it. They think that distance will keep their hearts secure, so they protect them like glass. But you can only be fully fulfilled if you let yourself love with both strength and gentleness. You begin to understand that love doesn't run out when you freely give it to your partner, family, friends, or even strangers. When you share it, it grows bigger. The more you love, the more you can love. Love is a subtle wonder that gets bigger the more you give it.

Chapter: 23

When you love someone profoundly, you begin to see things differently. You start to notice minute details that have deep significance, like the way someone laughs, the peacefulness of spending quiet time with someone, or the beauty of the morning sun. You become aware of how remarkable even the smallest things are when you are in love. It teaches you to be grateful for what you currently have rather than pining for what you lack. That metamorphosis changes everything. Instead of looking for perfect circumstances, you learn to enjoy the things that make life enjoyable. Being in a position of power is not a prerequisite for showing love; simply caring for someone is enough.

One further thing to know about wholehearted love is that it transforms how you interact with others. You stop judging someone and start caring about them when you really love them. You no longer monitor others' actions; instead, you focus on improving yourself. You begin to realize that everyone is battling their own conflicts that you can't see. Knowing that makes you more patient, kind, and understanding. You feel positive when you know you're spreading light into the lives of those around you instead of darkness. You choose to love, not because it's easy, but because that's who you are.

Loving someone fully also helps you feel more connected to your purpose. It makes you remember that your life has more value than just getting things done or gaining applause. When you love others deliberately, you connect with something that will stay forever. You begin to perceive your acts, like being kind, forgiving, and generous, as part of a larger flow of love in the world. Every caring choice you make leaves a mark that will last long after you're gone. Knowing this brings you peace. You recognize that your love has left an indelible mark that time cannot diminish, even during challenging moments or periods of uncertainty. Nothing else can take away the feeling of satisfaction that comes from loving truly.

Chapter: 23

Loving totally doesn't imply loving without bounds; it means loving without fear. It's about trying your best without losing who you are. Many people think that love and self-sacrifice are the same thing, but they are not. To love someone truly, you have to love yourself enough to be honest, take breaks when you need them, and let go of things that aren't beneficial for you. Undermining yourself for the sake of another is not genuine love; authentic love involves strengthening your hearts in ways that enhance both of you. When you love someone in a balanced way, your happiness lasts longer because it's grounded in reality rather than in needing them. When you contemplate it, the joy of loving someone fully often comes to mind.

When you look back on your life, you won't remember the items you bought or the prizes you received. You will recall the people you loved and the beneficial experiences you had with them. You will remember the laughter that shattered the silence in a room. The hug that conveyed everything without uttering a single word will be remembered. The forgiveness that restored a seemingly broken relationship will also be remembered. These are the things that a heart that loves fully holds dear. They are the things that make you remember that you lived, not merely existed.

It might hurt to love someone entirely at times. It could mean giving up what you want to keep, forgiving someone even when you don't want to, or choosing grace over pride. However, even in moments of pain, authentic love provides comfort by reminding you of the depth of your capacity to care. When you love sincerely, it shows that your heart is alive and open. People who love that way feel everything that makes us human: the joy, the pain, and the growth. Through all these experiences, they come to understand that love consistently restores their faith in hope, even when it faces challenges.

Chapter: 23

One of the best things about loving truly is that you learn to be present. Many of us worry too much about the future or reflect too much about the past. But wholehearted love only works right now. It is in the way you laugh, the way you touch others, and the silent support you offer during challenging times. When you're really present, you don't take love for granted; you relish it. You stop rushing through life and start seeing it with eyes of gratitude and connection. Providing support to someone is the most meaningful expression of love; it transforms each moment into a cherished memory.

When you love completely, you also fill empty spaces with happiness. When love is the most essential thing in your life, you start to notice how beneficial it feels to help, soothe, and lift others. Love is what keeps you going, even when things are tough. It enables you to figure out why you're going through something and what you should do about it. Those who love this way are confident because they know happiness comes from within, not from external events. A heart that loves completely carries light wherever it goes, even into the darkest periods of life.

Loving completely is the nicest thing about life. It's the peace of mind that comes from knowing you did your best, the freedom that comes from being true to yourself, and the joy that comes from giving your all to the people and things that mattered most. To love completely is to live completely. You should know that every connection, no matter how short, is vital for the rest of your life. When you love wholeheartedly, you leave behind a legacy that neither time nor space can diminish. Your love is like a thread that makes other people's lives more beautiful. That's what makes life worth living.

Chapter: 23

The Joy of Loving Fully
How love brings joy to both the giver and receiver

L ove is powerful because it alters both the giver and the receiver. Giving love openly and honestly makes both individuals pleased. It's not a transaction or a one-way exchange; it's an energy that flows back and forth, strengthening connections, healing scars, and giving life greater meaning. When you love from a place of honesty and kindness, you feel a level of satisfaction that nothing else can match. That's because giving, not having, is what makes you happy. Love is one of the few things in life that grows as you share it. When we love other people, we remember who we are and why we are here.

You cannot truly love someone if you do not feel alive, as love requires presence, openness, and the willingness to be vulnerable and hurt. It awakens your soul's holy side, which wants to connect with, give to, and care for others. When you love someone, you stop worrying about yourself and your issues and start viewing things from their perspective. You realize that love isn't about being flawless; it's about being there. It fundamentally involves supporting others, actively listening to them, and offering kindness during their most critical moments.

People change when they demonstrate love, and occasionally, they change more than the one who receives it. Think back to a time when you did something nice for someone, such as doing a small favor, saying something kind, or making a genuine gesture. Even before they say "thank you," you sense a quiet joy inside. You perceive it that way because you recognize that you have contributed, even if only to a minor extent. Love comes back to you as calm and joy. Love always comes back; back, that's the reality. When you express love without expecting anything in return, it comes back to you in ways you didn't expect. The fact is what it means to love fully: the delight that comes from your love being a bridge between spirits.

Chapter: 23

Love does not need to be grand or dramatic to bring happiness, which is a reassuring aspect of it. A tiny gesture of love can mean a lot. For instance, it can be as simple as offering someone a warm smile, reaching out to check on their well-being, or simply sitting beside a friend who is struggling. These little things may appear insignificant, yet they mean a lot. When you give selflessly, without anticipating anything in return, that is when love is at its most genuine. You recall that it's a beneficial thing to offer during those times. More than any success, loving others makes your spirit feel warmer and more whole. Even more astounding is the fact that love spreads.

When you love someone, they feel important, seen, and inspired to love others. It spreads on its own, like sunlight that touches everything in its path. A positive phrase can make someone feel better and encourage them to be nicer to others. A single act of love can move many hearts in a matter of minutes. The giver feels positive knowing that their acts have set off a chain reaction of wonderful things, and the receiver keeps it going. Love grows not by force, but by its own calm power. Science backs the idea up as well. Researchers have shown that when people are kind, their brains release oxytocin, the "love hormone" that makes us feel content and connected. It indicates that love is designed to suit both individuals in a relationship.

The person who gives feels positively about themselves because they've helped someone else, and the one who receives feels satisfied because someone cared enough to recognize them. This heavenly equilibrium is what makes love the strongest feeling. It starts over again. You don't lose love when you share it out; instead, you acquire more of it since every act of love makes you feel and experience greater delight.

Chapter: 23

When love flows freely between individuals, something profound happens: it gives life purpose. You understand that life extends beyond mere existence or survival; it encompasses forming meaningful friendships. Every time you show love to someone, whether it's a friend, family member, romantic partner, or even simply a stranger, you learn what really counts. The giver feels like they have a purpose, and the receiver feels like they belong. Both hearts remain joyful long after the interaction ends. People who put love at the core of their lives generally say they are always cheerful, even when things are challenging. But it isn't always straightforward to discover happiness in love.

When you love someone, you may have to wait to leave or forgive them when it seems unfair. Those gestures of love need both humility and courage, but they also produce a deeper form of delight. You discover strength you didn't know you possessed when you choose love, even when it's challenging. You feel pleased knowing that you decided grace over pride and kindness over fury. The person you present to may never fully understand how much you love them, but the act of giving changes you. That's the pure joy of unconditional love. It makes you feel more whole and improves your soul.

The individual who gains love has their strength. It can repair what years of pain or loneliness have broken. It offers people hope when they don't have any and reminds them that they matter. When someone feels sincerely loved, without any conditions or judgments, they feel more confident and acquire a sense of purpose. They begin to see themselves as cherished instead of terrified. The satisfaction they experience transforms them in numerous ways. They are reminded that compassion and kindness are genuine and that everyone may be saved or cared for.

Chapter: 23

When love is shared and returned, its excitement intensifies. Love is bright, much like light, regardless of how often you reflect it. When both the giver and the recipient are honest, their enthusiasm makes them happy. They get knowledge from each other. The receiver gains appreciation, while the giver gains kindness. Together, they create a circle of grace that sustains them during trying times. As a result, communities, friendships, and families can flourish through the sacred exchange.

Remember that love doesn't have to be flawless for you to be content. When things go wrong, real love is patient, compassionate, and forgiving. To be pleased in love, you don't need a perfect relationship. You need to remain committed to choosing love, even when circumstances are less than ideal. When both hearts are open, love becomes a journey of discovery. You realize how much happiness can come from little things, like a hug after a quarrel, a shared joke, or a simple word of support. These are the small wonders that make life worth living.

The best thing about love is that it makes people who are brave enough to accept it truly joyful again. The more you love, the more alive you feel. Love doesn't drain your vitality; it provides you with new life. It tells you that even when things look shaky, there is always something pure and lasting close by. Love makes everyone happy because it links hearts in ways that nothing else can. It turns ordinary days into gifts and ordinary individuals into vessels of grace. When you live a life built on love, you discover that happiness isn't something you seek; it's something you create, one loving act at a time.

Chapter: 23

The Joy of Loving Fully
Embracing the richness of love in daily life

The real beauty of love isn't in big gestures or life-changing events; it's in the little, quiet things that happen every day. To thoroughly enjoy the richness of love in your daily life, you need to learn to perceive it as a way of being, not just something that happens on special occasions. You can express affection by sharing laughter with someone, offering a kind word, or witnessing the sunrise. It's the smile you convey to a stranger, the patience you exhibit when someone bothers you, or the gratitude you feel when someone remembers your name. Love grows softly and thrives in these modest, often-ignored moments.

Love is rich not because it is rare, but because it is always there. We frequently forget to look at the little things in life. People seek love as if it were a distant treasure, yet love is already an integral part of our lives. Love is in the friends who listen, the people who care, and the problems that teach us patience. Love is in the friends who listen, the people who care, and the issues that teach us patience. When you choose to notice these simple things, life feels more complete. You start to recognize the extent of love that surrounds you, even during challenging times. You can see love in everything, and every moment is a symbol of it. To live in this manner, you need to be awake and stop hurrying through life. Instead, do one thoughtful thing at a time.

When we learn to accept love in our daily lives, we also realize that love isn't always about romance or excitement. It's about being reliable and being there for yourself and others, even when things are going well. A gentle touch, a kind word, or a quiet prayer are all small ways to show love. When you do it deliberately, love grows deeper. This phenomenon deepens not only during moments of passion but also during everyday moments of patience. Love is full of the little things that show caring, kindness, and faithfulness. It's not about being perfect; it's about being there.

Chapter: 23

Daily love has an impact on your perspective of the world. When love is your foundation, you see the world differently. You begin to understand people rather than pass judgment on them. Additionally, you become intrigued instead of critical. You are aware that even the smallest actions you take can make a big difference in the world. When done with love, tasks like cooking, cleaning, and going to work can all be considered sacred. All that is necessary for life to be beautiful is for it to be purposeful and kind.

Love often becomes lost in a world that values speed and getting things done. But love takes time to listen, watch, and connect. It blooms in solitude. When you take a moment to meet someone's gaze, genuinely listen to their words, or share a silent presence, you are demonstrating love in its most authentic form. Being fully present makes you happy in a way that nothing else can. It's knowing that this moment and this place are enough. When you stop wanting more and enjoy what you currently have, your love for it deepens. You have to accept the defects that come with love if you're going to love fully in everyday life.

People will let you down. Things will be different. Some days, your most excellent effort won't be enough. But when you love life, you learn to let go of anger, forgive fast, and see grace where others see failure. Love teaches you to accept things as they are while still hoping for better things to come. It is rich because it is strong. When things aren't perfect, love doesn't fall apart; it finds beauty in them. Every problem is an opportunity to learn something new, be kinder, and practice the patience that keeps genuine relationships going.

Chapter: 23

When you start contemplating love every day, your relationships begin to change. You stop wanting someone to meet all your needs and start liking them for who they are. Love is more about accepting someone than trying to control them. You stop trying to change other people and begin to appreciate them. This shift will make you and your relationships more peaceful. To love, you must learn that being kind is enough; you don't have to correct everything. You make others feel at ease when you treat them this way. Love is also complete on the inside.

People often forget that they have to love themselves first. It can be challenging to recognize the beauty in ordinary life if you are always hard on yourself or don't pay attention to your needs. To love oneself means to be kind to yourself by letting yourself relax, fail, and mend. When you love yourself, you can love other people more. You are less likely to respond, more patient, and more present. To love yourself every day, you need to be conscious of yourself and ask yourself how you can bring gentleness into your heart so that you may express it to others. A heart that is full of love is far stronger than an empty one. As you go about your day, you will discover love in places you didn't expect.

Occasionally, it's the laughter of a child, the advice of a grandparent, or the help of a friend. A stranger may surprise you with their generosity. Pay attention to the constant signs of love that life sends your way. Take the time to enjoy these small things instead of rushing through them; your days will feel longer. You can always count on love, even when things are horrible. It's the peaceful conviction that beauty still exists, that connection still matters, and that kindness still has worth.

Chapter: 23

You let love become your rhythm when you accept the richness of love in your daily existence. It's the first thing you do and the last thing you remember. That means I'm thankful every morning for another chance to love and be loved. It's about learning to discover the holy in everyday things, such as the sun's warmth, the comfort of routine, and the power of forgiveness. When love is a part of your life, your days don't feel empty anymore. They are filled. You cease waiting for happiness to arrive and instead begin to recognize that it is already present, concealed within the small details you often overlook. Living with love at the core of your existence makes your life calmer.

Love alters your heart such that worry, comparison, and anxiety don't have as much power over you anymore. Love makes labor meaningful, duty enjoyable, and faults beautiful. You make an imprint on the world with everything you do out of love. It reminds you that you matter and that your kindness has a greater impact on more people than you can see. That is what renders love so extraordinary: it develops in unseen ways and transforms lives in ways beyond your awareness. To truly accept love, you must be vigilant and cognizant of every opportunity to exchange, forgive, and grow.

Love makes the commonplace spectacular, the everyday sacred, and the fleeting eternal. If you think this way about life, you'll discover that love doesn't just fill your days; it changes them. You do not seek love; instead, you cultivate it through each decision, every word, and all acts of kindness. That's where real happiness is found in the end: not in what we obtain, but in how much we love along the journey.

Chapter: 23

Making the decision to love with all of your heart is really important. Love not only strengthens ties and promotes emotional growth, but it also gives life a meaning that nothing else can. This chapter explored the beauty of freely giving love, the joy that comes from doing so, and the depth of daily life when love acts as a compass. The following questions are designed to help you think about your own experiences with perfect love, how you give and receive it, and how it affects your daily life.

1. When you think about "loving wholeheartedly," what does that personally look like for you? Describe a moment when you loved without hesitation or holding back. How did that act impact your heart?

2. Reflect on a time when you felt deeply fulfilled by loving someone else. What about that experience brought you satisfaction or joy? How did it change the way you view relationships?

3. This chapter discusses how wholehearted love is often tied to vulnerability. What fears tend to hold you back from loving more openly? What steps could help you loosen those fears?

4. Joy often shows up unexpectedly through small loving gestures. What simple acts of love—either given or received—have brought you joy recently? How can you incorporate more of these into your daily life?

5. Think of someone in your life who loves wholeheartedly. What about their actions or attitude inspires you? How do they enrich the lives of others simply by the way they love?

6. Joy is described as something that returns to the giver of love. How have you personally experienced this? When you think of the moments you've given of yourself, what memories come to mind?

Chapter: 23

Love's ability to create joy is not limited to life-changing experiences; it may also be shown in ordinary deeds, such as small acts of kindness, patience, and thankfulness. To truly understand the depth of love, one must recognize that there are opportunities to promote warmth and connectedness in the world every single day. Taking these things into account will help you analyze how you currently show love and how you could develop a more profound sense of happiness that comes from unconditional, complete love.

7. How does giving love change your emotional or spiritual state? Do you feel lighter, more connected, or more grounded when you act out of love?

8. What daily habits or routines could help you stay more aware of opportunities to love others? How can you become more intentional about expressing love even in ordinary moments?

9. Consider how you receive love. Are you able to accept kindness, compliments, or support without discomfort? How does allowing others to love you increase joy in your life?

10. Reflect on how love shows up in your daily environment—your home, workplace, friendships, and routines. Where do you see love already present, and where might you want to add more of it?

11. Describe a moment in which someone's love helped you see life differently. How did their kindness or presence shift your perspective? What does that teach you about the ripple effect of love?

12. Thinking about your own life, what would embracing the "richness of love" look like on a practical level? What small commitments can you make to ensure love remains at the center of your words, decisions, and actions?

As you consider these questions, remember that love doesn't need perfection to bring joy; it only needs sincerity.

Chapter: 24

The Legacy of Love
How love leaves a lasting impact on future generations

L ove has a remarkable potential for endurance, in contrast to many other aspects of existence. True love endures and transcends our earthly condition, even as riches fade, achievements overshadow, and material belongings become less appealing. Our intangible inheritance is the lasting influence of love, which shapes people, influences choices, and influences generations to come, some of whom we may never meet. By fostering love, whether as a parent, spouse, friend, or mentor, people plant the seeds of influence that last long after their lives are over. Acts of generosity become treasured recollections of safety. In interpersonal relationships, compassionate behavior acts as a model. Being patient sets the standard for future interactions. Love thus quietly becomes a legacy unaffected by time.

Every family has a tradition of love, sometimes expressed and sometimes not. Consider the stories of sacrifice shared by older family members, which resonate throughout the family. A grandfather dedicated long hours to creating opportunities for his children, which he himself did not have. One mother kept the family together despite facing hardship. A sibling consistently demonstrated unwavering loyalty. These expressions of affection form the emotional legacy passed down through generations. Even those who never met its founders feel the legacy's impact through the values and stories passed down through the ages. Their devotion molded your family's culture, creating a foundation for your own.

What gives love its enduring power is its ability to educate by example. Receiving kindness in return creates an inbuilt desire to return the favor, but it is also possible to foster compassion. Deep forgiveness also encourages continued forgiveness. Love sets an example for future generations when it is shown consistently and publicly. More effective than verbal instruction, observable acts help children, in particular, internalize love. They watch how people behave, settle disputes, and show affection. These realizations significantly affect their capacity to love their family in the future. Our everyday acts, therefore, indirectly influence an invisible future.

Chapter: 24

The stories family members tell also carry on the family's history. These tales, whether they are about a parent's sacrifices, a grandparent's hardships, or how a couple met, are significant. Hearing about their forebears overcoming adversity with elegance and strength encourages young people to be resilient themselves. In this sense, love becomes a source of strength. They learn that they are descended from individuals who valued kindness, loyalty, and connection. Listening to these tales helps future generations understand their role in a larger story, a history of love that has overcome adversity and persevered. These memories serve as a reminder that love is always valued, even in the face of hardship.

Love has practical advantages for future generations in addition to its emotional ones. In addition to stronger ethical values, affectionate families tend to use more positive communication styles and have higher levels of trust. These qualities help youngsters interact with the world safely and securely. They learn to appreciate their viewpoints, their intrinsic worth, and the importance of work and openness in relationships. When love forms the foundation of a family, it fosters healthy relationships between generations. Conversely, dysfunctional families frequently perpetuate cycles of pain, miscommunication, or emotional distancing. Nevertheless, a single person consciously choosing love can break these patterns. A single heart committed to a different kind of love can radically change the course of a whole family's history.

Another example of the lasting impact of love is the ideals we pass on. Rather than being inherited, generosity, forgiveness, and empathy are developed through life events. Youngsters deeply ingrain these values when they witness adults who help others, show compassion, and respect human dignity. These early teachings remain a compass as they grow older and face the challenges of adulthood. Despite whatever deviations or challenges they may encounter, the love that first molded them never changes. This love then serves as their internal moral compass, guiding people to make better choices and engage in more sympathetic relationships. As a result, the love you provide now becomes a source of support for someone else later.

Chapter: 24

Love affects communities in ways that go beyond family bounds. Future leaders are created by teachers who are committed to their students. Similarly, a mentor's belief in a young person can have a profound impact on their life. The neighborhood as a whole can benefit from a neighbor's kind deeds. Numerous lives are profoundly impacted by such acts of affection. Compassion and the renewal of hope through forgiveness may impact lives in ways we will never fully understand, even though their repercussions are irreversible. Love lingers and permeates many people's lives, yet it does not always materialize. As a result, when people aid others with good intentions, they leave a compassionate legacy vital to a community's identity.

Even the tiniest acts of affection can have lifelong consequences. Someone might get closer to their objectives with a quick boost of encouragement. One act of forgiveness could stop hatred from spreading. An otherwise harsh personality could be softened by a brief act of kindness, even though it may not seem like much; many incidents have a big impact. People may forget their early years or past experiences, but they never forget how they were loved or how they were desired to be loved. They use love as their emotional rock when things get tough. This centuries-old foundation contributes to the resilience of future generations.

The capacity of love to heal is an integral part of its enduring influence. Love has the power to heal wounds that have endured for centuries. You can choose to be patient rather than irate. Rather than remaining mute, you might decide to comprehend. Compassion is an alternative to establishing distance. It is possible to alter your family's emotional history by consciously and deliberately choosing love. Your decision to love today may therefore bring more peace to future generations. A loving legacy has the capacity to change both the present and the future, which is its true beauty and power.

Chapter: 24

Being perfect is not necessary to leave an enduring legacy of love. Being present is crucial. Continually exhibiting humility, compassion, and sincere care creates a stronger impression. Instead of focusing on our mistakes, our spouses, children, and even individuals we hardly know focus on how we made them feel. They recall the hugs, encouraging words, the happiness we shared, and the sacrifices we made. They remember the unwavering love that saw us through the tough times, listening late into the night, and expressing that we were sorry when we were wrong. Love doesn't have to be flawless to be powerful; it just needs to be sincere.

Reflection reveals that love always serves as the foundation for the most meaningful events in a lifetime. The essential things are not the big successes or the cash amassed, but rather the times when one made a difference in another's life. These are the moments that endure. Therefore, when your descendants tell your story, in stories, character traits, or traditions, they will always emphasize the love you showed. Then, your lasting impact becomes a subliminal yet resolute message: "Embrace love. Spread and embody love. Ultimately, the only thing that can last beyond time is love. It manifests as a timeless gift, an unbreakable legacy, and an enduring influence that persists even after the absence of the individual.

By deliberately choosing love, people create a future that is kind, hopeful, and connected. Love has a lasting impact that sets in motion a chain of actions that goes beyond simple remembrance. It acts as the tenets that direct a child's development, the generosity that motivates others to take charitable action, and the support that uplifts people long after the initial act. That's what each individual can leave behind. Every act of love creates a narrative that reveals the eternal nature of love and cuts beyond time constraints.

Chapter: 24

The Legacy of Love
Stories of love's legacy in families and communities

T he enduring power of love frequently outlasts the lives of its original bearers. It quietly crosses generations, deeply entwined with traditions, choices, and memories. Long after the particular incidents have ended, the term "legacy of love" refers to the lasting effects of kindness, sacrifice, compassion, and dedication. These stories of love are the cornerstone of self-definition, resilience, and a sense of belonging in both familial and communal contexts. They impact the development of a sense of personal importance, the ability to overcome hardship, and interpersonal dynamics. It is not solitary incidents that create a legacy of love, but countless small actions that have an impact well beyond their immediate time frame.

Families that have endured hardship for centuries, supported by a caregiving tradition, provide a powerful example of the lasting power of love. Think of a grandma who lavished her children with love and care despite experiencing financial hardship. She taught them the values of generosity in times of need, faith in the face of difficulty, and the ability to forgive quickly. Her children later lived up to these values. Her ideals have shaped her grandkids, even though they never met her. The subtle power of a legacy steeped in love is best illustrated by how it transcends personal experience, becoming an essential component of the emotional makeup of everyone it touches.

Stories of enduring love strengthen community bonds. For instance, there are places where locals provide food during challenging times or where elderly individuals tend to the children of stressed-out, impoverished parents. Official history accounts may not document these acts, but they remain deeply ingrained in popular culture. Often remembered as "the good old days," the sense of care transcends family ties and extends to the larger community. This kind, nurturing environment created a sense of safety and acceptance that remains a source of inspiration for future generations to help, support, and shield one another.

Chapter: 24

Some households manifest the legacy of love by passing down goodwill, akin to a treasured family heirloom. One story describes the devotion of a father who, no matter how long his job kept him working, came home every night to read to his kids, even when he was exhausted. These kids learned that love is just being there, not a goal or a source of material wealth. Afterwards, they repeated this same technique once they became parents. These days, their grown children consider the deep sense of safety and value they felt, which stemmed only from the time someone spent with them. What began as a nightly ritual developed into a connection-based custom spanning several generations. The legacy of love is profoundly enduring: even the smallest deeds can influence lives long after the original act of giving ends.

Another illustration of this phenomenon is found in religious and cultural groups that build their identities on love and solidarity. Consider the numerous immigrant families who gave up all for their kids in the hopes of a better future. They led modest lives, accepted positions below their skill level, and dedicated themselves to creating opportunities they had never had. Their children go on to achieve success and show gratitude, recalling the love that shaped them. At social gatherings, family reunions, and celebrations, these tales of selflessness are shared to remind individuals that love is the foundation of their success, not to brag. As a result, these tales influence the next generation's conduct, social relationships, and values, shaping how they view their heritage. Additionally, there are love tales in communities that transcend local boundaries.

Under challenging circumstances, such as natural disasters, medical crises, or bereavement, love is what propels human behavior. Innumerable tales exist of neighbors providing food to those in need, volunteers repairing homes for strangers, and educators using their personal funds to assist their pupils. A community's character is woven together by such acts. Children who observe acts of kindness learn that kindness is required, normal, and expected. As a result, they propagate this idea, which initiates a domino effect of altruistic giving.

Chapter: 24

Each family has its story, told over and over again, often with laughter and sadness. Beyond simple memories, these stories develop into teaching tools, moral compasses, and moving reminders of core principles. Consider the tale of a couple who triumphed over years of adversity; it is a powerful illustration of human fortitude. An example of unselfish love is also provided by the tale of a mother's unwavering commitment to her child. These tales influence how people view their own interpersonal interactions. They develop into mental role models for forgiveness, love, and commitment. Through deeds and repetition, these stories demonstrate the enduring power of love.

Mentoring is one way that certain communities illustrate the long-lasting impact of love. Elders guide younger generations not via formal education but through their constant presence. When a senior community leader spends his afternoons teaching teens life skills, he not only helps the youth but also creates a lasting impression that will shape how they raise their children. He guides others, and his love has a cascading impact. With the person on the receiving end, it doesn't end there. Their influence ripples through every life they encounter. Communities go from merely surviving to truly flourishing in this way. Leaders are born of love. Generosity comes from love.

Love creates stable cycles that last despite social or economic difficulties. Even in families with complicated histories, love endures and leaves a legacy. Occasionally, a single individual serves as the catalyst, the one who prioritizes healing over resentment, forgiveness over resentment, and patience over anger. They leave a legacy to future generations by choosing to love differently. Think of a parent who breaks the pattern of emotional neglect; for example, this person provides their children with a priceless experience: fearless love. As a result, those kids build their own families on stronger foundations. One heart has the power to change the course of a whole family tree. This scenario best illustrates the unmatched impact of a love-infused legacy.

Chapter: 24

The eternal power of love is frequently amplified in our society. Through social media, storytelling platforms, and digital archives, people share tales of love, compassion, perseverance, and altruism with a global audience. A toddler may begin to think that people are naturally generous after viewing a video of someone doing something amazing. In a similar vein, a young adult may feel more hopeful about their future relationships after hearing a senior discuss decades of commitment. Love has always had a significant impact, but at a rate never witnessed before, it now spans national borders, cultural conventions, and generations.

One important insight is that the enduring power of love is independent of the perfection of people or families. Rather, it is created by individuals who genuinely care about it, despite their flaws. It is created by people who choose kindness over selfishness, compassion over anger, and patience when they are truly frustrated. Even after they die, a person's repeated decisions continue to influence their narratives about themselves. Rather than material possessions, love leaves a legacy of lasting emotions. It's evident in how others talk about you, how they remember you, and how your actions continue to influence their life. At the end, everyone leaves something behind. While some people give up their possessions, others give up their achievements. But love, the power that shapes personalities, strengthens familial relationships, and revitalizes communities, is the most significant legacy. Making love a priority in one's life has long-lasting consequences. Generosity becomes a story. It is educational to see patience in action. Charity acts give others hope. In the end, love creates a lasting legacy by laying the foundation for future generations to depend on.

Chapter: 24

The Legacy of Love
Building a life remembered for love

The idea of a legacy is often thought of in terms of material wealth, career achievements, or material belongings. But the lasting legacy, the one that endures beyond our lives, is essentially based on love. It is not a question of luck to cultivate a life known for love; instead, it is carefully crafted by our daily choices, the way we treat people, and the empathy we exhibit, even in secret. The accumulation of small deeds of kindness creates a legacy of love that eventually combines into a powerful and enduring force. Thus, making love a priority leads to a purposeful life that is marked by kind words, quick forgiveness, willing help, and profound relationships. These lasting characteristics are what people remember most about the influence you had on their lives.

Sincerity, not perfection, is what defines a life that is commended for its love. It is not your perfection that people remember, but the emotions you evoke. They recall the occasions when you supported them, paid great attention, and consoled them during their most trying moments. A loving legacy can be created by prioritizing understanding over pride, empathy over judgment, and generosity above self-interest. It grows by becoming a refuge for others, a source of solace, assurance, and hope. As a result, when you uphold these ideals, your name is linked to harmony rather than chaos, kindness rather than cruelty, and consolation rather than conflict.

When love becomes a way of life, it creates a permanent legacy. The way you respond, communicate, support, and care for others demonstrates your values. Every interaction, regardless of its magnitude, begins to shape people's perception of you. A legacy of love is created over many silent moments rather than in one. It can be found in your phone conversations, in the time you spend with people, in the support you offer, and in the patience you exhibit. The more you offer love, the more you build something that endures. In the end, what matters most to others is who you were, not what you owned.

Chapter: 24

Being present intentionally is also necessary to leave a loving legacy. Many of us walk through life in a daze, missing opportunities to show affection. Reflecting, however, reveals the impact of even seemingly insignificant activities. It could be remembering a birthday, offering a heartfelt remark, or simply praying with someone who is in pain. Being present is an invaluable gift. Making someone feel seen, valued, and significant leaves a lasting emotional effect. Being there becomes a memory; people will always remember how you made them feel less alone. A legacy of love is also fostered by having the guts to forgive.

Forgiveness is a powerful expression of love since it frees the forgiver as much as the forgiven. Resentment creates walls, while forgiveness builds long-lasting relationships, bridges that can last for generations. An individual's choice to prioritize forgiveness over resentment has led to healing within the family and the community. Forgiving shows others that love is stronger than anger and that pride shouldn't stand in the way of meaningful relationships. It's a timeless philosophy that spreads from person to person. This means that your ability to forgive becomes a central part of your story, a witness to love that is brave and humble. In addition, the ideals you pass on can influence your legacy.

The way you show love has a significant impact on what kind of love your kids, family, and community can have. Children develop patience by observing others demonstrate it. In the same way, showing kindness cultivates compassion. Treating others with dignity also fosters respect. A lifestyle that inspires others to develop their own capacity for love is essential to creating a life remembered for love. Your life is therefore a mirror of possibilities, demonstrating that love is a source of power rather than weakness. This impact transcends your life, persisting in the lives of people you have touched and extending farther than one may think.

Chapter: 24

If you want to create a life that is remembered for love, you must also embrace consistency. Even though breathtaking exhibitions can make an impression, it is the unwavering, unchanging love that truly transforms people. Your legacy is defined by your actions, like being there for others through life's ups and downs, staying reliable when busy, and showing kindness even when tired. Your love's constancy demonstrates its true nature. "You are worth my continued presence," is the message. People gradually come to believe that your love is a steady, sincere energy rather than a fleeting fad or contingent on external factors. Furthermore, once trust is built, it becomes a fundamental part of your legacy. Not only will people remember what you did, but they will also remember your constant presence.

Becoming generous is another essential part of creating a loving legacy. Giving is how love naturally shows up: making time, effort, money, and understanding available, and sometimes sacrificing something. Generosity is the willingness to share one's belongings, tend to a need as it emerges, and offer support when another's strength is weakened; it need not be flashy. People remember acts of generosity because they reach out to them in their most vulnerable moments. A person's generosity becomes a crucial part of their legacy, whether they offer words of encouragement, lend a hand, or offer a listening ear. It indicates that one can live a life that is open to investing in others, without reservation or guard.

Essentially, living an authentic life is the key to building a lasting legacy of love. It's about choosing integrity over fakery, genuine connection over theatrics, and significant action over short-lived celebrity. Genuine, welcoming, and palpable, true love doesn't put on a presentation. When people are comfortable being themselves with you, they remember you as someone who offered support rather than criticism. Being genuine improves your connections and increases your impact. People who feel safe and valued for who they really are in your presence will leave a loving legacy. You cultivate a personality that has a lasting effect on others.

Chapter: 24

In essence, a life characterized by love is based on humility. This quality allows love to be expressed without worrying about approval or recognition. People are freed from the need to be right, which leads to a focus on kindness. Honest listening, a readiness to apologize, and a commitment to harmony over selfish interests are traits of humble love. Thus, when love is infused with humility, it becomes powerful. Its appeal lies in the absence of hidden agendas. A humble person also makes their legacy approachable; people respect them and feel comfortable around them. Rather than intimidating them, your love moves them.

Rather than demeaning others, humility cultivates legacies that elevate them. After all, a life remembered for love requires one with meaning. Love serves as the guide for your choices, the lens through which you perceive adversity, and the driving force behind your actions. You know how desperately the world needs love, compassion, and optimism. Loving motivates you to solve the problem. The people you empower, the relationships you build, and the shared experiences you create shape the legacy you leave behind.

Your love leaves your stamp on the beings you have connected with. When your time here is over, the honors and worldly possessions will be forgotten. Your warmth, honesty, and love will last. They'll remember your understanding, generosity, compassion, and ability to make people feel valued. The result is the timeless present. Love remembers a well-lived life that inspires, heals, and uplifts others even after your departure. That is, after all, the most significant legacy anyone can leave.

Chapter: 24

The enduring power of love is not weakened by time or the ups and downs of life, but rather remains quietly in the people we affect, the choices we make, and the memories we leave behind. The transforming power of love was explored in this chapter, showing how it can influence not only our present experiences but also the paths taken by future generations. The following questions will help you reflect on the type of love you are, the love you give to others, and the love you hope to continue.

1. When you think about the people who loved you in ways that changed your life, who comes to mind? Describe what their love taught you, and how those lessons still influence the way you love others today.

2. Reflect on an act of love you received as a child or young adult that has stayed with you over the years. Why did it impact you so deeply? How does it continue to shape the kind of person you are becoming?

3. This chapter discussed how love can shape future generations. In your own life, what loving actions or habits do you hope to pass down to your children, grandchildren, or the people who look up to you?

4. Think about your family history. Are there stories of love, sacrifice, or resilience that have inspired you or helped you understand your roots? How do these stories influence the way you choose to love today?

5. Love creates ripple effects—small actions that turn into meaningful change. Can you think of a simple act of kindness from you or someone else that created a larger, lasting impact? What does this teach you about the hidden power of love?

6. Some legacies grow not from perfect people, but from those who loved through their flaws. Reflect on someone whose imperfect but sincere love shaped you. What about their love made it memorable, and how did it influence your own approach to relationships?

Chapter: 24

Through our ability to love, each of us is creating a legacy, whether we are aware of it or not. When we are gone, every act of compassion, every moment of letting go, and every nice word adds to the story that others will tell. One day, one choice, one act of love at a time: this next section invites you to go inward and reflect on the legacy you are creating.

7. If someone wrote a chapter about the way you love, what do you hope they would say? What qualities or behaviors would you want to be remembered for?

8. Think about how you show love in your everyday life—through service, encouragement, patience, or compassion. Which of these expressions feels the most natural to you, and which one do you feel challenged to grow in?

9. Sometimes, the legacy we leave begins with the healing we choose to do. Are there wounds, patterns, or fears you are trying to break so future generations can experience healthier love? How does this healing contribute to your personal legacy?

10. Consider the communities you belong to—your neighborhood, workplace, place of worship, or circle of friends. What kind of impact do you hope your presence and actions have on these groups? How can your love strengthen these communities in meaningful ways?

11. If you could pass down one lesson about love to the next generation, what would it be? Why does this lesson matter so deeply to you, and how can you embody it more intentionally?

12. Finally, imagine yourself many years from now, looking back on your life. What would make you feel proud of the love you gave? What changes can you make now to ensure that the legacy you leave behind is one defined by kindness, connection, and a heart that loved well?

Chapter: 25

Love Never Fails
Summarizing the timeless truth that love never fails

L ove is a fundamental reality that transcends time and cultural boundaries. Because it speaks to a profound human need for understanding, affirmation, and connection, this idea is relevant to people of many ages, cultures, religions, and personal histories. When people look back on their lives, they often regard their romantic experiences more highly than their material achievements; the relationships that shaped their lives are of utmost importance. What is really remarkable is that love is eternal; it does not fade with time. Love endures despite changing circumstances, growing older, or the intrinsic complexity of life. It offers steadiness in the face of uncertainty. As a result, the core of this timeless reality is that love, in its purest form, is spontaneously strong.

One reason why love never fails is that it has the power to change things. What seems hopelessly shattered can be repaired, and even the hardest hearts can be softened by it. Love illuminates the darkness, offers hope, and comforts the emptiness. Love continues to have an impact, working quietly beneath the surface, even when its expressions diverge from our expectations. The victories of love are not always apparent; they frequently appear in the subtle processes of healing, forgiveness, and human development. Its endurance, not its perfection, is what defines love. It continues to prove itself time and time again, and it does not give up when giving up would seem like a more practical course of action.

The enduring quality of love is discernible everywhere. Love from the parents' end lasts long after children grow up. Long-term friendships withstand time and distance. Couples overcome obstacles that could have brought them apart in the first place. Communities come together during difficult times. All these examples show that the resilience of love is not due to a lack of hardship but to a deliberate choice to persevere. The tenacity of love is guaranteed because it always resurfaces, sometimes slowly, sometimes suddenly, but always with a faint, unflinching power that defies disintegration.

Chapter: 25

Another factor in love's enduring strength is its knowledge, which goes beyond transient feelings. Even though feelings may change drastically, true love results from a deliberate decision. It is a decision to be caring, compassionate, to reach out, and to be loyal even when feelings fade. Love may endure adversity because it is grounded in a deliberate aim rather than in fleeting moments. A link that cannot be broken by time is strengthened when someone chooses love above pride, anger, and distance. These qualities grow into something deeper and more stable, guaranteeing that love lasts long after the initial emotional rush has passed.

Love finds ways to make an impression that lasts, even in partnerships that experience hurt or separation. A message from the past can still be consoling. Kindness can inspire others for a long time. A moment of forgiveness can heal a wound even after the talk has ended. In this sense, love creates a legacy that endures, influencing others long after a relationship ends. Love's enduring power is often underestimated, but it has a slow, steady, and indisputable impact. Love's influence endures even when human endeavor fails.

Love never fails because it offers us things that last a lifetime. It instills patience, humility, bravery, and resilience. Love acts as a mirror, pointing out our shortcomings and motivating us to improve ourselves. It challenges us to evolve while demonstrating our potential for profound empathy. Love strengthens us when it challenges us, shapes us when it confronts us, and highlights our core values when it consoles us. Like no other force, love has the capacity to strengthen the heart, mend emotional scars, and develop character. As so, it affects us for a long time and becomes a part of our identity.

Chapter: 25

One of love's most important characteristics is its enduring nature, which endures despite life's inherent fragility. Seasons fluctuate, people can disappoint, and situations are constantly changing; thus, life is by its very nature vulnerable to the whims of change. Nevertheless, love remains a constant component. It endures despite being lost. The love given by the deceased does not fade; instead, it becomes a treasured memory that provides comfort, directs choices, and strengthens subsequent generations. Additionally, the lessons learned from love hold even after relationships end. The impact of love is always significant. Love has a tenacity that goes beyond the current experience and often serves as a trigger for eventual healing, even after grief.

Love's enduring power comes from its ability to bring hope to situations that seem hopeless. A single act of kindness can lift someone out of despair. Similarly, a heart that is willing to forgive can restore an apparently damaged connection. In addition, a loving presence helps calm the inner turmoil of someone feeling too much emotion. What makes love unique is its capacity to bring light back into gloomy circumstances. It offers the strength to face life's inherent challenges, but it does not eliminate them. Thus, love makes things easier, more transparent, and better.

Love provides a sense of security even amid widespread uncertainty: "You are not alone." When we say that love is unfailing, we mean that love sometimes fails to achieve the outcomes we desire. Love sometimes requires us to navigate situations we would rather avoid. It could call for release, patience, forgiveness, or sacrifice. But love is unwavering, supporting us, guiding us, and revealing the truth even in these trying times. Love is steadfast because it consistently invests in our growth, especially during difficult times. All acts of love ultimately lead us to the fulfillment of our innate potential.

Chapter: 25

Its ability to transcend situational limitations and to express itself verbally is what gives love its enduring quality. It appears throughout the threads of all human relationships, across the phases of human life, and in every act of selfless deed. People acknowledge the enduring influence of love when they claim that it is eternal. Many years from now, people may still discover resonance in the affection shown. An act of forgiveness can free one person. The extended grace can change a person's life path. Love has the exceptional capacity to transcend time, to resolve past wrongs, and to uphold cultural or familial customs. Its tenacity stems from its constant motion through time, through people's hearts, and through memories of the past.

Fully loving someone despite their imperfections creates a lasting impression that is impossible to replicate. Choosing compassion over apathy, understanding over judgment, and love over bitterness all lead to a higher goal. Every act of love contributes to a larger narrative that continues long after the moment has passed. Your love will impact the people you touch, even though it may not be immediately apparent. Consequently, love is more resilient than failure. The impact of love is assessed in subsequent generations rather than in individual moments.

In the end, the notion that love never fails is a way of life rather than merely a statement. It reminds us that love is the most valuable gift we can offer, regardless of what else occurs in the world. Love has the power to restore, to rebuild, and to renew. Love strengthens connections, elevates the human experience, and leaves behind a legacy that surpasses monetary prosperity. When everything else fades, love remains. Even after words are lost, it endures. It adapts when conditions change. Love is unfailing, symbolizing the one power that can overcome every challenge. A life with love at its core is one with true meaning.

Chapter: 25

Love Never Fails
Reflecting on how love endures all challenges

L ove has the natural ability to withstand all efforts to weaken it. "Love never fails" is a statement that goes beyond transitory feelings or ephemeral attractions. It is about a deep love that endures all of life's hardships, including storms, heartbreaks, disappointments, miscommunications, and even the passing of years filled with change. Instead of giving in to the pressures of the outside world, this everlasting love finds new ways to adapt, rebuild, and flourish. Love is resilient in the face of hardship because of unwavering dedication rather than perfection. It is choosing every day to accept love once more, regardless of what the outside world may say. An enduring love recognizes that obstacles are a chance for progress rather than a sign of failure. When love encounters hardship, it undergoes a remarkable transformation, revealing its actual potential.

When circumstances are favorable, falling in love can seem effortless. However, love truly reveals its nature when faced with challenges such as disagreements, financial troubles, or mistakes. The power of love is found in preserving the relationship in the face of adversity rather than avoiding it. People discover new facets of themselves and grow stronger, more patient, more resilient, and more compassionate when they decide to love throughout difficult circumstances. Love shows us that enduring adversity is only one aspect of perseverance; another is having faith that the relationship is worthwhile. For love to last, one must be humble. Challenges frequently highlight disparities, worries, fears, and weaknesses. Love endures because its partners are committed to each other's development rather than because they are perfect.

Humility promotes understanding, forgiveness, compromise, and candid communication. However, challenges could be written off as pointless debates if one lacks humility. A modest person, however, views challenges as chances for development and education. A long-lasting love learns from its mistakes, avoids repeating them, and looks for answers rather than placing blame. This humility serves as the cornerstone that keeps love strong in trying times.

Chapter: 25

One fundamental fact about enduring love is that challenges enhance it rather than diminish it. Sometimes adversity reveals the actual worth of love. Beyond appearances, challenging circumstances can compel individuals, families, or groups to confront their fundamental beliefs. Love frequently sheds impatience, pride, selfishness, and irrational expectations when it encounters difficulties. What remains is a love that has matured into something more stable and real. Refinement is unquestionably a transformative process, though it is frequently difficult. The lesson demonstrates that love is not brittle. Instead, it is robust enough to endure hardships and stay intact.

Love's enduring power also stems from its association with a higher cause. Purpose provides a sense of direction when emotions fluctuate. A sense of purpose provides a strong foundation amid fluctuating emotions. Love develops when you act with a purpose, whether that purpose is to protect your loved ones, fulfill a vow, or foster a common spiritual path. It develops into something more than a transient attraction. Your purpose is what keeps you going when times are challenging. Your feeling of purpose acts as a reminder of the firm foundation you've built when self-doubt arises. When times are difficult, love with a purpose doesn't run away. Instead, it reaches deep, looking for insight, recovery, and the opportunity to begin again. Long-lasting love ceases to be merely consoling and instead becomes a symbol of courage.

Another factor contributing to its resilience is the fact that love doesn't exist in isolation. Patience, empathy, forgiveness, and candid communication are all necessary for true love. These are the resources that enable love to persevere through difficult circumstances. When two individuals, or perhaps an entire community, adhere to these principles, their relationship becomes unshakable. In a sense, patience slows down our quick reactions. Empathy can dissolve barriers. Forgiveness restores trust. Assumptions can be clarified through communication. Even amid a dense atmosphere, they create an environment conducive to love. Without these attributes, problems can quickly destroy relationships. But with them, obstacles become chances for love to grow and strengthen the connection.

Chapter: 25

Courage is necessary to endure love. It requires bravery to remain open and vulnerable after experiencing harm, to maintain trust after disappointments, and to exhibit compassion. Durable love is daring, not irresponsible. Even when you are tempted to retreat, you quietly choose to believe in the goodness of the link. Love needs courage to recognize possibility rather than failure, to try again rather than give up, and to confront challenging conversations rather than avoid them. This bravery lets love guide the relationship, even while acknowledging grief. Love endures because it holds onto the hope that something worthwhile is still achievable.

The memory consists of mutual laughter, the forming of hopes, the easing of grief, the promises made, and the prayers prayed throughout hardship. In times of adversity, memory may be a source of strength. Love chooses to keep a wider view rather than letting fleeting adversity mask lasting importance. Resilient love doesn't lessen pain; it keeps the relationship's experiences from drowning out the hurt. Hope, which is essential to enduring relationships, is based on memory. It is the conviction that things will become better in the future than they are now. Love often perseveres even in the face of obstacles such as separation, illness, grief, financial difficulties, or emotional conflict.

Despite the misconception that love is brittle, it is actually one of the most powerful energies in the universe. Love withstands miscommunications, errors, and vulnerable moments. Change, disillusionment, and silence can all contribute to its persistence. Love is destroyed by the decision to call off an engagement, not by the challenges encountered. When two people consistently choose each other, love persists. As long as there are close family links, it endures. When friendships are restored through effort, they endure. Love endures not because of fortunate circumstances but because individuals strive to maintain it.

Chapter: 25

The most fundamental aspect of eternal love is its capacity to change people. Adversity shapes love by increasing giving, sensitivity, and insight. When love perseveres through hardship meant to shatter it, it is a monument to resilience. Couples who have conquered adversity frequently claim that their most difficult times served as catalysts for a deeper connection. Adversity also seems to make families stronger and closer. Enduring love is a constant source of consolation and an anchor, even in the most challenging circumstances. It provides sanctuary not because life gets easier but because hearts are fortified.

Beyond that, enduring love leaves a mark. Future generations are profoundly taught the value of dedication by the unwavering love that endures through hardship. The tenacity and acts of compassion that children witness are absorbed by them. Stories of reconciliation and resiliency bolster communities. In addition to influencing the present and the future, strong love triumphs against hardship. When people witness love triumph over hardship, their relationships grow more optimistic. They understand that love is a commitment that lasts a lifetime and transcends transient emotions. Consequently, your perseverance inspires others. The main argument of this last chapter—that love is unfailing—is finally confirmed by looking at how resilient love is in the face of adversity.

Love endures not because people are perfect, but because it surpasses our frailties. It lights the shadows and endures beyond pain. What makes love so unflinching is that it is based on hope, strengthened by forgiveness, guided by purpose, and protected by humility. Love endures even when all else fades. When this idea is the foundation of one's life, it is clear that love not only endures hardship but also transforms it into experiences that strengthen its base and show its strength.

Chapter: 25

Love Never Fails
Encouraging readers to embrace a love that lasts forever

The idea of eternal love has a powerful influence. It's a strong, unwavering tie that remains even when the world around it changes, not the kind that breaks down under stress or dwindles with the seasons. To cultivate lasting love for yourself and those you care about, you must first understand that it doesn't happen overnight. Conscious choices, unselfish deeds, and the little, commonplace acts of compassion are how it grows. You develop resilience to confront life's unavoidable changes by continuously choosing love, even when it's challenging. Adversity is something that eternal love faces head-on with courage, compassion, and composure. Perfection isn't the goal of a lasting relationship.

Being present is the key to lasting love. Often, people lose hope because they think long-term love requires either perfect behavior or constant emotional highs. But enduring love is really made up of everyday events: the quiet support, the gentle prodding, and the willingness to listen when it would be easier to avoid. Its tenacity is based on commitment rather than expediency. Because love was never entirely dependent on feelings, it endures throughout emotional ups and downs. It takes dedication to continuously exhibit humility, compassion, and purpose to cultivate this kind of love.

To accept lasting love, one must admit that it surpasses fleeting annoyances and misunderstandings. It goes beyond arguments to the innermost parts of the heart, where understanding and forgiveness thrive. Love's dedication to the person, the relationship, and the future is what makes it unwavering. This steadfast love acts as a reminder that optimism persists in the face of adversity. Developing a mindset that prioritizes growth over abandonment is essential to creating enduring love. This shift in viewpoint significantly alters the dynamics of the relationship.

Chapter: 25

It is necessary to recognize the intrinsic beauty of the shared experience in order to cultivate lasting devotion. A lasting love is not defined by the absence of hardship, but rather by the way two people overcome obstacles together. Adhering to a lifetime of love means accepting that both joyful and challenging times are inevitable and that each one teaches us something. Happiness highlights the benefits of perpetual commitment, serenity cultivates thankfulness, and adversity builds resilience. These diverse experiences form the foundation of this enduring love, each adding to its profundity, insight, and importance.

The first step in cultivating a commitment to eternal love is realizing that love is a continuous, daily endeavor. Instead of being a spontaneous feeling that overtakes you, it is an active participation. Taking responsibility for your actions, keeping the lines of communication open, and showing kindness when you're feeling down all need effort. Nevertheless, each time you make such choices, you fortify the basis of your love. You strengthen the foundation of your faith and purpose against temporary problems. Long-term love requires intentionality, including being mindful of your words, deeds, and the provider's care. It takes bravery to be in love for a long time.

To be vulnerable, to forgive sincerely, and to keep an open heart in the face of hardships takes a great deal of strength. Developing this kind of love requires understanding that vulnerability is not a sign of weakness but an opening to more profound relationships. This kind of sincerity creates a link that is resilient to the effects of time. Allowing oneself to love fully also fosters self-understanding. One brave choice at a time, enduring love is built via the bravery of love, which will enable people to say, "I am present, even amidst hardship. I choose you, not only today but also in the days to come."

Chapter: 25

The practice of thankfulness is vital for building long-lasting love. Gratitude softens the heart and cultivates an attitude that recognizes the beneficial things in life despite flaws. The emotional connection that sustains love is strengthened by actively identifying the little deeds of kindness, the dedication that endures, and the shared moments of happiness or comfort. Gratitude transforms ordinary days into meaningful ones and cultivates an attitude that views the partnership as a treasured experience rather than a right. As a result, enduring love blossoms in hearts that are constantly grateful.

Another crucial element of cultivating enduring love is shielding the relationship from external influences that could endanger it. Life usually goes by faster. The obligations accumulate. Stress can easily impair judgment. However, enduring love requires conscious attempts to reestablish contact. Emotional closeness can be fostered by scheduling time for talking, paying close attention, sharing quiet moments, or just being there. Cultivating a lifelong love requires dedicating oneself to the moments that strengthen your relationship. You still choose each other today because of these circumstances.

Understanding the normal developmental phases of relationships is essential to accepting lasting love. Change will inevitably occur for everyone involved, including oneself; this is something to welcome rather than fear. When a group develops, learns, and surpasses the sum of its members' abilities, it is said to be growing. A lasting love leaves an impression that endures, encouraging tolerance, wisdom, and personal growth. Therefore, establishing a lasting love requires a joyful embrace of this changing experience rather than a resistant attitude. Love's ability to transform and uplift others is what gives it its enduring power.

Chapter: 25

Finding a permanent love requires effort, understanding, and faith, as it is a promise rather than a mere fantasy. To encourage others to seek this type of love, we must first recognize that it is difficult to break. It's a power that, with time and nurturing, grows more resilient. True love endures challenges and grows stronger, learns from them, and undergoes transformations. With this knowledge, you can see challenges as opportunities to strengthen your bond rather than threats. Committing to a lasting relationship means valuing what you share. It involves protecting your relationship from the damaging impacts of uncertainty, impatience, or fear and maintaining it with utmost respect.

Making the conscious decision to choose love promotes harmony in your relationships. You create a protected space where both people can thrive and feel safe. This viewpoint inspires others to see love as something that grows stronger with every act of devotion rather than as brittle. Avoiding arguments is not the goal of enduring love; rather, it is a firm commitment. After all, one of the best gifts you can offer yourself and the world is lasting love.

Loyalty over convenience, hope in the face of uncertainty, and compassion in difficult situations are examples of acts of love. Love has an enduring quality since it is based in the soul and is not just a feeling. When you choose to love sincerely, you leave an enduring legacy. Your love then serves as a source of guidance, inspiration, and comfort for others. Therefore, the greatest reward for living with this reality is eternal love.

Chapter: 25

The one thing that endures in the face of the most significant hardship is love. This chapter explored the enduring quality of love, its ability to overcome seemingly insurmountable obstacles, and the need for people to develop a long-lasting bond. As you reflect on this chapter, consider how love has helped, challenged, or changed you. These questions are intended to encourage an intimate and meaningful interaction with the main idea.

1. When you think about the phrase *"love never fails,"* what does it mean to you personally? How has this truth shown up at different points in your life?

2. Reflect on a moment when love carried you through a difficult challenge. What did that experience teach you about the strength and resilience of love?

3. Love doesn't always remove challenges, but it gives us the courage to endure them. In what ways has love helped you stay grounded during stressful or uncertain seasons?

4. Think about a situation where you witnessed love triumph, even when the odds were against it. What impact did that moment have on your view of relationships, commitment, or faith?

5. This chapter encouraged readers to see love as something more profound than feelings. What difference do you notice between "feeling love" and "choosing love," and how have you practiced that difference in your own relationships?

6. In your own words, describe an example of love that refused to fail, whether from your family, friendships, community, or spiritual life. How did that example shape your understanding of unconditional love?

Chapter: 25

This book has been filled with the triumphs, sacrifices, challenges, and beauty of love in every chapter. Love is the one force that is always powerful, meaningful, and capable of change. As we inch closer to the end, this truth becomes clearer than all the others you have looked at. You've seen in these chapters how love brings light even into the darkest times of life, mends relationships that seemed irreparable, strengthens families across generations, and heals wounds that seemed unhealable. You have seen how love can be strong when it is vulnerable, forgiving, and kind. Love has consistently demonstrated its resilience in the face of fear, failure, and any challenges life may present.

You have been inspired by this book to consider love from a variety of angles, such as sacrificial, romantic, spiritual, familial, and unconditional love. Every chapter revealed the more profound significance of love, which transcends feelings, situations, and limitations. This journey shows that choosing to love is a daily choice. You don't have to wait for it. It grows via deeds, service, humility, and consistency. Love can blossom whenever you have the opportunity to listen more than you talk, forgive more than you judge, and give more than you take. Rather than its perfection, its true strength lies in its capacity to endure hardship. Remember that your most significant legacy is love as you move on.

Your love will remain a quiet presence in the lives of those you touched long after you are gone. Even if you are no longer physically present, your deeds of kindness will continue to guide others. You have what it takes to heal, to offer hope, and to promote peace. Make your life an example of enduring love, a love that chooses empathy even when it's difficult, sees the good in everyone, and extends forgiveness. You will alter the environment around you and your connections if you live this way. As a result, the main takeaway from this book endures: no matter the challenges or the situation, love always triumphs, and true "Love Never Fails".

www.ingramcontent.com/pod-product-compliance
Lightning Source LLC
Chambersburg PA
CBHW062155270326
41930CB00009B/1544